Tourism and Recreation in Rural Areas

Tourism and Recreation in Rural Areas

Edited by

RICHARD BUTLER, C. MICHAEL HALL
AND JOHN JENKINS

JOHN WILEY & SONS
Chichester · New York · Weinheim · Brisbane · Singapore · Toronto

National   01243 779777
International   (+44) 1243 779777
e-mail (for orders and customer service enquiries): cs-books@wiley.co.uk
Visit our Home Page on http://www.wiley.co.uk
                or http://www.wiley.com

Reprinted October 1999

Other Wiley Editorial Offices

John Wiley & Sons, Inc., 605 Third Avenue,
New York, NY 10158-0012, USA

WILEY-VCH GmbH, Pappelallee 3,
D-69469 Weinheim, Germany

Jacaranda Wiley Ltd, 33 Park Road, Milton,
Queensland 4064, Australia

John Wiley & Sons (Asia) Pte Ltd, 2 Clementi Loop #02-01,
Jin Xing Distripark, Singapore 129809

John Wiley & Sons (Canada) Ltd, 22 Worcester Road,
Rexdale, Ontario M9W 1L1, Canada

Library of Congress Cataloging-in-Publication Data

Tourism and recreation in rural areas / edited by Richard Butler, C.
    Michael Hall, and John Jenkins.
        p.   cm.
    Includes bibliographical references and index.
    ISBN 0-471-97680-6 (cloth)
    1. Tourist trade. 2. Farms—Recreation use. 3. Rural
development. I. Butler, Richard, 1943– . II. Hall, Colin
Michael, 1961– . III. Jenkins, John, PhD.
G155.A1T58935   1997
338.4′791–dc21   97-25520
                                                                        CIP

British Library Cataloguing in Publication Data

A catalogue record for this book is available from the British Library

ISBN 0-471-97680-6   ✓

Typeset in 10/12 pt Times from the authors' disks by BookEns Ltd, Royston, Herts.
Printed and bound in Great Britain by Bookcraft (Bath) Ltd, Midsomer Norton
This book is printed on acid-free paper responsibly manufactured from sustainable forestry,
in which at least two trees are planted for each one used for paper production.

To the Barkers, of Fields Farm, Coningsby, Lincolnshire,
for their generosity in allowing me to experience the pleasure
of holidays on a real farm for many years

To the Springetts for their own little bit of New Zealand rurality

To Julie for what we share away from urban life, and to Schaapie my
friend and colleague

Finally, this work is dedicated to *The Archers*; for many urbanites the only
contact which they have with rural life

Contents

Contributors

Richard W. Butler, Department of Management Studies, University of Surrey, Guildford, Surrey, United Kingdom

Jean-Michel Dewailly, University of Science and Technology, Lille, France

Patricia L. Drews, Department of Geography, University of South Carolina, Columbia, South Carolina, United States

Alison Gill, Department of Geography, Simon Fraser University, Burnaby, British Columbia, Canada

C. Michael Hall, Centre for Tourism, University of Otago, Dunedin, New Zealand, and the New Zealand Natural Heritage Foundation

Jeffrey Hopkins, Department of Geography, The University of Western Ontario, London, Ontario, Canada

Robert L. Janiskee, Department of Geography, University of South Carolina, Columbia, South Carolina, United States

John M. Jenkins, Centre for Tourism and Leisure Policy Research, University of Canberra, Belconnen, Australian Capital Territory, Australia

Geoffrey Kearsley, Centre for Tourism, University of Otago, New Zealand

Niki Macionis, Centre for Tourism and Leisure Policy Research, University of Canberra, Belconnen, Australian Capital Territory, Australia

Martin Oppermann, Centre for Tourism Studies, Faculty of Commerce and Tourism, Waiariki Polytechnic, Rotorua, New Zealand

Evi Prin, Centre for Tourism and Leisure Policy Research, University of Canberra, Belconnen, Australian Capital Territory, Australia

Donald G. Reid, University School of Rural Planning and Development, University of Guelph, Guelph, Ontario, Canada

Jens Aarsand Saeter, Research Fellow, Eastern Norway Research Institute, Lillehammer, Norway

Michael Troughton, Department of Geography, The University of Western Ontario, London, Ontario, Canada

Preface

Western nations have experienced major structural change in rural areas as a result of global economic, political, social and technological change. This structural change has led to a number of responses in government policy which have often focussed on attempts to generate new patterns of economic activity in order to diversify the rural economic base. Tourism has been hailed as a panacea for rural redevelopment for almost 30 years, but little critical evaluation of the effectiveness of tourism as such a tool has been undertaken. Many of the problems and difficulties inherent in using tourism as such a tool appear to be common throughout the Western world. In order to explore this further the editors commenced a detailed comparative study of tourism and recreation in rural areas in 1994.

With the assistance of funding from the University of Canberra, the Social Science and Humanities Research Council (Canada), and a Canadian Government Programme for Institutional Research Linkages Grant, a series of seminars and workshops were held on rural tourism and recreation and related issues at the University of Canberra, Australia, in November and December, 1994; Trent University and the University of Western Ontario, Canada, in July 1995; The Hague, The Netherlands, August, 1996; and the Victoria University of Wellington and the University of Otago, New Zealand, in November and December 1996. Meetings focussed on identifying common themes and issues in rural tourism and recreation in western nations. Out of the initial discussion, five major areas emerged as being central to the changing nature and role of tourism and recreation in rural areas: the economics of rural restructuring, public sector rural policies, imaging and reimaging, the social dynamics of rural change, and the over-arching issue of sustainability of tourism and recreation in rural areas. This book is, in great part, a reflection of the centrality of these issues in contemporary rural tourism and recreation and is designed to bring together a range of authors from Australasia, North America and Europe to critically evaluate the enthusiasm of much of government and the tourism industry for promoting rural tourism.

The editors would like to gratefully acknowledge a number of people and institutions who assisted in the preparation and development of this book. The assistance of the funding bodies noted above was clearly invaluable for providing a framework for the book and further ongoing research. Angela Elvey, Gary Johnson, Micaela Saint, and Rachel Samways assisted in the preparation of the manuscript, while the tremendous ongoing research assistance of Dave Crag must also be noted. The final editing stage also received considerable support from Bruce Cockburn, Neil and Tim Finn, Sarah McLachan, Don McGlashan and Natalie Merchant. We would also like to thank Iain Stevenson and John Wiley for the ongoing support for this project. Finally, we would like to give our thanks to our families, and especially to Margaret and Kirsten, for their love and patience, particularly when fellow editors come visiting.

| Richard W. Butler | C. Michael Hall | John M. Jenkins |
| Cranleigh | Brooklyn | Melba |

Part One:
Continuity and Change in Rural Tourism

1   Introduction

RICHARD BUTLER, C. MICHAEL HALL AND JOHN M. JENKINS

Rural areas have long been seen and used as appropriate locations for recreation and tourism activities (Towner, 1996). In the post Second World War period, however, the relationships between the rural setting and the leisure activities engaged therein have changed significantly (Cloke, 1993). Recreation and tourism in many rural areas have gone from being primarily passive and minor elements in the landscape to become highly active and dominant agents of change and control of that landscape and of associated rural communities. These changes in nature and significance have drawn increasing attention to the role of leisure in rural areas, sometimes resulting in rather overstated estimates of likely effects, such as the claim 'Rural tourism to the rescue of Europe's countryside' (World Tourism Organisation (WTO), 1996). Despite such hyperbole, the changing nature of rural areas in many parts of the world and the often expanding role of recreation and tourism in those areas deserve careful consideration. While much has been written on the subject of the changing character of rural areas, of agriculture, and of the countryside (e.g., Bowler, Bryant & Nellis, 1992; Ilbery, 1997), relatively little has been written on the linkages between leisure and the social, cultural and economic elements of rural areas. The central focus of the discussion which follows is the dynamics of the relationships between leisure (which incorporates tourism and recreation) and the traditional, modern and postmodern elements of rural areas. Much of this discussion is in the context of rural areas in the developed world (in particular, Europe, North America and Australasia) where such use of the countryside is a well established and accepted, if often controversial, fact of life.

Leisure, recreation and tourism

It is perhaps appropriate to define, in the context of this volume, some of the key terms which are used. Leisure, recreation and tourism are closely interrelated, and at times are used in the literature almost interchangeably (Burton and Jackson, 1989). Leisure is a complicated concept, and can be envisaged as both a state of mind and as a form of activity, or as both a subject and a descriptor. As a state of mind it implies freedom from obligations, and leisure time is that time which has no claims to it. Recreation is normally thought of as activity (or deliberate inactivity) that is voluntary and which is engaged in for the purposes of enjoyment and satisfaction during time which is free from obligations, i.e., during leisure time. It can be engaged in at any location, including the home. Tourism, on the other hand, whatever definition is used, implies travel away from home, and frequently implies a time involvement of at least 24 hours.

In many cases, however, the specific activities which are engaged in during leisure, recreation and tourism are identical, the key differences generally being the setting or location of the activities, the duration of time involved, and, in some cases, the attitudes, motivations and perceptions of the participants. In recent years the differences between recreation and tourism in particular, except at a philosophical level, have become of decreasing significance and distinctions increasingly blurred. As noted below, changes in the economic and social fabric of society have meant that once traditional timing, setting and patterns of work and leisure activities have often become indistinguishable, and similarly, the boundaries between the different elements of leisure become frequently meaningless.

Rural areas are now host to an almost infinite variety of activities engaged in during participants' leisure time, and to attempt to determine whether participation in an activity is of a recreational or touristic nature is not only difficult but, to some, increasingly irrelevant (e.g., Hall, 1995). Moreover, in many situations, participants will be made up of both recreationists and tourists, and while there may be differences in their motivations, travel patterns and origins, there may be no differences at all in their actual participation in the activity or the resources which that demands. As the rural population itself has changed, so too has the leisure use of rural areas also changed. Thus a rural festival may have an audience of local residents, visitors on a half day trip, and visitors from abroad on a lengthy vacation (see Chapter Ten), and although each may have different expectations, perceptions, and satisfactions from the experience, the major feature is participation at the festival itself.

As will be noted below, there have often been major differences in the policy objectives of many public sector agencies with respect to recreation and tourism in rural areas. Recreation has tended to be viewed as a social service and policies have been primarily geared to securing access to resources and providing opportunities for locals and visitors, while tourism has generally been seen as an agent for stimulating economic development or redevelopment, rather than something which the public sector should provide directly (see Chapters Two to Five). These traditional policy distinctions are also becoming less applicable because of the way in which the leisure use of rural areas has become more ubiquitous and varied. These uses now vary from a brief sojourn in the local neighbourhood by rural residents to a lifetime of retirement to a country residence by a former urbanite, with day trips, vacations and second home visitation in between. The emphasis is, therefore, better placed on the activities and their participants, the demands they place on the rural areas and the changes they cause, rather than on any differentiation between recreation and tourism.

Change in rural areas

As noted above, the literature on rural change is large, and this volume is concerned primarily with only one element of that change. It must be stressed, however, that the changes which have taken place in the recreational and tourist use of rural areas are both a result of, and a factor in, the wide range of other changes that have and are

Figure 1.1. The oast houses of south-east England have been abandoned as mechanisation and competition from overseas grown crops have affected the hop growing industry. Although a defining element of the rural landscape, they have increasingly been either demolished or converted into housing. (C.M. Hall)

occurring in rural areas throughout the world (see Chapter Three). Rural societies and economies have been restructured extensively since the 1950s (Ilbery, 1997), but the process of change has been continuous since mankind first abandoned the nomadic way of life. Rural to urban migration, the enclosure of open fields, the commercialisation of agriculture, the impacts of technology (from improvements in transportation and mechanisation to refrigeration and chemicals) and changes in the political and economic arrangements at a global level have all played significant roles in changing rural areas over several centuries (see Chapter Three) (Figures 1.1 to 1.3). Fewer people work on and live off the land, and yet more live in rural areas than ever before.

Many of these same forces which have changed the face of agriculture in most of the developed world have also contributed to making it possible and attractive for many individuals not involved in agriculture to make a living in rural areas, or simply to live in a rural setting. Improved accessibility has meant that people can live in rural areas but work in urban centres. Widespread mechanisation has reduced the need for

Figure 1.2. The reality of the rural landscape. Richborough Castle near Sandwich, Kent, with the towers of Richborough power station in the distance. (C.M. Hall)

labour, in some areas making properties available for other uses than for housing for rural workers (see Chapter Eight). Centralisation of functions has seen the decimation of services in many small rural communities, which, combined with a decreased permanent population, has meant that many villages could no longer function as a conventional residential settlement. These factors, coupled with a rise in demand for retirement, commuting and holiday or amenity properties in rural areas, have resulted in dramatic changes in the demographics and socio-economic composition of the population of many rural settlements throughout the developed world (Pahl, 1965).

These changes have been reflected in changes in ownership and management of many rural areas. The appearance of agribusinesses and the decline of the traditional family farm have meant major differences in the appearance and operation of farms, and hence the landscape of rural areas. The appearance of both large corporate and small individual ex-urban property owners has resulted in changes in attitudes towards not only the control of the rural landscape but also of access to it by non-property owners. In many locations what was once *de facto* widespread public access to rural land and water has now become a *de jure* issue of restriction, liability and litigation (see Chapter Eleven).

Thus at a time when demands on rural areas are not only becoming more complex and varied, but also increasing very rapidly, the resources and the opportunities to meet these demands are changing and often shrinking. It is against this backdrop of

Figure 1.3. Increased traffic, often from tourists, in many English villages, has led to damage to the very cottages which visitors regard as the essence of the village landscape. (C.M. Hall)

a rapidly changing rural environment that attention now shifts to a brief review of the development of recreation and tourism in rural areas and the way these uses have evolved.

Changing patterns of recreation and tourism in rural areas

Historical patterns

For many centuries the traditional image of leisure in the countryside was bipolar. The bulk of the population had little leisure time and was too busy with survival and production to place great demands for leisure on the rural environment. Leisure activities were generally confined to the mimicking of urban leisure in the rural settlements, with activities being focused on the church, the tavern, and the market. Holy days, fairs, and agricultural events, generally governed by the seasons, dominated most communities (Armitage, 1977). Travelling shows, coinciding with festivals and special events would be occasional highlights of the year. Otherwise leisure was home and family based and related to the social events of births, marriages and deaths. For many years harsh restrictions were applied to hunting or fishing by most rural residents and such activities were not part of the recreational pastimes of most of the rural populations.

There was, of course, a small minority of the population of most rural areas who had a vastly different pattern of leisure activities, and which set the fashion for subsequent generations. This was the landed gentry, the social and economic elite of the day. While in Europe this was mostly the aristocracy, in the New Worlds it also included military personnel (Wolfe, 1962), bureaucrats, and successful entrepreneurs. Almost irrespective of origins and lineage, however, this group utilised their own and neighbouring properties for a wide variety of recreational activities, many of which depended on carefully managed rural resources for their successful execution.

Hunting and fishing were some of the earliest of these activities, along with walking, riding, and lawn sports. Over the years, specific forms of these activities developed, and with them, unique landscapes. Deer hunting in medieval England saw the establishment of the deer parks on many estates, while fox hunting, perhaps the quintessential recreational activity of the rural landed elite, depended on a mix of agricultural and timbered land to which there was unlimited access, as well as a supply of foxes. The demands of specific forms of shooting, for example of red deer and grouse, saw the development of land management techniques which have not changed much in two centuries (Orr, 1982), while in other parts of the world such as Australia and New Zealand, species such as rabbit and deer were imported to provide similar opportunities for sport (Crosby, 1986).

In addition, from the time of the development of large urban centres, there has always been the use of rural areas for leisure by the urban elite, on a more temporary basis. Ranging from summer palaces of eastern potentates, a very few have consistently found rural settings highly attractive for ex-urban leisure diversions. Lack of easy accessibility, requirements of considerable wealth and time, and the ability to leave one's urban base of power and security for lengthy periods meant that the numbers of such individuals were always limited.

Democratisation and commercialisation of leisure

While a few landed estates were always maintained simply for leisure and escape from the urban setting at the appropriate time of the year or 'season' (Towner, 1996), many were part of working farms and estates, and the recreational activities were integrated to a high degree with the overall operation of the property. Changes in the nature and economics of agricultural and forestry operations, particularly in the last half century, have meant that many such estates have become uneconomic. Many have been broken up and subdivided, lands being sold to agribusinesses and properties to corporations, educational, health and other enterprises. Of those that remain, many have found that economic survival has been aided by an expansion of the recreational elements of the operations. Conversion of properties to hotel, health, sporting, retirement, and other leisure related accommodation purposes, and the use of the grounds for various activities (including golf, survival games, equestrian events, game parks and zoos, and theme parks) have proved the salvation of some estates. The commercialisation of what were personal leisure pastimes, such as shooting and fishing can provide lucrative alternatives to sheep farming and forestry (Cherry, 1993).

As a result of these changes, the old established pattern of large zealously guarded private islands of leisure in a sea of agriculture no longer exists to any degree, except perhaps in parts of Scotland. An ever increasing number of smaller, often commercial recreation areas dot the rural landscape, along with a vastly greater number of extremely small private individual leisure properties, normally centred on a residence, frequently a part-time one. As numbers of practising farmers in rural areas have declined, the numbers of practising recreational residents have increased.

This is not to suggest that elitism is now absent from rural areas. As Clarke and Little (1996) have pointed out, the predominant culture of the countryside is still based on traditional perceptions of what is or should be rural and preserved. Marginalised groups have little, if any, status with respect to policy formulation, landscape management or the provisions of recreational opportunity. It is fair to say that many of the current notions of rurality have been created and maintained to fit the preferences of those who own and use such rural areas (Murdoch and Marsden, 1994).

Recreation and tourism activities

One of the major elements of change in rural areas has been the changes within recreation and tourism. Until the last two decades or so, recreational and tourist activities in rural areas were mostly related closely to the rural character of the setting. They were primarily activities which were different to those activities engaged in urban centres, and one of the reasons for the difference was the setting in which they occurred. They could be characterised, at the risk of generalization, by the following terms: relaxing, passive, nostalgic, traditional, low technological, and mostly non-competitive. The list of activities included walking/rambling, picnicking, fishing, sightseeing, boating, visiting historical and cultural sites and festivals, horse-riding and nature and farm based visits.

Figure 1.4.   Cycle touring, Norway (C.M. Hall)

In the past two decades, while the above activities are still common and frequently practised in rural areas, there are many other activities now engaged in which are quite different. These could be characterised as: active, competitive, prestige or fashionable, highly technological, modern, individual, and fast. They include trail biking, off-road motor vehicle riding, orienteering, survival games, hang gliding, parasailing, jet boating, wind surfing, gentrification of properties, adventure tourism, snow skiing, 'hard' ecotourism, and fashionable shopping.

There is, therefore, a far wider range of leisure activities being engaged in within rural areas in many parts of the world (Figures 1.4 to 1.7). This pattern has brought with it a requirement for the establishment of specific facilities and settlements (resorts) to cater to the increasingly more sophisticated demands being placed on resources (see Chapters Five and Six). The simple traditional rural setting is no longer suitable for the highly specialised contemporary, perhaps postmodern, forms of recreation and tourism. Purpose built facilities, often only usable for a single activity are regarded as essential, thus placing new demands on the rural resource base and bringing with them the likelihood of new forms of impact and conflict.

Figure 1.5. Wilderness regulations, Indian Peaks Wilderness, Colorado (C.M. Hall)

Figure 1.6.   Gambling as a form of rural tourism development, Colorado (C.M. Hall)

Figure 1.7.   The selling of rurality, handicrafts shop, rural Ontario (C.M. Hall)

Conflicts

One of the features of rural areas in the last half century has been the difficulty of accommodating not only the structural changes which have occurred (see Chapter Three) but also the much greater range of uses to which the areas have been subjected. Conflicts have arisen not only between recreation and tourist uses and other forms of land use, but also between the various forms of recreation and tourism. Conflicts between motorised and non-motorised recreational users of the same area can be severe and often agreement and compromise is difficult to achieve, as can be seen with disagreements between cross-country skiers and snowmobilers, between non-mechanised trail users and off-road vehicle drivers, and between yachtspersons and water skiers. Conflicts also exist between non-mechanised users of the same facilities, as witnessed by conflict between pedestrian trail users and mountain-bike riders, between canoeists and anglers, and between ramblers and hikers and hunters.

Such conflicts can only be expected to become more severe as the overall demand from recreational and tourist use of rural areas increases, along with a widening of the range and types of uses. Compounding this problem is the one noted above, of decreasing public access to parts of the rural estate because of the changing pattern of ownership and, with it, an increasing reluctance of many landowners to accept traditional access to their property by the recreating public at large (see Chapter Eleven). Problems of liability, of property damage and vandalism, and of a loss of privacy are all factors involved in this changed attitude. As increasing numbers of urbanites acquire leisure or retirement properties in rural areas, they regard and treat those properties as private preserves, just as the landed elite zealously guarded their own leisure estates centuries before.

As well, agribusinesses, adopting a corporate outlook, are also less likely to accept informal and unpaid access to their lands by the public for recreation than was the traditional farming landowner, who probably had to deal with far fewer, and less impacting visitors. In addition, the landscapes produced by many agribusinesses do not lend themselves as suitable for leisure activities as did traditional mixed farming, neither from an aesthetic nor a functional viewpoint (see Chapter Seven).

Changing image of rural areas for leisure

Not all new forms of agriculture provide no opportunity for leisure pursuits, but the activities provided may be different and not meet the demands of many participants. The growth of wineries has seen the development of a new form of landscape to many rural areas which has a high tourist potential (Chapter Twelve), but in a passive rather than an active form. The increasing opportunities for visitors to pick their own produce have provided other forms of attractions encouraging urbanites to visit rural areas and combine a range of activities with shopping. As Hopkins points out (Chapter Nine), many rural areas are now changing their image and aggressively marketing aspects of their rural heritage, authentic or otherwise, to would-be urban purchasers. A similar pattern can be seen in the marketing of rural festivals (Chapter Ten) and the farm image (Chapter Thirteen).

Increasingly rural areas and the governments which control and serve them have come to realise the economic benefits which can accrue to rural areas from tourism and recreation development (Chapter Fourteen). It is ironic that after many years of neglect, tourism and recreation have quickly become seen as major agents of economic redevelopment for rural and other areas. Government policies at all levels have begun to appear in recent years in efforts to increase access to rural areas for urban and rural residents, coupled with a realisation that some reallocation of wealth can also occur through such activity (Chapter Four).

The importance of the image of rural areas has only recently been appreciated, and major efforts have been made in a variety of settings to deliberately improve, establish and change the allure of rural areas through the creation and recreation of specific images (Chapters Seven and Eight). As Dewailly points out (Chapter Eight) not all of these images are authentic or correct, but many of them are effective and accepted, and in a highly competitive environment truth in advertising is not always maintained. The fact remains that the overall image of rural areas is a very positive one in most of the developed world. Rurality may be a myth in the terms that many people regard it, a peculiar blending of nostalgia, wholesomeness, heritage, nature and culture, combining the romantic combination of man and nature working in harmony, captured on calendars and Christmas cards throughout the developed world, but it is a powerful myth that has created a demand for access to, and in some cases, acquisition of parts of the rural landscape. The icons of rural areas range from fruit and sausages (Chapter Five) to squirrels and kitchens (Chapter Nine) and a range of ethnic activities (Chapter Ten), but almost all represent a combination of rural people and the landscape and its elements. Given the rate and extent of change in that landscape throughout the developed world, it is highly questionable whether that landscape can live up to its image for much longer.

Conclusions

Several major themes run through the above discussion. The key one is change, and as has been shown, both the rural landscape and the activities which take place there have changed and are changing at a rapid rate and on an extensive scale. The processes driving these changes are global in scale and relate to societal and economic forces. While there are an infinite range of local variations, the overall effects have been similar in all rural areas. Most of these changes show few signs of ceasing, and as the population at large increases in affluence, mobility and the amount of leisure time it has available, the recreation and tourism demands on rural areas and the changes they bring about can be expected to continue.

A second important theme is the relationship between the leisure use of rural areas and the other, often more traditional, uses of those areas. The old established patterns of recreation and tourism in rural areas were relatively complementary, or at least not in conflict with traditional activities. The newer forms of recreation and tourism are less complementary and in many cases highly competitive, not only with other forms of land use but with other forms of recreation and tourism, thus increasing the potential for conflict in rural areas. While a century and a half ago the urban park movement was striving to bring the countryside in the form of large natural parks into the city for the welfare of the residents, now increasingly, large leisure developments are taking place in rural areas, also for the welfare of the urban residents. Many rural areas are the scene of recreation and tourist activities not because of their rural attributes, but simply because such activities cannot take place within urban areas because of lack of space. In such instances, rural areas have become a location and a backdrop for the activities, rather than a key setting.

Finally, there is the response of residents of rural areas to the growth in demand for recreation and tourism in those areas. In some cases this has been positive, as expressed in the establishment of festivals, of other attractions, of the provision of accommodation on farms, and the conversion of facilities for leisure functions. Resorts and facilities have been developed, sporting facilities have been improved and created, landscapes and communities enhanced aesthetically, cultural facilities restored and interpreted, and natural features protected. On the other hand, an increasing trend towards agribusiness, corporate farming and forestry, institutional ownership of land, and the growth in numbers of retirement and leisure homes in rural areas have resulted in the denial of access for the public to a greater number of resources and the privatisation of an increasing proportion of the rural landscape.

The future of recreation and tourism in rural areas depends heavily upon the successful integration of the traditional and the new forms of leisure with the traditional and new forms of other economic activities in these areas. To make recreation and tourism sustainable in rural areas over the long term (Chapter Fifteen) will require negotiation, compromise, and a willingness of all parties to participate in dialogue on future directions and emphasis. Solutions to potential conflicts and problems will need to reflect local conditions and preferences as well as the overall global trends noted above.

References

Armitage, J., 1977, *Man at play*, Frederick Warne, London

Bowler, I., Bryant, C. and Nellis, M., eds., 1992, *Contemporary rural systems in transition*, 2 Vols., CAB Press, London

Burton, T.L. and Jackson, E.L., eds., 1989, *Understanding recreation and leisure*, State College PA: Venture Publisher

Cherry, G.E., 1993, Changing social attitudes towards leisure and the countryside 1890–1990. In *Leisure and the Environment*, S. Glyptis, ed., Belhaven Press, London, pp. 22–33

Clarke, P. and Little, J., 1996, *Contested countryside cultures*, Routledge, London

Cloke, P., 1993, The countryside as commodity: new spaces for rural leisure. In *Leisure and the Environment*, S. Glyptis, ed., Belhaven Press, London, pp. 53–70

Crosby, A.W., 1986, *Ecological imperialism: the biological expansion of Europe, 900–1900*, Cambridge University Press, Cambridge

Hall, C.M., 1995, *Introduction to tourism in Australia: impacts, planning and development*, Longman Australia, South Melbourne

Ilbery, R., ed., 1997, *The geography of rural change*, Longman, London

Murdoch, J. and Marsden, T., 1994, *Reconstituting rurality: class, community and power in the development process*, U.C.L. Press, London

Orr, W., 1982, *Deer forests, landlords and crofters: the Western Highlands in Victorian and Edwardian times*, John Donald, Edinburgh

Pahl, R.E., 1965, *Urbs in rure*, Weidenfeld and Nicolson, London

Towner, J., 1996, *An historical geography of recreation and tourism in the western world 1540–1940*, John Wiley, Chichester

Wolfe, R.I., 1962, The summer resorts of Ontario in the nineteenth century, *Ontario History*, **54** (3): 149–160

World Tourism Organisation (WTO) 1996, Rural tourism to the rescue of Europe's countryside, *WTO News*, **3**, August/September: 6–7

Part Two:
Tourism and Recreation Policy Dimensions

2 The policy dimensions of rural tourism and recreation

C. MICHAEL HALL AND JOHN M. JENKINS

Introduction

Tourism and recreation offer many prospects for rural areas. They are geographically widespread, offering employment and income opportunities, often repeatedly utilising the same resources, and possessing the potential to conserve rather than destroy assets. In addition, other industries (e.g., aviation and transport, entertainment, construction, agriculture, horticulture, and manufacturing) benefit from tourism and recreation. Nevertheless, inevitably, there are and will continue to be contested opinions on what is desirable in recreation and tourism development in specific rural places (Bramwell, 1994, p. 5).

The purpose of this chapter is to present an overview of the rationale for government intervention in rural recreation and tourism, and thus reasons for the development of associated public policies. A key theme underpinning the discussion in this chapter is that rural areas are economically, physically, socially and politically diverse, and suffer from varying interpretations and a lack of integrated planning and policy-making. As Pearce (1989, p. 77) noted: 'Tourist development in rural regions is characterized by a multiplicity of small-scale, independent developers and diffuse developments'. The discussion also notes: (1) the lack of attention to tourism and recreation in rural areas as far as research programs and government policies and action have been concerned; (2) the lack of understanding of the institutional arrangements and policy instruments most suitable for rural tourism development; and (3) the frequent failure of the public and private sectors to tackle the problem of integrating tourism activities with the more traditional uses of rural areas and with other policy initiatives.

Government intervention in rural recreation and tourism

The basis for government intervention in rural tourism and recreation lies within the philosophical and ideological debate as to the appropriate role of government and the state in society (Hall, 1994a; Hall and Jenkins, 1995). Within the former state socialist countries of Eastern Europe, and the Asia state socialist countries of North Korea and, to a lesser extent, China and Vietnam, the state has supremacy over the economy and the lives of individuals who make up the state. Government not only decided when people could go on holiday but, also, for how long and where. In this context, government not only significantly influenced people's travel decisions but also supplied much of the tourist experience through, for example, the provision of cheap worker and union rural holiday resorts as existed throughout Eastern Europe (Hall, 1991). However, with the end of the Cold War and the demise of state socialism, such centrally-planned approaches to economic and social development and, therefore, tourism development, are less numerous and significant in global terms. Thus, in an increasing number of instances, rationales for government involvement in rural tourism and recreation should be examined with reference to the appropriate role of government in market-driven economies.

Within Western society, considerable debate has emerged in the past two decades over the appropriate role of the state in society. Throughout most of the 1980s and the early 1990s, 'Thatcherism' (named after Conservative Prime Minister Margaret Thatcher) in the United Kingdom and 'Reaganism' (named after Republican President Ronald Reagan) in the United States, saw a period of retreat by central government from active intervention. At the national level, policies of deregulation, privatisation, free-trade, the elimination of tax incentives, and a move away from discretionary forms of macro-economic intervention, were and have been the hallmarks of a push towards 'smaller' government and lower levels of government intervention.

As noted above, tourism is not immune from changes in political philosophy. Tourism is subject to direct and indirect government intervention often because of its employment and income producing possibilities and therefore its potential to diversify and contribute to rural economies. Given calls for smaller government in Western society in recent years, there have been increasing demands from conservative national governments and economic rationalists in the public and private sectors for greater industry self-sufficiency in tourism marketing and promotion, often through the privatisation or corporatisation of tourism agencies or boards (Jeffries, 1989). The implications of such an approach for the tourism industry are substantial. As Hughes (1984, p. 14) noted with respect to tourism in the United Kingdom, 'The advocates of a free enterprise economy would look to consumer freedom of choice and not to governments to promote firms; the consumer ought to be sovereign in decisions relating to the allocation of the nation's resources'. Such sentiments are far away from ideas of the role of the state in tourism espoused by the International Union of Official Travel Organizations (IUOTO), the forerunner to the World Tourism Organization (WTO), who, in the 1970s, argued that tourism was such an important sector that in order to foster and develop tourism

> on a scale proportionate to its national importance and to mobilize all resources to that end, it is necessary to centralize the policy-making powers in the hands of the state so that it can take appropriate measures for creating a suitable framework for the promotion and development of tourism by the various sectors concerned (IUOTO, 1974, p. 71).

Over 20 years later, the comments of IUOTO are far removed from contemporary debates concerning the role of the state and government in tourism.

The doyens of free-market economics, Friedman and Friedman (1979, in Veal,

1994, p. 32), advocate three essential duties of government espoused by the economist Adam Smith:

> ... first, the duty of protecting the society from the violence and invasion of other independent societies; secondly, the duty of protecting, as far as possible, every member of the society from the injustice or oppression of every other member of it, or the duty of establishing an exact administration of justice; and, thirdly, the duty of erecting and maintaining certain public works and certain public institutions, which it can never be for the interest of any individual, or small number of individuals, to erect and maintain; because the profit could never repay the expense to any individual or small number of individuals, though it may frequently do much more than repay it to a great society.

A fourth duty recognised explicitly by Friedman and Friedman is 'the duty to protect members of the community who cannot be regarded as "responsible" individuals' (1979, in Veal, 1994, p. 32). Less technical reasons for intervention, include: equity, economic management and development, tradition, and incidental enterprise (Lipsey *et al.*, 1985; Veal, 1994; Hall and Jenkins, 1995).

Much intervention in tourism and other public policy arenas (e.g. education, health and welfare) is related to market failure, market imperfection and social need. The market method of deciding who gets what and how is not always adequate, and therefore government often changes the distribution of income and wealth by measures that work within the price system. Across the globe almost every industry has been supported at various times by subsidies, the imposition of tariff regulations, taxation concessions, direct grants and other forms of government intervention, all of which serve to affect the price of goods and services and therefore influence the distribution of income, production and wealth. The size or economic importance of the tourism industry, so commonly emphasised by the public and private sector sectors (e.g., World Tourism Organization, 1996), is no justification in itself for government intervention; within market-driven economies justification must lie in some aspect of: (i) market failure; (ii) market imperfection; or (iii) public/social concerns about market outcomes. In other words, 'implicit in each justification for political action is the view that government offers a corrective alternative to the market' (Hula, 1988, p. 6).

Market failure takes many forms. For instance, the market often fails to protect adequately the environment on which much of the tourist industry depends for its survival. One would expect that a business or industry that receives income from environmental quality would largely maintain that quality. However, there is a real risk that, where several businesses rely on the same environmental space or where others are competing for resources, that the 'tragedy of the commons' (Hardin, 1968) – the inability of individuals or the private sector on many occasions to come together to coordinate a strategy to protect (or enhance) the environment because they regard it as a 'free' resource to which their own individual activities do little harm – will emerge. This arises for such reasons as the inclination of businesses to free-load on the activities of others, and the difficulty in getting private interests to pool their resources. In addition, business is rarely interested in long-term social and environmental need as opposed to short-term revenue and profits, and yet tourism development may impact adversely on some sections of the community to the extent that government has to step in to rectify the problem. Infrastructure supply is another avenue for market failure, market imperfection or social need. This is illustrated in the manner in which governments in many parts of the world usually find themselves as the main providers and managers of roads, airports, railways, power supply, sewage and water supply, although increasingly infrastructure is being provided by way of public-private sector partnerships or statutory or corporate authorities in which government is a major shareholder.

Market imperfections can be found in areas where the market does not cater to the needs of individual citizens. In many countries, government, in consultation with industry, unions and other interests, has established equal employment opportunity legislation, anti-discrimination legislation, occupational health and safety practices, minimum wage structures, the provision of facilities for disabled people, and other workplace and social/cultural arrangements. Public consensus may also deem that a particular market outcome is unacceptable. A prime example is social welfare policy because there is usually a political consensus that aid ought to be targeted to those who are unable to compete in the market (see Hula, 1988).

Tourism, like any other industry, has problems which stem from market failures and imperfections and from subsequent government responses. However, as an industry, tourism is poorly understood, as are its various impacts. Hard to define, tourism is consequently beset by problems of analysis, monitoring, coordination and policy-making. Moreover, until recently, tourism research (Faulkner, 1991), and notably tourism public policy (Hall and Jenkins, 1995), has been a low priority, with the tourism industry more often concerned with promotion and short-term returns than strategic investment and sustainability. The major focus of the tourism industry and even government tourism agency research has therefore been on understanding the market and the means by which potential consumers can be persuaded to buy tourism products. Understanding of (1) the dynamics of the tourism destination system in terms of the most appropriate set of supply-side linkages to maximise the returns from visitor expenditure, (2) the long-term effects of tourism on the socio-cultural and physical environment, and (3) the relationship of tourism to other industries, is minimal. In site-specific instances, such issues are frequently ignored.

All these factors mitigate tourism in some degree. When market failure, market imperfections or public concerns are raised, there is, then, of course, not only the problem of identifying which level of government should intervene but also the problem of determining the nature of intervention. Moreover, as cynicism toward government decisions and actions has increased in western societies in recent years, the utility of much government corrective action, at all levels, has also been questioned, particularly as governments often seem to find it increasingly difficult to make consensus decisions which satisfy the wide range of interests in policy matters (e.g., Hula, 1988; Hall and Jenkins, 1995). As governments seek to address these problems, the following questions should be addressed:

- are the returns from public assistance greater than the cost?
- is there an alternative source of private sector assistance that could be delivered at less cost to the community or with better returns?
- is it possible that public assistance will generate negative effects (e.g., the moral hazard whereby the industry becomes lazy and sits back waiting for assistance

from external sources and in particular the public sector)? There is, for instance, an expectation in the industry that national, regional or local governments will fund a considerable component of international and intranational marketing and promotion (e.g., see Craik, 1991; Jenkins, 1993b);

- what are the opportunity costs of public assistance (i.e. could the money be better spent on investments other than tourism)?; and
- is there detailed and widespread understanding of tourism planning and development issues and problems?

Given the downturns in rural economies over the past three decades, it is perhaps understandable that much government attention has been given to the economic benefits of tourism, particularly in those rural areas struggling to keep pace with and adapt to the vagaries of a globalised economy. Tourism development has therefore received increasing recognition as a regional and national economic development tool over this period. In Japan, long held as a model economy for many of the developed nations of the West, the countryside has suffered from rural outmigration. As a result, 'It is the policy of the national and regional governments as well as business to hold the line on population loss by replacing the declining industries – forestry, farming and fishing – with rural tourism' (Graburn, 1995, p. 57).

Government intervention in tourism and recreation is widespread. In particular, tourism is being promoted as a source of rural economic growth and employment generation at all levels of government in developed nations (e.g., Australia, Canada, the European Union, New Zealand, the United Kingdom and the United States) (Cabinet Office, 1985; Williams and Shaw, 1988; Hall and Jenkins, 1995; LEADER, 1995), the former state socialist countries of Eastern Europe (Hall, 1991), less developed countries (e.g., Kenya, Cuba and Sri Lanka) (Harrison, 1992), and the Pacific region generally (Hall, 1994b; Hall and Page, 1996). For example, the opening line of the Albertan tourism policy in the mid-1980s stated: 'As a lead player in the provincial economy, Tourism means jobs, commercial stability and economic diversity' (Government of Alberta, 1985, p. 1). The Australian Commonwealth Department of Tourism (1994, p. 2) argued: 'Tourism creates jobs, stimulates regional development and diversifies the regional economic base. With the decline in many traditional industries in rural and regional areas, tourism offers an opportunity to revitalise regional Australia and spread the social benefits of tourism'. Similarly, according to the Rural Tourism Theme Group of the Finnish Rural Policy Committee:

> Rural tourism is a means of exploiting the resources of the countryside in an all-round manner in order to create exportable products. By increasing development efforts both quantitatively and qualitatively, rural tourism can be made into a substantial source of employment and income throughout the Finnish country-side. The goal is to double the rate of utilisation of accommodation capacity and to increase turnover in the sector ten-fold by the year 2005. By then, employment in the sector would correspond to around 5,000 person years (Rural Tourism Policy in Finland, 1996).

However, there is a longstanding, widespread, but erroneous, perception that tourism offers salvation from local economic crises (e.g., Clout, 1972). Indeed, optimism over the potential employment and economic benefits of tourism 'owes much to a policy climate that has been uncritical over a range of issues' (Hudson and Townsend, 1992, p. 50). This is not surprising because few strong theories, concepts or studies exist to guide the development, role and management of tourism in rural areas (Butler and Clark, 1992; Jenkins, 1993b). Nevertheless, cautionary comments regarding tourism development in rural areas have existed for almost as long as government has promoted rural tourism development. For example, as Baum and Moore observed in the United States in the 1960s:

> ... there are and there will be increasing opportunities for recreation [and tourism] development, but this industry should not be considered to be a panacea for the longstanding problems of substantial and persistent unemployment and under-employment besetting low-income rural areas... The successful development of a particular recreational [and tourism] enterprise or complex of enterprises requires the same economic considerations as the planning and development of economic activities in other sectors (Baum and Moore, 1966, p. 5).

And, as the Canadian Council on Rural Development (1975, p. 5) reported:

> Tourism and recreation demands for rural resources can provide income and employment opportunities for rural people and therefore assist in a 'stay' option for those who prefer rural living. The supply and demand relationship however remains a controlling factor underlining that tourism and recreation are not a panacea to the economic problems of depressed areas but that they can be an important supplement to existing economic activities...benefits are likely to accrue only to those with the necessary imagination, managerial skills and financial capability. Other factors identified which determine the degree to which rural communities can be expected to benefit from tourism and recreation are: the diversity of recreational facilities available; accessibility to markets; and the retainment locally of tourist expenditures.

The formulation and implementation of rural tourism and recreation public policies present several conundrums. Unrealistic expectations of tourism's potential are unfortunately combined with ignorance or wilful neglect by decision-makers of the potentially adverse economic, environmental and social consequences of tourist development that threaten to curtail its benefits. Yet, as Duffield and Long (1981, p. 409) observed, 'Ironically, the very consequences of lack of development, the unspoilt character of the landscape and distinctive local cultures, become positive resources as far as tourism is concerned'.

Rural tourism and recreation are now invariably subject to government intervention. That intervention can restrict, create or maintain (at times simulta-neously because government policies across sectors are not always coordinated or complementary) rural tourism and recreation opportunities. The actual extent of government intervention in rural tourism will vary from country to country and within nation states according to various conditions and circumstances peculiar to each country and region (e.g., politico-economic-constitutional system, socio-economic development, degree of tourism development). Tourism and recreation are ultimately located according to such factors as inherent locational features, the number and spatial distribution of attractions and their accessibility, but governments and developers exert some control over development processes through, for example, decisions to build or not to build infrastructure. Several important and explicit reasons as to why governments may care to intervene in rural tourism and recreation specifically may be identified:

- the political and organisational aspects of leisure behaviour, recreational choice, access and participation, and tourism planning and development;
- the economic significance of rural recreation and tourism as emphasised in government publications. Rural tourism policies are often formulated and implemented with a view to creating jobs, diversifying the economic base, and facilitating greater economic activity generally;
- the broader socio-cultural goals of government policy – better quality of life for rural residents, health and fitness, personal and professional attainment and education (e.g., training programs; increasing environmental awareness), and equity in access to recreational resources (including private lands);
- the protection of attractive areas;
- environmental conservation and pollution control;
- infrastructure investments and development;
- the development of tourist services; and
- the marketing and promotion of tourism (e.g., Greffe, 1994; Bramwell and Lane, 1994; Hall, Jenkins and Kearsley, 1997).

Broader concerns are related to whether to implement policies on a sectoral or a spatial basis.

Thus there is a substantial range of important domestically driven reasons for government intervention in rural tourism and recreation. However, many of the problems and opportunities associated with rural recreation and tourism have an international and therefore multidimensional (including multi-cultural) character. The factors which affect rural tourism and recreation planning and policy-making cannot be understood by focusing solely on the level of the nation-state. Some account must be taken of the globalisation of economies, and the concomitant changing trade-relations in the world-economy and power shifts within the system of national states (see Chapter Three). For example, within the global economy the sub-national or local state is becoming increasingly important and has led to the recognition that places and regions are in competition with one another for global capital and the consequent capacity to generate employment and economic growth (see Chapter Three). Accounts of the development of rural regions which explicitly recognise local to global contexts and issues:

- add to knowledge of political, social, technological and economic developments within and among nation-states;
- provide a more comprehensive picture of why rural areas are in such a state of flux and the decisions and actions taken with respect to their economic, physical and social development; and
- are more likely to provide understanding for integrating tourism planning and development with local, regional and national planning schemes.

Further complicating the global, national and local dimensions are the different agencies, and even sections and cultures within agencies, whose value sets, and therefore agendas and priorities, differ (Pearce, 1992; Hall and Jenkins, 1995). The following section discusses the extent and nature of government involvement in rural tourism and recreation planning and policy-making.

The policy dimensions of rural recreation and tourism

While the direct interest of government in rural tourism is a relatively recent phenomenon, many rural recreation areas were established long ago as governments intervened by developing policies and programs for land and water management, and by providing human and financial resources to manage associated natural resources. Of particular note were the establishment of national parks, the reservation of public lands, the protection of coastal lands and waterways, and other valuable conservation and recreational assets. In contrast to such public assets, private land ownership generally conveys special privileges to landowners and developers (e.g., restrictions on recreational access) (see Chapter Eleven).

Government intervention in rural recreation and tourism was initiated for different reasons in different countries, though some common elements may be noted. For instance, in the United Kingdom and some parts of mainland Europe, tourism has played a role in the countryside for several centuries (Butler and Clark, 1992). In Australia, Canada, New Zealand and the United States, the establishment of national and state/provincial parks for recreational and tourism opportunities and the protection and maintenance of representative environments came about in the nineteenth century. Interestingly, the first national parks in all four countries were set aside for conservation and recreation purposes because the land was worthless for such rural activities as intensive agriculture, lumber, mining and grazing. National parks were therefore seen as a mechanism for rural economic development through tourism, with the development process usually occuring with the government working in partnership with railroad companies who used natural images in their advertising to help promote visitation to the newly established national parks (Hall, 1992).

Following the Second World War, rapid urbanisation and greater personal mobility through increased car ownership led to further demands from urbanites for increased access to rural recreational resources. Subsequently, as governments throughout the western world established more national and recreational parks, they gradually provided easier access and a greater number of recreational facilities to the extent that such parks are perhaps now an even more integral element in the images presented by promotional agencies in numerous countries and regions.

More generally, the economic, physical and social environments of rural areas around the globe have undergone dramatic changes. Institutional, socio-economic and technological forces, together and separately, have clearly had a significant influence on the emergence of recreation and tourism patterns in the developed world. Therefore, primarily because of pressures from outside of rural areas, recreation and tourism are becoming increasingly important economic, environmental and social elements of rural regions and communities. Growth in rural recreation and tourism, and escalating pressures on resources stemming from these forces have necessitated closer examination of planning, development and management of the recreational and tourist resource bases of countries and regions. However, as noted above, such pressures are only poorly understood by policy-makers. According to Craik (1991, p. 8), many

> governments are embracing tourism as the industry of the future and hoping that the benefits will outweigh the costs. The reality is that, as tourism becomes part of

more local, regional and national economic strategies, the range and degree of impacts is increasing... Inevitably, changes attributable to – or coinciding with – tourist development are becoming more intense and increasing in scope. Over time, this phenomenon transforms the amenity, culture and lifestyle of destinations.

The increasing demand for rural recreation and tourism, and the social and institutional forces leading to greater rural recreation opportunities are well documented. Rural recreation has been dealt with at length by several authors, particularly since the 1970s (Groome, 1993), with a limited, and at times implicit, tourism focus (Patmore, 1983; Lavery, 1974; Coppock and Duffield, 1975; Pigram, 1983; Glyptis, 1992). There is considerable evidence that more and more people in Western industrialised nations are visiting and appreciating rural areas (e.g., Patmore, 1983; Pigram, 1983; Butler and Clark, 1992; Commonwealth Department of Tourism, 1994), and that many more people are ready to use it as a recreation resource if it is accessible. However, as many people utilise rural areas for recreational activities, competition between resource users and economic, physical and social impacts on the rural environment are inevitable. Nevertheless, as Hudson and Townsend (1992, pp. 52–53) observed:

> Non-tourist activities that are incompatible with one type of tourism may be perfectly compatible with another. Thus, the broader question of the relations between tourism and other economic activities could be related to segmentation of the tourist market and to policy choices to develop one sort of tourism rather than another. Exploring possible combinations of activities, relative to the specific attributes of particular places, could identify windows of opportunity to which local authority policies might respond in formulating an overall programme for local economic development and employment.

Moreover, balance of payments anomalies, public goods and notional prices, environmental impacts and their associated costs, notional costs, the opportunity costs of allocating or redistributing resources to tourism, social impacts (e.g., crime and social dislocation), international capital flows, overseas borrowings on capital, foreign ownership and the offshore distribution of domestic/local profits, all serve to impact on the tourism industry's regional contribution (e.g., Bull, 1995), but many of these factors are not widely reported in the popular press or in government publications. In many cases, tourism's net benefit/cost to national and regional economies is far from clear.

In the United States, for example, 'there has been growing concern about rural economic problems, and a survey in 1991 of state tourism agencies there found that 60 per cent had made increased efforts in rural tourism and 30 of 50 states had tourism programs specifically targeted for rural areas' (Luloff et al., 1994, in Bramwell, 1994, p. 2). This is not surprising. Over 70 per cent of all United States citizens recreate in rural areas, while figures for other countries reveal similar, if not slightly smaller, participation rates (Lane, 1994, p. 8). Enjoyment of the countryside in the United Kingdom 'has become a mass activity with over 900 million day visits to the countryside (including the coast) in 1993...and an estimated 84 per cent of the population participating in at least one countryside activity per annum' (Bishop, 1996, p. 254). Moreover, and perhaps 'Most important of all, tourism has developed away from spectacularly scenic areas into countryside of all types. It has broken free

of large and specialised resorts into small towns and villages to become truly rural'
(Bramwell, 1990, in Lane, 1994, p. 8). Nevertheless, a critical mass of recreational
activity in a region may be lacking. 'Most rural communities are too small or too
remotely located and have too few resources to create this all too important critical
mass of recreational activity on their own' (Subcommittee on Procurement, Taxation
and Tourism of the Committee on Small Business, House of Representatives, 1993,
p. 15).

The role of tourism and recreation in rural regional development is a complex and
pressing issue. However, management decisions for the allocation of related outdoor
recreation resources are seldom guided by strategic policy frameworks. Decisions are
typically made in a reactive manner in response to various pressures from groups
competing for the same resource or lobbying for different management of a
particular resource (Bryan and Taylor, 1991). Even in Europe, where rural tourism
has been increasingly promoted over the last decade as an important mechanism for
regional economic development and European integration, substantial problems
have emerged with respect to policy formulation and implementation. For example,
according to the LEADER II rural development program (discussed in more detail
in Chapter Three):

> Unfortunately, there are numerous instances, particularly in Mediterranean
> Europe, where over-estimation of the contribution which tourism can make to the
> process of local development has led to stagnation, regression and even total loss
> of profitability of local tourism and its authenticity. This over-estimation leads to
> excessive creation of tourist accommodation, speculation by local people and
> outsiders, environmental degradation and the deadening of the human element
> and the personal touch which are features most sought after by real rural tourism
> enthusiasts.
>
> This over-estimation of tourism potential is often aggravated by a lack of the
> appropriate institutions at local level, the reckless and headlong rush to make a
> profit, a level of vocational training and management well below the requirements
> of a quality tourism services, on both individual and collective levels (this is
> particularly true of areas 'deep in the country' in Southern Europe). On top of
> this, there is a lack of planning and tangible objectives. All of these factors
> [weaken] this development model and all are possible causes of failure, even in
> areas with numerous natural and cultural assets (LEADER, 1995).

Tourism and rural development: policy foci

Tourism is widely regarded as a tool in rural development. This implies the selective
expansion of tourist flows designed to achieve one or more of the following goals:

• to sustain and create local incomes, employment and growth;
• to contribute to the costs of providing economic and social infrastructure (e.g.,
  roads, water, sewage and communication);
• to encourage the development of other industrial sectors (e.g., through local
  purchasing links);
• to contribute to local resident amenities (e.g., sports and recreation facilities,
  outdoor recreation opportunities, and arts and culture) and services (e.g., shops,
  post offices, schools, and public transport); and

- to contribute to the conservation of environmental and cultural resources, especially as scenic (aesthetic) urban and rural surroundings are primary tourist attractions.

Government has a variety of policy instruments to try and achieve these goals. Policy instruments are government actions which influence the behaviour of economic agents by providing incentives, usually financial, for appropriate behaviour and activities, and disencentives for inappropriate behaviour and activities. Examples of policy instruments for rural tourism development are illustrated in Table 2.1.

Five different categories of policy instruments are identified, although several instruments could fall into more than one category (see Jacobs, 1993, and Roseland, 1996, for the application of similar categories in the area of sustainable development):

- regulatory instruments – regulations, permits and licenses that have a legal basis and which require monitoring and enforcement;
- voluntary instruments – actions or mechanisms that do not require expenditure;
- expenditure – direct government expenditure to achieve policy outcomes;
- financial incentives – including taxes, subsidies, grants and loans, which are incentives to undertake certain activities or behaviours and which tend to require minimal enforcement; and
- non-intervention – where government deliberately avoids intervention in order to achieve its policy objectives.

Government, at all levels, therefore has a substantial number of instruments available to achieve desired policy outcomes. However, while the goals of rural tourism development are fairly clear at the regional level, little research has been conducted on the most appropriate policy mix to achieve such objectives and there is often minimal monitoring and evaluation of policy measures (Hall and Jenkins, 1995; Hall, Jenkins and Kearsley, 1997). As a component of regional planning, rural tourism, where it is championed, should simultaneously:

- stimulate local business;
- create employment opportunities;
- be a recognised and understood factor in regional social and economic development;
- be clearly positioned in terms of its contribution to the various components of regional development; and
- be identified as a means of developing regional infrastructure, facilities and services; including recreational facilities that can be used by rural residents and tourists.

Unfortunately, the latter receives very scant attention save for a limited number of studies (e.g., Clark, 1988; Craik, 1991). Furthermore, relatively little is known about the most appropriate set of institutional arrangements to achieve the goals of rural tourism development. Institutional arrangements for rural recreation and tourism may be extremely complex, especially when they seek to integrate national, regional and local concerns (e.g., see the discussion of the European Union rural development

Table 2.1 Rural tourism development policy instruments

Categories	Instruments	Examples
Regulatory instruments	1. Laws	Planning laws can give considerable power to government to encourage particular types of rural tourism development through, for example, land use zoning
	2. Licences, permits and standards	Regulatory instruments can be used for a wide variety of purposes especially at local government level, e.g., they may set materials standards for tourism developments, or they can be used to set architectural standards for heritage streetscapes or properties
	3. Tradeable permits	Often used in the Unites States to limit resource use or pollution. However, the instrument requires effective monitoring for it to work
	4. Quid pro quos	Government may require businesses to do something in exchange for certain rights, e.g., land may be given to a developer below market rates if the development is of a particular type or design
Voluntary instruments	1. Information	Expenditure on educating the local public, businesses or tourists to achieve specific goals, e.g., appropriate recreational behaviour
	2. Volunteer associations and non-governmental organisations	Government support of community tourism organisations is very common in tourism. Support may come from direct grants and/or by provision of office facilities. Examples of this type of development include local or regional tourist organisations, heritage conservation groups, mainstreet groups, tour guide programs, or helping to establish a local farmstay or homestay association
	3. Technical assistance	Government can provide technical assistance and information to businesses with regard to planning and development requirements
Expenditure	1. Expenditure and contracting	This is a common method for government to achieve policy objectives as government can spend money directly on specific activities, this may include the development of infrastructure, such as roading, or it may include mainstreet beautification programs. Contracting can be used as a means of supporting existing local businesses or encouraging new ones
	2. Investment or procurement	Investment may be directed into specific businesses or projects, while procurement can be used to help provide businesses with a secure customer for their products

3. Public enterprise	When the market fails to provide desired outcomes, governments may create their own businesses, e.g., rural or regional development corporations or enterprise boards. If successful, such businesses may then be sold off to the private sector
4. Public–private partnerships	Government may enter into partnership with the private sector in order to develop certain products or regions. These may take the form of a corporation which has a specific mandate to attract business to a certain area for example
5. Monitoring and evaluation	Government may allocate financial resources to monitor rural economic, environmental and socio-economic indicators. Such measures may not only be valuable to government to evaluate the effectiveness and efficiency of rural tourism development objectives but can also be a valuable source of information to the private sector as well
6. Promotion	Government may spend money on promoting a region to visitors either with or without financial input from the private sector. Such promotional activities may allow individual businesses to reallocate their own budgets by reducing expenditures that might have made on promotion
Financial incentives	
1. Pricing	Pricing measures may be used to encourage appropriate behaviour or to stimulate demand, e.g., use of particular walking trails, lower camping or permit costs
2. Taxes and charges	Governments may use these to encourage appropriate behaviours by both individuals and businesses, i.e., pollution charges. Taxes and charges may also be used to help fund infrastructure development, e.g., regional airports
3. Grants and loans	Seeding money may be provided to businesses to encourage product development or to encourage the retention of heritage and landscape features
4. Subsidies and tax incentives	Although subsidies are often regarded as creating inefficiencies in markets they may also be used to encourage certain types of behaviour with respect to social and environmental externalities, e.g., heritage and landscape conservation, that are not taken into account by conventional economics
5. Rebates, rewards and surety bonds	Rebates and rewards are a form of financial incentive to encourage individuals and businesses to act in certain ways. Similarly, surety bonds can be used to ensure that businesses act in agreed ways, if they don't then the government will spend the money for the same purpose.

Table 2.1 *cont.*

Categories	Instruments	Examples
	6. Vouchers	Vouchers are a mechanism to affect consumer behaviour by providing a discount on a specific product or activity, e.g., to shop in a rural centre
Non-intervention	1. Non-intervention (deliberate)	Government deciding not to directly intervene in sectoral or regional development is also a policy instrument, in that public policy is what government decides to do and not do. In some cases the situation may be such that government may decide that policy objectives are being met so that their intervention may not add any net value to the rural development process and that resources could be better spent elsewhere

project, LEADER, in Chapter Three). For example, in the western United States, federal lands are an important tourism and recreational resource. At the 1992 Interagency Conference on Tourism on Federal Lands, the Bureau of Land Management, Bureau of Reclamation, Fish and Wildlife Service, National Park Service, Forest Service, Department of Army, and the United States Travel and Tourism Administration (which has now been abolished), signed a Memorandum of Understanding (MOU) which outlined a framework of cooperation and commitment to work with each other, and with local, regional and state agencies in promoting tourism on federal lands. At the State level, a similar MOU was signed in Arizona in 1993 as an extension of the federal MOU. The Arizona MOU included all the State representatives of the federal agencies plus Arizona's departments and offices of Tourism, Game and Fish, State Parks, Lands, Commerce, Transportation, United States Department of Agriculture (USDA) Soil Conservation Service, Bureau of Indian Affairs, Navajo Nation, and the University of Arizona Cooperative Extension Service. The State MOU also established the Arizona Council for Enhancing Recreation and Tourism (ACERT) to provide coordinated planning services and leadership in developing recreation and tourism in Arizona. The MOUs state that:

> the common goal of the agencies is to advance the domestic and international public's awareness of tourism opportunities on the Federal Lands, and to market these tourism opportunities in an environmentally sensitive manner to produce economic, educational, and recreational benefits for the United States with emphasis on assisting rural communities. The Arizona MOU also seeks to harmonize, to the extent possible, all Federal and State activities in support of tourism and recreation with the needs of the general public, local communities, and the public and private tourism opportunity (Rural Tourism Development Program, 1996).

At the local level, ACERT is running the Arizona Rural Tourism Development Program to provide unified agency assistance to rural communities to develop tourism. The USDA Cooperative Extension Service is, in turn, using the ACERT program as part of its own six State 'Communities in Economic Transition' program. Six communities were selected to take part in the initial phase of the program, two of them Native American communities which had been nominated by the Arizona American Indian Tourism Association.

As the above example demonstrates, such regional approaches to the implementation of rural tourism development policies on a spatial basis may prove extremely complex as they reflect the diffuse nature of the relationship between government institutions and tourism. However, in such a complex policy environment as tourism, the set of linkages and relationships reflected in the Arizona situation may assist in the development of strategic alliances between the various interested parties, thereby increasing the likelihood of policy goals being met.

The establishment of cooperative structures is recognised as being extremely important in policy areas, including tourism and rural development, which may cover a range of traditional administrative and ministerial boundaries. For example, in 1995, the Finland Government established a Rural Policy Committee, which included members from various ministries as well as government and non-government organisations. 'The work of the Committee represents new thinking –

Table 2.2.   Tasks of the Finnish rural tourism theme group

1. To draft a long-range rural tourism strategy and action programme in collaboration with enterprises and development and marketing organisation in the sector.
2. To support the regional and national development of rural tourism by arranging the compilation of statistical material on the sector, customers and competitors as well as on projects to develop rural tourism on a regional basis, and to mediate the information thus generated for use in various projects.
3. To put together a national product development plan for rural tourism. The emphasis in the customer-centered development of services is on all-round exploitation of the natural attractions of the countryside, such as forests, water bodies, peatlands and rural culture. The product packages available are being developed systematically, respecting the principles of sustainable tourism, as village-level cooperation and transcending the boundaries between different sectors of the economy.
4. To assist in the compilation of a national rural programme and in gathering together those sections of EU programmes with a bearing on rural tourism.
5. To promote cooperation in both domestic and international marketing of rural tourism and to put together, as an umbrella project, an export marketing programme for tourism of this kind.
6. To launch, as necessary, national development projects for rural tourism. The most urgent projects in the current year are restructuring of training for advisers and entrepreneurs as well as development of quality-management instruments.
7. To produce proposals and initiatives for solving problems affecting rural tourism.

Source: Rural Tourism Policy in Finland, 1996. Reproduced with permission.

of a kind that transcends the demarcation lines between sectors of administration – in Finnish rural policy. The task of the Working Group is to harmonise rural development measures and promote the efficient use of resources allocated for the countryside' (Rural Tourism Policy in Finland, 1996, np). In order to promote rural tourism development the rural policy committee appointed a Rural Tourism Theme Group with members coming from both government and non-government sectors. The tasks of the Group are listed in Table 2.2.

While the goals of rural tourism development, e.g., economic growth and adaptation, employment generation, increased investment, population retention, infrastructure and facility provision, and conservation, are fairly standard policy goals, the actual policy process by which they can be achieved is not. Little attention has been given to the objective setting process, the selection of policy instruments and the most appropriate policy mix, the design of institutional arrangements, and the implementation of monitoring and evaluation programmes which measure policy effectiveness in terms that relate to the quality of life of those who the policies are meant to assist, e.g., in terms of recreational access and opportunity or housing and social welfare, rather than in terms of how much money was spent. As the Rural Development Commission (1996a) stated with respect to the British Government's White Paper, Rural England (Department of the Environment and Ministry of Agriculture, Fisheries and Food, 1995): 'Monitoring progress in the countryside also calls for the development of better information. We have precise figures for changes in the area of broadleaf woodland and species diversity in hedgerows, but no official estimates of rural housing need'.

Rural tourism and recreation: access and opportunity for all?

Not everyone has equal opportunity to access their rights to rural tourism and recreation opportunities. Many areas are inaccessible because of management attitudes to recreational access, or because of limited accessibility (e.g., costs of entry, and extent, cost and nature of transportation and supporting facilities). For instance, approximately 25 per cent of British people, largely affluent with one or more cars in their household, are the most frequent visitors to the countryside, visiting several times per annum; approximately 50 per cent (mainly adults with young children) are occasional visitors and 25 per cent visit rarely or not at all. The latter include people characterised by one of the following: poor access to private transport; disabled; ethnic minorities; international visitors; or live in deprived areas (Countryside Commission, 1990a, in Jones and Crowe, 1996, pp. 238–239; Countryside Commission, 1991c, in Bishop, 1996, p. 268). Participation in rural recreation in the United Kingdom is related to social class, with professional and higher managerial occupations being the most frequent trip-makers, although the actual volume of trip-making is dominated by clerical and skilled manual workers (Groome, 1993). Nevertheless, more local research indicates that 'variations in the social class of visitors emphasised the tendency for visitors' characteristics to mirror the social composition of neighbouring areas, particularly where catchments are quite local' (Groome, 1993, p. 24).

Throughout the developed world, recreation and tourism policies which cater to disadvantaged groups have been formulated and implemented, but they are generally one-off policies initiated by public or private agencies and which are poorly integrated with wider economic and social programs. The countryside is not accessible to everybody who wants access. Tourism policies emphasise economic outcomes with little consideration of those who lack such access, perhaps because, increasingly, market and economic issues have primacy over social concerns in terms of encouraging demand for tourism and recreational opportunities (Lane, 1994). Research concerning the allocation and distribution of outdoor recreations' benefits and costs across society is far from comprehensive, yet access and use by low income groups, ethnic minorities, indigenous groups, the aged, persons with disabilities, and women is lacking. In short, recreational participation and access to recreation and tourism opportunities has substantial inequities.

If rural tourism and recreational policy is designed to achieve quality of life outcomes for rural residents then greater attention needs to be paid to integrating social and economic goals in public policy. However, for this to be achieved those groups which are at present under-represented in recreational use patterns will have to be incorporated into the process by which recreation and tourism policies are formulated. Therefore, issues of equity in recreational opportunity serve to highlight areas in which recreation and tourism policies could have much greater impact as part of the wider planning environment, e.g., facilitating the role of local communities in policy-making and planning, and the retention of local characteristics which could provide a competitive edge in marketing tourist destinations.

Local community involvement: widely advocated but lacking in application

Tourism is often seen by government as a mechanism to implement redistribution policy (i.e. the spatial redistribution of incomes, and economic and amenity development activity). However, residents of an area will gain unequally, if they gain at all, and some may even be harmed. Some may not want to see development of any kind (Hall, 1995). A number of issues therefore need to be addressed in rural tourism community planning, including:

- seasonality in visitation rates, visitor expenditures, employment and incomes;
- development of infrastructure and tourist related services;
- the recreational needs of the local residents;
- positive and negative economic, physical and social impacts on host communities;
- conservation of natural and cultural heritage; and, ultimately
- the development of a sustainable tourist industry.

While community tourism planning (Murphy, 1985, 1988) has become something of a "catch-cry" for academics and politicians alike, the political dynamics and realities of community planning are often ignored. Public participation refers to 'decision making by the target group, the general public, relevant interest groups, or other types of decision making by the target group, the general public, relevant interest groups, or other types of decision makers whose involvement appeals to our desire to use democratic procedures for achieving given goals' (Nagel, 1990, p. 1056). However, as Hall and Jenkins (1995, p. 76) ask with respect to public participation, 'to which public are we referring?'

Awareness of the political dimensions of tourism, and more particularly the uneven allocation and distribution of power in a region or a community, should caution us about the representativeness of outcomes of rural planning and development exercises. Certain interests are often better able to achieve their objectives than others not only because of their greater resources, but also because of their ability to influence the direction of tourism policy in terms of access to power, e.g., rural business groups. In tourism planning and policy-making it is inequality rather than equality that is the order of the day (Hall and Jenkins, 1995).

Public participation in tourism planning may be more a form of placation than a means of giving power to communities to form their own decisions (Haywood, 1988). In addition, participation ought not to be assumed to affect planning outcomes. Alternatives may have already been defined before public participation began, while any changes which do occur may simply be changes at the margin. Therefore, notions of representation and responsiveness in tourism planning and policy-making need to be assessed in the light of the reality or unreality of participation (deLeon, 1994).

Fishkin's (1991) three dimensions of democracy: deliberation, nontyranny, and political equality, provide a basis for assessing the adequacy of exercises in public participation. However, in order for such dimensions to be achieved, tourism policy analysts and planners will need to be both proactive in their design of planning systems and understand the political structure they are operating in. Urban planners have described such systems as 'participatory design' or 'advocacy planning' (Forester, 1988), and these may well be usefully applied to the rural sphere. Advocacy planning means speaking for those who will actually live in rural areas, 'instead of doing research about them for those who hold the power. It means helping people in a community do their own planning' (deLeon, 1994, p. 205). This type of approach will challenge many ideas about the role of government in the tourism planning and policy process, particularly with respect to the roles of the bureaucratic 'expert' and interest groups. Linked to the institutional change required are changes in attitudes and perceptions of both the planners and the planned, but particularly by government policy-makers. Citing several authors, Bramwell (1994, p. 5) points to an increasing prominence being given to rural communities and individual local residents and businesses and to their role and degree of control in shaping rural tourism in the context of rural forces. If members of rural communities are to be engaged in rural policy, planning and development processes, then the development of policy needs and instruments needs to be an exercise not only in information, but also in consensus building, deliberation and negotiation with the community. This process will depend upon a relationship of trust being developed among the partners who formulate and implement rural development policy; and any such trust building measures take time. However, the history of rural development initiatives is littered with enough examples to indicate that such time is a resource well spent in terms of effective policy outcomes.

Any area which attempts to attract tourists needs to examine its rural community, environmental situation and productive capacities. Not all areas possess the inherent or collective resources and capacities to attract tourists and generate repeat visits, and what is successful in one location may not prove successful in another. Therefore, comprehensive research into the role of rural tourism is needed to determine whether tourism can be benefited from, and, if so, to help develop favourable economic and social situations while retaining the region's desirable social and cultural conditions.

For better or worse, the deregulation of markets, technological developments (e.g., in agricultural production, recreational activities, communications and transport), multinational corporations, the growth of agribusinesses and the reduction in the number and size of family farms are going to significantly influence the face and structure of rural communities for many years. They will also have significant influence on the decision-making powers of traditional rural families/ farmers and many local residents. Some areas will become more like the larger cities exhibiting and experiencing similar benefits (e.g., economies of scale, infrastructural development and provision of social services) and costs (e.g., crime, congestion and pollution). Many smaller and/or remote areas are likely to continue to decline unless they are able to regenerate or develop productive activities such as mining, high technology or tourism, or unless these public policies are developed as a means of decentralising a range of social services and infrastructure, including communication technologies, and educational, health and transport services. In rural England, for example, according to the Rural Development Commission:

> The poor provision of local services makes it difficult for people to get to shops, doctors, schools and other essential facilities, especially those who do not have the use of a car and where public transport is limited and expensive. Our 1994 survey found that: 41% of parishes had no shop, 43% no post office, 52% no school,

29% no village hall and 71% no daily bus service (Rural Development
Commission, 1996b).

In this environment, which is probably typical of many rural areas in western
countries, policy-makers cannot afford to see tourism in splendid isolation. Tourism
must be contextualised and integrated into the wider rural setting and must be seen
as a means to an end rather than an end in itself.

Can tourism contribute to regional development?

> Rural recreation and tourism planning needs to be integrated with wider concerns
> (e.g. economic growth and development, social change, public policy develop-
> ments) in the pursuit of some future goals with respect to the physical
> construction of the countryside and the achievement of defined national, regional
> and local social and economic objectives. In addition, planning for rural
> recreation and tourism needs to take account of wider patterns of participation in
> leisure in society as a whole (Groome, 1993, p. 13).

Tourism can contribute greatly to rural development and prosperity, but is often
misunderstood. Many public and private sector interests erroneously consider
tourism to present an easy path to economic development and restructuring.
Unrealistic expectations of tourism's potential in rural areas are often combined with
ignorance or wilful neglect by planners, decision-makers and developers, of adverse
environmental and social impacts of tourist development. Adverse impacts may, of
course, destroy or curtail tourism's benefits. In short, it is not easy to plan high
quality and sustainable tourist developments that balance (1) the economic and
social needs of local residents with tourists' needs and expectations, and (2) tourism
with environmental (namely, conservation and preservation) concerns. In other
words, sustainable tourism is not an easily achieved goal.

Tourism can help diversify, and therefore stabilise, a local economy, create
business opportunities (both within and outside the industry), jobs and incomes (and
the subsequent multiplier effects), and contribute to the tax base. Nevertheless, faced
with limited resources and already over-extended leaders and volunteers, many rural
communities now must compete with a rapidly growing number of rural areas which
are also attempting to develop resources for tourism.

Conclusion

> As a society grows wealthier, the value placed on improvements in the quality of
> life relative to material gains may rise. Poor communities may welcome new
> industries for the employment and tax revenues they bring, while richer
> communities may seek to remove these same industries in order to avoid the
> unpleasant social [and other] costs they bring (Lipsey, et al., 1985, p. 507).

Despite the focus on tourism as a tool for regional development, rarely is there a
clear concept in policy or planning terms of rural tourism or of the role of tourism in
rural regions or local communities. The situation has changed little from what
Balmer Crapo Associates described in 1975, when they noted the ignorance of

impacts, a non-rural focus, a lack of framework, policy and planning, and institutional complexity (in Butler and Clark, 1992). In part, this stems from (1) different attitudes towards rural areas, and (2) attitudes towards tourism. Interest in rural tourism has been largely spasmodic (Blacksell and Gilg, 1981; Pigram, 1993). Many studies focus narrowly on the specific economic (e.g., employment and incomes), physical (e.g., environmental) or social (e.g., crowding) impacts of tourism development at a local or regional level. Others (1) examine minor aspects of tourist motivations and decision making that provide little insight into tourist behaviour in complex environments; and (2) centre on aspects of farm tourism, with other forms of rural tourism largely ignored (e.g., Oppermann, 1996).

Troughton et al. (1975) noted that the countryside is poorly developed in terms of its image and its functional relationships. This observation is probably still valid not only for Ontario, but for most of the developed world. As the Countryside Commission (1996) reported in a press release on the November 1996, European Conference on Rural Development in Cork, Eire, 'Europe's countryside needs a fully integrated rural policy instead of a Common Agricultural policy with environmental measures tacked on as an afterthought'. However, tourism is also promoted in the absence of a clear understanding by many elected officials and entrepreneurs which has meant it has often been encouraged and supported in ignorance of its likely effects. Nevertheless, there has been a shift in the appreciation of rural areas for tourism. Rural resorts have been rejuvenated and communities revitalised because of the rise of environmental concerns and related desires for fresh and organic products, and the current trend to shorter and more frequent vacations (Butler and Clark, 1992).

It is essential that tourism be planned and integrated into the pattern of normal activity; which is obvious and easily stated but rarely successfully achieved in the long term. Effective rural recreation and tourism planning has been hampered by a lack of understanding of the political processes of planning and policy-making which include numerous stakeholders: government agencies at all levels, conservation groups, developers and local communities. The range of interests and conflicts has led to the advocacy of 'alternative', 'cultural', 'soft' and 'sustainable' tourism policies, many of which have received little critical attention even though they tend to be long on vision and short on implementation strategy (Pigram, 1993; Jenkins, 1993a, b; Hall, 1995). Increased focus therefore needs to be given to the formulation of the goals, institutional arrangements, instruments, and monitoring and evaluation of rural policy if it is to become more effective in meeting the needs and aspirations of rural communities. As Richter commented, 'tourism policymakers have been far more ready to inventory sites than inventory the political factors that could support or strangle the industry' (1991, p. 191).

Tourism is a complex, dynamic, highly competitive and very fragmented industry that is notoriously difficult to control and set appropriate policy for. The issues of capacity and limiting its development are crucial to destination areas (Butler and Clark, 1992). The chances of conflict between tourism and other business and social activities are high, often because of the lack of understanding by policy makers and planners of the complexity of tourism.

Local control of tourism is critical. Whether control rests with the local community may determine the success of tourism in rural areas. That is not to say that local control will necessarily result in appropriate tourism development, nor that local control will be permanent. However, if local control is absent or lost, the chances of development not being compatible with local preferences and needs are much greater (Butler and Clark, 1992). Thus, if rural recreation and tourism policies are to help rural communities in achieving sustainable futures as they adapt to dynamic global and local forces, an implicit assumption, and what should be an explicit objective of rural policy-making and planning, is that the local people in question will have a say in development, and an opportunity to lead a fulfilling and satisfying lifestyle in the community in which they have, and continue to choose, to reside.

References

Baum, E.L. and Moore, E.J., 1966, Some economic opportunities and limitations of outdoor recreation enterprises. In *Guidelines to the planning, developing, and managing of rural recreation enterprises*, G.W. Cornwall and C.J. Holcomb, eds., pp. 52–64, Bulletin 301, Cooperative Extension Service, Virginia Polytechnic Institute, Blacksburg

Bishop, K., 1996, Sustaining enjoyment of the countryside: The challenges and opportunities. In *Rights of way: Policy, culture and management*, C. Watkins, ed., Pinter, New York

Blacksell, M. and Gilg, A., 1981, *The countryside: Planning and change*, Allen and Unwin, London

Bramwell, B., 1994, Rural tourism and sustainable tourism. In *Rural tourism and sustainable rural development*. B. Bramwell and B. Lane, eds., Channel View, Clevedon

Bramwell, B. and Lane, B., eds., 1994, *Rural tourism and sustainable rural development*. Channel View, Clevedon

Bryan, H. and Taylor, N., 1991, Resource policy and outdoor recreation. In *Outdoor recreation policy: Pleasure and preservation*, Greenwood Press, New York

Bull, A., 1995, *The economics of travel and tourism*, Longman, Melbourne

Butler, R. and Clark, G., 1992, Tourism in rural areas: Canada and the United Kingdom. In *Contemporary rural systems in transition: vol 2, Economy and society*. I.R. Bowler, C.R. Bryant and M.D. Nellis, eds., CAB International, Wallingford

Cabinet Office, 1985, *Pleasure, leisure and jobs: the business of tourism*, Enterprise Unit, HMSO, London

Canadian Council on Rural Development, 1975, *Economic significance of tourism and outdoor recreation for rural development*, Working paper, Canadian Council on Rural Development, Ottawa

Clark, L.A., 1988, A local government view — planning for tourism in Far North Queensland. In *Frontiers in Australian tourism: The search for new perspectives in policy development and research*, B. Faulkner and M. Fagence, eds., Bureau of Tourism Research, Canberra

Clout, H.D., 1972, *Rural geography: an introductory survey*. Pergamon Press, Oxford

Commonwealth Department of Tourism, 1994, *National rural tourism strategy*. Commonwealth Department of Tourism, Canberra

Coppock, J. and Duffield, B., 1975, *Recreation in the countryside*, Macmillan, London

Countryside Commission, 1996, *Facing up to the future — a vision for a living countryside*, Countryside Commission News Release 96/68, 7 November

Craik, J., 1991, *Government promotion of tourism: the role of the Queensland Tourist and Travel Corporation*, The Centre for Australian Public Sector Management, Griffith University, Brisbane

deLeon, P., 1994, Democracy and the policy sciences: aspirations and operations, *Policy Studies Journal*, **22** (2): 200–212

Department of the Environment and Ministry of Agriculture, Fisheries and Food (DoE/MAFF), 1995, *Rural England: a nation committed to a living countryside*, HMSO, London

Duffield, B.S. and Long, J., 1981, Tourism in the highlands and islands of Scotland: rewards and conflicts, *Annals of Tourism Research*, **8**(3): 403–31

Faulkner, B., 1991, Tourism bureau hits ad fundamentalism, *Australian Financial Review*, October 18

Fishkin, J.S., 1991, *Democracy and deliberation: new directions for democratic reform*, Yale University Press, New Haven

Forester, J., 1988, *Planning in the face of power*, University of California Press, Berkeley

Glyptis, S., 1992, The changing demand for countryside recreation. In *Contemporary rural systems in transition: Vol 2, economy and society*, I.R. Bowler, C.R. Bryant and M.D. Nellis, eds., CAB International, Wallingford

Government of Alberta, 1985, *Position and policy statement on tourism, policy statement #1 in response to the white paper: an industrial and science strategy for Albertans 1985–1990*, Government of Alberta, Edmonton

Graburn, N.H.H., 1995, The past in the present Japan: Nostalgia and neo-traditionalism in contemporary Japanese domestic tourism. In *Change in tourism: People, places, processes*, R.W. Butler and D.G. Pearce, eds., Routledge, London

Greffe, X., 1994, Is rural tourism a lever for economic and social development? In *Rural tourism and sustainable rural development*. B. Bramwell and B. Lane, eds., Channel View, Clevedon

Groome, D., 1993, *Planning and rural recreation in Britain*, Avebury, Aldershot

Hall, C.M., 1992, *Wasteland to world heritage: preserving Australia's wilderness*, Melbourne University Press, Carlton

Hall, C.M., 1994a, *Tourism and politics: policy, power and place*, John Wiley, Chichester

Hall, C.M., 1994b, *Tourism in the Pacific rim: development, impacts and markets*, Longman Australia, South Melbourne

Hall, C.M., 1995, *Introduction to tourism in Australia: impacts, planning and development*, 2nd ed., Longman Australia, South Melbourne

Hall, C.M. and Jenkins, J.M., 1995, *Tourism and public policy*, Routledge, London

Hall, C.M., Jenkins, J.M. and Kearsley, G., eds., 1997, *Tourism planning and policy in Australia and New Zealand: cases, issues and practice*, Irwin, Sydney

Hall, C.M. and Page, S.J., 1996, *Tourism in the Pacific: issues and cases*, International Thomson Business Press, London

Hall, D.R., ed., 1991, *Tourism and economic development in Eastern Europe and the Soviet Union*, Belhaven Press, London

Hardin, G., 1968, The tragedy of the commons, *Science*, **162**: 1243–48

Harrison, D. ed., 1992, *Tourism and the less developed countries*, Belhaven Press, London

Haywood, K.M., 1988, Responsible and responsive tourism planning in the community, *Tourism Management*, **9** (2): 105–118

Hudson, R. and Townsend, A., 1992, Tourism employment and policy choices for local government. In *Perspectives on Tourism Policy*, P. Johnson and B. Thomas, eds., pp. 49–68, Mansell, London

Hughes, H.L., 1984, Government support for tourism in the U.K.: a different perspective, *Tourism Management*, **5**, 1: 13–19

Hula, R.C., 1988, Using markets to implement public policy. In *Market-based public policy*, R.C. Hula, St Martin's Press, New York

International Union of Official Travel Organizations (IUOTO), 1974, The role of the state in tourism, *Annals of Tourism Research*, **1**, 3: 66–72

Jacobs, M., 1993, *The green economy: environment, sustainable development and the politics of the future*, University of British Columbia Press, Vanvouver

Jeffries, D., 1989, Selling Britain – a case for privatisation?, *Travel and Tourism Analyst*, **1**: 69–81

Jenkins, J.M., 1993a, Tourism policy in rural New South Wales: policy and research priorities, *Geojournal*, (May): 281–290

Jenkins, J.M., 1993b, An alternative economic base: tourism and recreation development and management. In *Prospects and policies for rural Australia*, A.D. Sorenson and W.R. Epps, eds., Longman Cheshire, Melbourne

Jones, M. and Crowe, L. 1996, Local countryside = accessible countryside? Results from a countryside recreation survey in Wakefield Metropolitan District. In *Rights of way: Policy, culture and management*, C. Watkins ed., Pinter, New York

Lane, B., 1994, What is rural tourism? *Journal of Sustainable Tourism*, **2** (1/2): 7–21

Lavery, P. ed., 1974, *Recreational geography*, David and Charles, London

LEADER, 1995, Marketing quality rural tourism: rural tourism and local development, harmful effects of too much tourism, In *LEADER technical dossier*, LEADER II library

Lipsey, R.G., Langley, P.C. and Mahoney, D.M., 1985, *Positive Economics for Australian Students*, 2nd ed., Weidenfeld and Nicolson, London

Murphy, P.E., 1985, *Tourism: a community approach*, Methuen, London

Murphy, P.E., 1988, Community driven tourism planning, *Tourism Management*, June, pp. 96–97

Nagel, S., 1990, Policy theory and policy studies, *Policy Studies Journal*, **18** (4): 1046–1057

Opperman, M., 1996, Rural tourism in southern Germany. *Annals of Tourism Research*, **23** (1), 86–102

Patmore, J.A., 1983, *Recreation and resources: leisure patterns and leisure places*. Basil Blackwell, Oxford

Pearce, D., 1989, *Tourist development*, Longman Scientific and Technical, Harlow

Pearce, D.G., 1992, *Tourist organisations*, Longman Scientific and Technical, Harlow

Pigram, J.J., 1983, *Outdoor recreation and resource management*. Croom Helm, London

Pigram, J.J., 1993, Planning for tourism in rural areas: Bridging the policy implementation gap. In *Tourism research: Critique and challenge*, D.G. Pearce and R.W. Butler, eds., pp. 156–174, Routledge, London

Richter, L.K., 1991, Political issues in tourism policy: a forecast. In *World Travel and tourism review: indicators, trends and forecasts*, Vol. 1, F. Go and D. Frechtling, eds., pp. 189–193, CAB International, Wallingford

Roseland, M., 1996, Economic instruments for sustainable community development, *Local Environment*, **1** (2): 197–210

Rural Development Commission, 1996a, *Country people take centre stage: post white paper views – Richard Butt, chief executive*, Rural Development Commission, Salisbury

Rural Development Commission, 1996b, *Rural issues and facts*, Rural Development Commission, Salisbury

Rural Tourism Development Program, 1996, *http://www.state.az.us/ep/commasst/tour-dev.shtml*, 30 September

Rural Tourism Policy in Finland, 1996, *http://www.mmm.fi/maasmatk/enggroup.htm*, October

Subcommittee on Procurement, Taxation and Tourism of the Committee on Small Business, House of Representatives, Wilmington, NC., 1993, *Effects of tourism as a tool for rural economic development*, U.S. Government Printing Service, Washington D.C.

Troughton, M.J., Helson, J.G. and Brown, S., eds., 1975, *The countryside in Ontario*, University of Western Ontario, London

Veal, A.J., 1994, *Leisure policy and planning*, Longman, Harlow

Watkins, C., ed., 1996, *Rights of way: Policy, culture and management*, Pinter, New York

Williams, A.M. and Shaw, G., eds., 1988, *Tourism and economic development: Western European experiences*, Belhaven Press, London

World Tourism Organisation, 1996, *Tourism Trends 1995*, World Tourism Organisation, Madrid

3 The restructuring of rural economies: rural tourism and recreation as a government response

JOHN M. JENKINS, C. MICHAEL HALL AND
MICHAEL TROUGHTON

Introduction

Much is said and written about change in rural areas. Rural areas have been changing, sometimes quite rapidly, as a result of endogenous (e.g., reduced protectionism, policies supporting multiculturalism, population loss – especially of younger and skilled people – or gain, ageing populations, increased leisure time, changing family structures) and exogenous (e.g., transnational corporations, technological innovation, global money markets and economic restructuring) forces. Some changes, though, are not easily categorised (e.g., the greening of politics, levels of foreign investment, industrial and occupational developments, residents' levels of living and well-being) (Walmsley, 1990).

As argued in Chapters One and Two, any examination of rural tourism and recreation policies must be integrated with developments in rural areas generally. Rural areas around the globe are markedly different from what they were less than a generation ago, with many rural areas becoming more and more urban-like. Changes to rural areas have been inextricably linked to developments in both global and local economies, and tourism has emerged as one of the central means by which rural areas adjust themselves economically, socially and politically. In short, global and regional economic, political, social and technological developments have dramatically affected rural areas and led to their restructuring, usually involving attempts to widen their economic base in which turning to tourism is often seen as part of a 'natural' progression towards a tertiarised economy (Hudson and Townsend, 1992, p. 64).

This chapter presents a brief overview of the economic, political and social restructuring of western rural areas. As noted in Chapter Two, rural development policy, often developed with at least some recognition of the potential of rural tourism, is a popular response to restructuring processes (Marsden, Lowe and Whatmore, 1993). But, rural restructuring is enmeshed in the process of globalisation, and as places adapt to increasingly competitive and complex market situations, they cannot help but reinforce the effects of the vagaries of the global economic system to which they are increasingly tied. This chapter provides the context in which rural tourism and recreation are being actively encouraged. In addition, it details the regional, national and international public policy issues and initiatives identified in the previous chapter, as central governments respond to what amount to substantial challenges to planners, policy-makers and diverse rural communities. The chapter concludes with a case study of LEADER (*liaison entre actions de développement de l'économie rurale*), a European strategy for rural development. LEADER is a 'Community initiative' launched in 1991 as part of the major 'cohesion' policies of the European Union (EU).

Rural change and restructuring

The issue of restructuring, both generally and in the rural context, is a widely and vociferously debated issue, largely because it has been apparent at the global and local levels virtually everywhere in the industrialised world since the late 1970s (Clark *et al.*, 1992). During the last 20 years in particular, rural areas have experienced numerous, often far-reaching economic, social and political/institutional changes which have had profound effects on the ways in which people in rural areas live and govern themselves (Marsden, Lowe and Whatmore, 1993). The nature and processes of change continue to present significant challenges to the formulation and implementation of public policies for rural areas (e.g., OECD, 1990; Sorensen and Epps, 1993; Bramwell and Lane, 1994; Fagan and Webber, 1994).

However, change is not new. During the last 250 years rural economies and societies in developed countries have undergone a series of fundamental restructurings, beginning with the impacts of the so-called Second Agricultural and the Industrial Revolutions of the eighteenth and nineteenth centuries, and thence the general shift from predominantly rural to urban societies in the twentieth century. Most recently, in the period since the Second World War, increasing urban dominance has been accompanied by further major rural restructuring centred on the processes of industrialization of primary rural economies, especially agriculture, and their impacts on rural communities. This latest phase has been among the most disruptive to the rural system as a whole and to its more traditional landscapes; the latter have undergone physical transformation, linked, in many cases, to the fragmentation of relatively homogeneous rural systems into several parts as distinct among themselves as with the wider urban system (Bowler *et al.*, 1992).

This section provides a brief review of the major developments up to the Second World War, including some distinctions between the older European and more recently established North American and Australasian rural systems. The purpose is to provide a better understanding of the context within which tourism and recreation become part of the restructuring process by (1), establishing the continuity of change, and (2), identifying the situations which the most recent restructuring has altered.

The period of absolute or relative rural dominance

Despite the impact of the Industrial Revolution, rural systems in most developed countries held a dominant place in both landscape and socio-economic terms up until the Second World War. Even in the cradle of the industrial revolution, Great Britain, the effects of the second agricultural revolution were to establish an extensive agricultural landscape based on commercial farming, in which the traditional rural villages and even some market towns retained their rural service functions including labour supply. Whilst the initial transformation in Britain and adjacent areas of Western Europe was of established land-based owner-tenant (peasant) societies, the tenure systems of which evolved slowly during the nineteenth and early twentieth centuries, the rural economy quickly became organized to supply the urban-industrial labour force. While some of the latter was drawn from surplus rural populations, remaining large rural farm and non-farm populations continued to support a distinct rural system in which the linkages between the extensive land use, notably farming, and rural settlement remained strong. A still relatively labour intensive and local rural economy retained strong elements of rural culture manifested in both social (including recreation) and political contexts (Beresford, 1975) .

In contrast, the majority of the landscapes and economies of the North American and Australasian regions of rural settlement were fashioned during the nineteenth and early twentieth centuries basically 'from scratch' and with an initial commercial orientation as the primary element in the various settlement models. This led, among other things, to a more comprehensive pattern of private land ownership based on the primacy of the individual owner-operated family farmstead. Granting or sale of farm parcels were the means of settling huge areas and were established within regular, surveyed land allocation systems. This process determined rural settlement based on dispersed farmsteads, interspersed with non-farm rural service centres. Commonly, this mode of settlement, without the need to accommodate pre-existing human landscape features, created a more regular, utilitarian and homogeneous rural landscape (Fuller, 1985; Troughton, 1982).

The scale of land allocation varied with respect to physical conditions, notably moisture availability, but in North America especially led to the rapid occupance and settlement of the agriculturally suitable parts of the continent in both the United States and Canada. In both cases, the system aimed at shifting as soon as possible from a subsistence to a commercial mode. In this endeavour, it was aided by the rapid development of railway transportation which, by mid-nineteenth century, was guiding westward expansion, and linking the newly established farming communities to their urban industrial markets, both in Europe and, increasingly, in North America itself (Fowke, 1957; Zimmermann and Moneo, 1971).

Whereas expansion of the rural systems of North America and Australasia was accompanied by active urban development, the rural systems maintained a high degree of relative autonomy. In many regions, the rural population remained in the majority well into the twentieth century, and in countries like Canada the rural settlement frontier was still expanding. Agriculture, and other rural economic activities (forestry, fishing and even mining) were still very labour intensive and many rural labour forces continued to expand at least until the 1930s. Even

mechanization of farming, which was already under way by the 1850s, was locally based, utilizing horse drawn implements and transportation. General ownership of the internal combustion engine powered cars, trucks and tractors, was still relatively restricted until the Second World War, and even expanding urban places tended to be constrained by the need for workers to live close to their place of employment and the limits of public transit development. In this context, rural communities, farm and non-farm populations remained closely linked in economic, social and political terms. The rural economy emphasized small-to-medium sized farms and firms, the latter based on rural input supply or output processing. Social life, including recreation, was also local within rural regions, and the degree of rural community solidarity was emphasized by the rural political structure and its propensity to coalesce around rural populist causes (Fuller, 1985).

While there is no doubt that by the Second World War many older and newer rural systems had developed their own distinctive characteristics, some more viable than others, some more closely integrated into wider economic systems, one can suggest that nationally and even throughout the developed countries of Western Europe, North America and Australasia, rural systems had been created, based predominantly on commercial agriculture operated by large numbers of individual farm family and hired labour, that remained relatively, if not absolutely dominant in their respective national, provincial or state systems and exhibited a high degree of common rurality of lifestyle and outlook (Troughton, 1997).

On the other hand, one must recognize that changes were occurring already in the first decades of the twentieth century that would be the basis of more radical transformation after the Second World War. In addition to the inexorable growth of the urban population and its gradual assumption of numeric advantage and cultural dominance over the rural population, the structure of the rural economy also began to experience new inputs and to develop new structures and relationships. Three major strands can be identified, with somewhat different geographic foci; namely, intensification of inputs to land, the initial substitution of capital for labour, and the beginnings of the consolidation of agriculturally related activity beyond the farm gate.

Intensification, based on measures to improve crop and livestock yields, naturally was first in evidence in areas where a real expansion was no longer possible and where large numbers of small farms looked to increase farm income. Consequently, in Western Europe, to earlier initiatives in land drainage and reclamation and fallow reduction, were added improvements to fertilization, weed control and plant and animal breeding, which within predominantly intensive mixed farming systems, gave major yield increases and greater productivity (Grigg, 1992). On the other hand, these systems remained labour intensive, and in many cases (e.g., Scandinavia) farmer-based cooperative purchase and marketing arrangements were the dominant institutions.

Labour substitution, on the other hand, began to be developed in the more extensive landscapes of North America, in particular. In many areas, marginal physical conditions demanded larger farms to secure adequate production and income, but these, in turn, required greater energy inputs. Initially, these were supplied by large numbers of men and horses, especially at harvest. Gradually, however, steam and then gasoline powered machines were introduced. The invention of the internal combustion engine and its application to tractors, was the key innovation. Tractors began to appear in larger numbers in such locales as the US Midwest and the Canadian Prairies, and to initiate the shift to fewer, larger farms and reduced labour inputs. However, it may be noted that in the Prairies, peak farm horse populations were only reached in the 1920s and tractors were present on less than a quarter of all farms before 1940 (Vogeler, 1981).

Finally, the first decades of the twentieth century also witnessed the initial stages in the shift from local, often rural, processing of agricultural produce, to its concentration in fewer, larger and increasingly urban-based manufacturing plants. The process began with the application of factory processing to livestock in the US meat packing industry. It spread through the consolidation of grain milling, often at ports or other transhipment points. Much of this early growth represented regional bulking of extensive production. In the early 1900s processing to supply domestic markets with both canned and fresh fruits and vegetables, and dairy products, began the transfer from large numbers of small local plants to the large plant agribusiness sector. The latter, essentially developed in the US, also began to develop the institution of corporate or temperate plantation farming (Vogeler, 1981). Nevertheless, before the Second World War agribusiness and corporate farming was generally confined to a few specialist crop regions such as California. Input supply of farm machinery was also beginning to become consolidated, but still only supplied a minority of farmers. Fertilizer, the manufacture of which became concentrated among the large chemical companies was, likewise, limited in its purchase and application. Intensification was largely based on inputs of animal manure and crop rotation. Although there was some regional overlap, there was greater contrast between regions modernizing in specific rather than overall terms.

In summary, the period up to the Second World War included a critical shift from a previous traditional rural economy in Europe, and the development of huge new agricultural regions of up to 300 million hectares of additional settled farmland. Except for extensions in eastern Europe, the latter was increasingly dominated by very large numbers of individual farm enterprises, involved in small to medium scale commercial production for a generally expanding urban-industrial market. Modernization was ongoing but mechanization, capital intensification and the role of agribusiness (and governments) was generally modest. It followed that agriculture was often at the heart of a well-populated and still somewhat self-sufficient rural system and provided the basis for the majority of the settled ecumene and its rural landscape.

One might just note that other extensive economic activities, notably forestry, mining and fishing were more important in some rural regions. Mining and fishing tended to be highly localized; mining giving rise to many small and often short-lived settlements; fishing, concentrated in many small, often isolated marine communities, the activity generally labour intensive and with modest technological inputs. Forest economies were (and are) more widespread, especially in the boreal forest zone. Prior to the Second World War, however, despite the existence of large lumber and pulp mills, the forest activities were also still unmechanized and labour intensive and many logging settlements also were relatively small, somewhat isolated and self contained communities.

Rural restructuring in the modern era

The situation with respect to most rural economies in developed countries has altered radically since the Second World War, but not all in the same direction. The first characteristic to be noted is that a combination of circumstances began to effect a basic fragmentation of many rural systems which had been remarkably homogeneous at the national scale up to the war. A major contributing factor which pre-dated the war was the economic Depression of the 1930s. This major economic downturn had particularly severe consequences both in older and newly established rural regions. The collapse of primary commodity markets including those for grain, timber and pulp, affected all developed economies. In some regions, like the US plains states and Canadian Prairie provinces, the collapse of markets for grain was exacerbated by the incidence of severe drought and soil erosion, and led to widespread farm abandonment and partial collapse of the overall rural system (Buckley and Tihanyi, 1967). In the Prairies it brought a sudden end to immigrant-based settlement and expansion; in the US it created westward migration and social disruption on a large scale (Vogeler, 1981). More broadly, the Depression emphasised the growing weakness of many marginal and/or peripheral rural regions, for example Maritime Canada and, in the US, rural New England, the so-called 'cut-over' Great Lakes states, and Appalachia, including the Tennessee watershed. However, whereas high overall levels of unemployment and the generally depressed economy kept many 'on the farm' during the 1930s, the wartime recovery and the post-war boom and its demand for labour in urban-manufacturing and service industries, fuelled massive rural out-migration from those areas that remained economically disadvantaged (Buckley and Tihanyi, 1967). This contributed to the emergence of the marginal peripheral regions as a major rural sub-type, increasingly distinct from the more viable core rural regions.

The rural periphery   Among the problems faced by the peripheral regions was the fact that in many areas, physical conditions that had allowed, if not favoured, modest activity based on human and animal labour, could not be converted to or make use of new mechanical and chemical inputs. Thin, stony soils, and marginal climates for intensive crops, could not generate the capital for or from inputs of tractor power and applications of fertilizers. The result was depressed farm incomes, inability to compete with physically better areas, and a search for other sources of income. In some cases part-time farming emerged as a solution, but in many more remote areas off-farm employment was not available.

   In some regions, for example in the boreal forest zone in North America, forestry and mining had provided some alternative rural or regional employment. However, these two activities rapidly became more mechanized. An overall decrease in labour demand also included a shift from seasonal to full-time jobs which severed some of the links that had operated between farming and forest employment. Elsewhere, large areas of former farmland were more or less abandoned. In eastern Canada for example 50 per cent of all farmland and 35 per cent of improved farmland was lost primarily after 1950, and in some areas the losses were as high as 80 per cent of farmland and 90 per cent of farm population (Troughton, 1983).

   In older settled areas, which often retained a greater density of population, the results were mixed. The same problems of low productivity and farm income were widespread in many areas of western Europe (e.g., highland Britain, central France, southern Germany, southern Italy, northern Scandinavia). In these areas, while there was considerable out-migration and a switch to part- time farming, some of the absolute losses were mitigated by the rural policies of the European Community which, through various subsidy and rural development initiatives, sought to lessen the impact of absolute change. By and large, such programmes were either not attempted or were less successful in North America and, in consequence the retreat and associated rural decline was more precipitous (Bowler, 1979; Grigg, 1992).

Overall, therefore, we can see emerging already in the first post-war decades, a distinction between rural regions that were unable to modernize in this, the first phase of intensive capitalization of agriculture, based on increased mechanization and fertilization, and those that were able to take advantage of the increasingly available inputs. An often extensive rural margin or peripheral rural zone persists in many countries today, exhibiting distinct and problematic characteristics. There are often large expanses of former farmland, reverting to forest or bush, dotted with abandoned farmsteads with just the occasional surviving farm family, usually dependent on off-farm employment.

The former rural service centres have often experienced similar decline; the reduced population, income and demand for services resulting in reduced activity, even ghost towns and villages. The exceptions to this situation are most often where the former economic landscapes are also recreational amenity areas. Here the emphasis is on the lakes and rivers and cottage and resort development. However, only certain regions are either suitably located or especially attractive to the extent that recreation and tourism can offset the decline of the former economy. Generally, the periphery represents an area where the traditional rural economy has failed and where restructuring in economically viable terms has not been possible. In many cases peripheral regions continue to be zones which demand transfers of public funds and where many rural development alternatives are attempted but where few have proven sustainable.

The rural-agricultural hinterland In contrast to the collapsing periphery, the majority of the remaining rural regions were able to participate in the post-war economic recovery. Physically productive areas were able to realise the gains attendent upon the new capital inputs. As such, the emphasis was largely on capital intensification rather than a real expansion. Indeed, intensification often included reduction of the settled and/or farmed area. The new emphasis was on productivity of land and labour, which was generally achieved, but which brought its own problems. At the same time these remaining rural areas were also further sub-divided into two separate rural regional types, namely, the remaining agricultural hinterland or countryside, and the zone of exurban activity or the 'rural-urban fringe'.

Despite their general suitability for agriculture, the two zones experienced increasingly distinct rural restructuring. The agricultural hinterland was affected primarily by agricultural restructuring, specifically its industrialization. The 'fringe' was also affected by agricultural change but this was/is often secondary to the impacts of urban expansion. This latter zone, which also emerged and grew rapidly soon after the war, reflected the growing dominance of urban populations and activities which directly affected those rural areas closest to them (Russwurm, 1977).

The rural farm and related economy of the more or less viable hinterland agricultural regions has undergone a series of restructuring over the last 50 years. The details have varied with respect to major regions and political jurisdictions, but there have been some common features. As noted, in the aftermath of war came the shift to increased mechanization. This reflected two inter-locking factors; one, the shortage of farm labour, initially due to wartime duties, thereafter to the competition from urban employment, so that farmers had to mechanize to function; secondly, the emphasis on increasing land and labour productivity. The shift to larger farms was usually at the expense of former farmers, beginning the trend to reduced farm numbers in the core regions (Johnson and Quance, 1972).

The shift to large scale raising of housed livestock, the so-called 'factory farming', began in the 1950s with poultry in the US and was attendent upon large surpluses of corn and soybeans which could be utilized in the conversion process. This led, in turn, to expansion of specialized livestock in the hog and cattle sectors and to increased emphasis on cash cropping of food and feed grains and oilseeds. Building upon this came a general shift to greater farm level specalization and even greater capital intensification (Gregor, 1982).

A key to the shift and an increasingly controlling ingredient was the rapid growth of the agribusiness sector. In the post-war era agribusiness grew rapidly and at the same time consolidated into increasingly larger corporate entities. Its various sectors were able to dominate both the input and output sectors of the agricultural system. Inputs of farm machinery, fertilizers and the new set of agricultural chemicals, notably various tyes of pesticides, came increasingly from a narrow set of farm machinery manufacturers and large chemical companies. Similarly, the various output processing and distribution sectors were increasingly dominated by large corporations in such fields as milling, oilseed crushing, meat packing, dairy products, and fruit and vegetables processing (Wallace, 1985; Vogeler, 1981). In both the input and output sectors the company plants were mainly located in urban centres and this shift contributed to a further drastic erosion of rural employment (e.g., Mitchell, 1975).

Overall, this set of processes constituted the industrialization of agriculture. Industrialization creates farms that are capital intensive and specialist enterprises but also reduces the farm production unit to just one stage on a set of commodity based assembly lines, with the demand for the product determined by the agribusiness sector and based on a strict set of input requirements. The effects of agribusiness on the rural economy include a selective reductionist approach to the farms and a reduction in and separation or decoupling of the linkages between the farm and non-farm components of the rural system (Troughton, 1985). In many nations and regions, this has now resulted in the situation whereby not only have farm numbers been halved but a minority of those remaining (as low as 25–30 per cent) contribute 75–85 per cent of total farm production by volume and value. The remaining, non-industrial farms tend to be either low income or hobby operations and/or heavily dependent on non-farm employment to maintain farm family income (Troughton, 1997).

In turn, industrialization has had a twofold weakening effect on the overall rural community, including both the farm and non-farm sectors (see below). Reduced numbers of farms and farm population weaken the community. Reduced agriculturally related employment reduces the rural employed labour force. Together, these impact on the ability of the community to sustain the range of goods and services and, thereby, significantly reduce the level of community sustainability (Stabler, 1993). These impacts are general throughout the hinterland agricultural regions, but vary in terms of the ultimate result. In older, more densely populated and accessible rural areas, the decoupling of farm and non-farm components may be somewhat offset by some degree of rural repopulation by non-farm populations. Elsewhere, however, in more extensive and less densely populated areas the impacts may be devastating for the majority of erstwhile rural settlements. In parts of North America there are literally hundreds of abandoned or almost totally reduced rural settlements. Thus, although the regional farm economy may be more productive than ever, the rural community system is in general disarray, often as devastated as in any peripheral rural area. In some of the worst affected and physically more marginal areas it has even been suggested that these should revert to 'buffalo pastures' (Paul, 1992).

The rural-urban fringe The effects of industrialization are in evidence in all intensive agricultural regions, but from a rural economy and societal standpoint, they are somewhat masked or overlain within many near urban or fringe zones. In these areas, the impacts on the rural system are predominantly those of competition for and conversion of land, attendant upon the processes of urbanization. In the agricultural context, the pressures are those identified by Von Thunen and others, notably the competition for farmland from higher economic rents generated by urban land uses (Russwurm, 1977; Bryant *et al.* 1982). There is still some opportunity in the fringe for intensive urban-oriented production (e.g., orchards, nursery operations), but in many cases crop and livestock operations face pressures that result in widespread temporary land rentals, or exclusion of livestock in the face of urban objections to problems such as odour and waste disposal. In some instances, farmers in the fringe are diversifying into a range of non-agricultural activities in order to maintain livelihood and income (Bryant and Johnston, 1994).

Most marked, however, is the transformation of the former farm and non-farm rural landscape into urban uses, especially exurban residential and commercial activities. Whereas in some jurisdictions, growth has been planned and contained, generally, actual expansion was haphazard and accompanied by speculative activity which created a much more extensive 'urban shadow' zone, affecting broad zones of rural territory (Russwurm, 1977). Paradoxically, in the areas beyond actual urban boundaries, and which are still nominally rural in political and administrative terms, there has occurred population growth which masks the overall decline in rural population elsewhere. However, this growth in 'rural' population is largely of ex-urban newcomers. Despite the fact that many seek a 'rural lifestyle' and amenities, most are commuters to employment in the cities and towns, for whom the rural residence represents a dormitory function. Besides the competition for agricultural land and farm properties which is reducing the traditional economy, the newcomers are transforming rural communities (Walker, 1987). In some cases, their numbers contribute to the ability of the community to retain functions, including schools, churches, and stores, in other cases villages are transformed into extensions of suburban sub-divisions and boutique areas. In many cases it is arguable that, despite claims to be retaining a rural community and lifestyle, that the fringe is really an extensive urban zone.

The social and economic dimensions of restructuring and rural change

Despite a lingering image of stability and tranquillity, and a traditional way of life, the reality of the rural sector in all developed countries is of rapid and disruptive change (Troughton, 1990), especially in the most recent decades. According to Middleton (1982, p. 54), 'the pace of change in rural areas is accelerating and largely irrevocable'. Industrialisation, free or less restricted trade (with policies of high and extensive protectionism being abandoned), widespread growth in wealth and leisure, increased environmental awareness, growing conflict among competing land use interests, ageing populations, faster and more comfortable transport, inconsistent farm incomes and declining agricultural/farm employment, population decline or growth, and many other factors have served to change the face and structure of rural economies, and the lifestyles of rural people. Production processes have become increasingly integrated across national boundaries (OECD, 1990; Troughton, 1990; Sorensen and Epps, 1993; Fagan and Webber, 1994; Lane, 1994), the significance of multinational corporations is increasing, 'the pace of change in the direction and composition of world trade has quickened' (Fagan and Webber, 1994, p. 26), and the international mobility of financial capital and people continues to escalate. In brief, the patterns of economic development for rural areas have changed, and therefore so, too, have the ways in which communities operate in order to adapt and survive (Troughton, 1990, p. 23). England provides a case in point for these changes which are occurring throughout the developed world.

One-fifth of the population, or just over 10 million people, live and work in rural England, where there have been substantial changes since the early 1980s, including:

- Between 1981 and 1991 the population of remoter rural districts rose by 6.4 per cent;
- Between 1981 and 1989 employment in high technology industries grew 12 per cent in the most rural counties and fell by 16 per cent in conurbations; and
- In 1993 employment in manufacturing accounted for a similar proportion of the labour force in rural districts as in urban districts (Rural Development Commission, 1996).

However, such 'improvements' in economic performance in many rural areas in England tend to simplify or mask the economic reality and dimensions of restructuring that are actually occurring in that country, and particularly in the more remote regions, where there are continuing problems of limited job opportunities, high levels of unemployment and under-employment, outward migration of young adults and decline in traditional employment sectors. For example, according to the Rural Development Commission (1996):

... nearly 60,000 jobs have been lost in rural collieries since 1984; and rural jobs are also disappearing as a result of change in the agriculture sector, defence restructuring and the decline of seaside tourism and fisheries. There has been a continuing decline in the agricultural labour force during the 1990s and it is likely that a further 65,000 full-time jobs in farming will have been lost by the end of the decade.

This more detailed picture of change in rural England is mirrored in Australia (see Sorensen and Epps, 1993; Fagan and Webber, 1994) and Canada (Troughton, 1990, 1991), much larger countries with more physically remote and marginal rural settlements. As Troughton (1990, p. 25) noted with respect to the Canadian situation:

> In many areas, even of viable agriculture, villages and towns are stagnating or in decline due to losses of populations, and, in turn, of basic functions such as transportation links, schools, doctors, and churches, as well as rural industry. The situation is generally worst in physically poor and/or isolated 'marginal' areas, where outmigration has been highest and dependency in all senses is most pronounced. The only exception is in the rural–urban fringe zone, close to urban centres, where repopulation by exurbanites is universal.

In Canada, despite some recent attention to programmes for local community development (e.g., the Canadian Federal Government's Community Futures Programme), 'There is no clear, focused or coordinated national or Provincial rural or small town community development policy. Fragmentation and segmentation dominate the policy and programme environment for rural and community development' (Dykeman, 1990, p. 12).

It is therefore not surprising that in this economic climate many local authorities have turned to tourism as a last resort in the face of falling agricultural and industrial employment and, in many instances, in light of a failure to attract high-technology industry (Hudson and Townsend, 1992). Yet, such shifts have much more than economic consequences. Social and cultural change in individual localities can be traced, in part, to changes in the means and modes of production or in service orientation, e.g., developments in manufacturing, mining, high technology, tourism, and infrastructure. All of these will lead to changes in occupational and social structures, which, in turn, help to transform the nature of communities (Day *et al.*, 1989; Yarwood, 1996). Structural change can also be seen at different physical scales from changes in the spatial arrangement of fields comprising individual farms, to the number and size of individual farms, to changes in settlement patterns and land use policies (e.g., Pacione, 1984; Mather, 1986). Clearly, new population, demographic and spatial arrangements arising out of restructuring may have a dramatic impact on rural social coherence (e.g., Cloke and Thrift, 1987).

People's expectations and images of rural areas are also changing (see Chapter Seven), while greater emphasis is being given to the conservation and maintenance of natural and cultural heritage (including the rights of indigenous people) and the marketing and promotional potential of heritage. As noted in the previous chapter, people may want development and employment but many also want traditional images of the countryside to be retained (also see Chapter Eight). Unfortunately, legislation and planning laws are often inadequate to control or influence landscape quality. Indeed, they are notoriously poor in the United Kingdom (Middleton, 1982) and more generally around the world (e.g., Jenkins, 1995; Mather, 1986). In short, economic, environmental, political, social and technological developments and issues are putting increasingly varied and complex pressures on rural areas in many countries, but the planning and policy responses are generally mixed, if not inadequate, and lacking in coordination in scale and structures.

The changes that have occurred in rural areas in western countries are complex and diverse, with recognition of global developments clearly demonstrating that domestic challenges and transformations have not occurred in isolation (e.g., Champion, 1987; Lawrence, 1987; Day *et al.*, 1989; Cloke and Goodwin, 1992, 1993; Lawrence *et al.*, 1992; Pawson and Scott, 1992; Marsden *et al.*, 1993; Cloke *et al.*, 1995; Pawson and Le Heron, 1995). Broader analytical perspectives, often lacking in tourism research and planning (Hall and Jenkins, 1995), link domestic transformations with changes in the world economy. At the macroeconomic level, the patterns of change in rural areas reflect global pressures towards policy convergence, driven largely by the power and policy preferences of global financial markets. Microeconomic reform has, to a large extent, been forced on rural areas in many countries by changes in the world economy. There is also considerable evidence of a weakening capacity of the nation state to influence or control local patterns and processes, while the sub-national or local state is correspondingly gaining in influence. Therefore, the ability of governments to influence local fortunes may be somewhat limited, and recognition of the interplay between macro and micro-economic forces is critical to analysing rural issues. As Fagan and Webber (1994, pp. 91–92) noted:

> Different sectors are important for employment and exports; different groups of people have prospered or suffered from the relative growth and decline of sectors; and the detailed geography of production has altered perceptibly ... new forms of global integration – of finance, trade and tourism – have generated new kinds of activities ...

Changes in the world economic and financial systems, improvements in technology, and recent developments in political philosophies, are major forces behind economic globalisation and subsequent restructuring. Among other things, the financial systems of many countries have been at least partially deregulated, currencies have been floated, foreign investment encouraged, tariffs reduced and companies encouraged to look to new markets, such as Asia and the Pacific and other regions rather than Europe or North America for economic growth (Hall, 1994). For both Canada and the United States, countries of Asia and the Pacific Rim now constitute their major trading partners rather than Europe. Similarly, Australia, South Korea and Japan have emerged as major export markets. These developments reflect important changes in the nature of the global economy.

> Japan and the Newly-Industrialising Countries (NICs), especially those on the Asia-Pacific Rim, have emerged as major players in the world economy. In contrast to the experience of these NICs, several developing countries have proved unable to support their citizen's lives. The industrial changes have had quite different impacts on particular groups of people. The contribution of women to paid employment around the globe, for example, has expanded dramatically often within new forms of employment [such as tourism] (Fagan and Webber, 1994, p. 25).

The emergence of international regional trade associations also contributes to increased economic turbulence and place competition as some firms relocate to lower cost regions to minimise production costs. Australia, building on its experience with the Closer Economic Relationship (CER) with New Zealand, was instrumental in launching the Asia Pacific Economic Cooperation forum, which is the main platform for trade and tariff cooperation in the Asia-Pacific region (Hall, 1994). However, a number of other trading associations including the Association of South East Asian Nations (ASEAN) Free Trade Area, the Central Asia Free Trade Area, the North American Free Trade Area (NAFTA), and, most significantly, the European Community (EC) have all contributed to reductions in protection for traditional rural producers with consequent exposure to the dynamic nature of the international marketplace. In addition, microeconomic reform, including such mechanisms as changes to industrial relations and welfare policies, particularly for the unemployed and socially disadvantaged, has been attempted at various levels to make business, industry and government more efficient and globally competitive. However, the impact of economic restructuring and associated policy responses has been very uneven (Fagan and Webber, 1994).

Policy concerns and issues

Around the globe, recent government programs have sought to address rural problems and imbalances by way of rural and/or regional development programmes targeted at such industries as 'tourism'. However, simultaneously, governments have adopted restrictionist economic policies which have compounded the difficulties of rural areas adjusting to structural shifts in their economies and social infrastructure (e.g., by way of centralisation of health and transport services). Policy-makers appear to be struggling with national versus local priorities (e.g., the restructuring and deregulation of agriculture and other industries versus subsidised benefits by way of taxation policy), a point which raises the issue of conflict in the values and objectives of the nation state as opposed to the local state. Policy-makers are also confronted with inadequate (and sometimes misleading) information on rural issues, and therefore a restricted capacity to identify appropriate policy instruments to select, promote and support traditional industries and other productive capacities as viable and sustainable alternatives. Many industries appear to present opportunities to diversify the economic base of rural areas, and to stem the leakage and transfer of labour and capital (and thus community services and infrastructure) from rural economies. Tourism is one such industry, which has the added benefit in that it frequently makes use of existing resources (Bull, 1995). Of course, part of the inherent appeal of rural areas is their aesthetic landscapes, their lack of congestion, and the accessibility of open, undeveloped space.

Debate concerning rural prosperity and regional development should also explicitly recognise the uneven spatial impact of factors affecting rural areas. Rural regions are not uniform. They vary in their economic base, their population dynamics and social and political networks, and in their inherent natural (e.g., soil and climate) and human (e.g., leadership and workforce) qualities. Where large differences in wealth and opportunity exist, planning and development strategies may be formulated and implemented to reduce regional disparities. Undeveloped and underdeveloped resources sometimes attract special attention and are powerful incentives for government investment in rural/regional planning and development policies and programs. Once resource development opportunities are perceived, planning is undertaken to:

- decide which resources to develop (or not to develop) and how they should be developed;
- decide which resources to conserve or protect and how they should be conserved or protected;
- decide in what order of priority projects should be undertaken and when they should be undertaken; and
- ameliorate or solve conflicts which emerge between stakeholders (i.e., potential and actual resource users).

Ultimately, policies, plans and programs may be sectoral (applied across the community with consequences for particular places) or spatial (applied to specific places) (see Chapter Two). Whatever strategies are adopted, the roles of each level of government will be critical. Indeed, as noted in Chapter Two and to some extent in this chapter, there is scope for considerable debate about the appropriate roles of government and means of coordinating public policies and programs.

Many rural areas in western countries are markedly different from what they were only a generation ago. Rural economies are much more open to global forces, they are more economically, culturally and environmentally diverse, and their populations are becoming more concentrated in larger centres (e.g., see Sorensen and Epps, 1993). Rural areas are continuing to evolve. Little wonder, then, that although 'rurality varies as a concept from region to region and through time' (Lane, 1994, p. 18), it remains an important foci for government action. Regardless of present government activity in rural regional development generally, and in the development and promotion of rural tourism specifically, competition between places will probably continue, some regions will be better suited to global and national development, new areas will rise, and some presently strong regions will fall.

Development processes will thus probably continue to exhibit a 'Darwinian' flavour (Sorensen, 1990). Government funding of industry development grants and other support mechanisms is closely linked to perceived gains and likelihood of programme/project success. Government intervention is rarely linked directly to the degree of economic and social need of specific areas (see Chapter Two). Public policies and programmes are influenced by economic concerns and accountability measures that relate to desired outcomes and impacts which are economically rather than socially driven. As a result, tourism public policies and programs will struggle to counter processes in which place prosperity is strongly influenced by exogenous events (e.g., changing lifestyle preferences, infrastructure investment, technological innovation, currency movements (a major factor affecting farm profitability and the flow of overseas tourists), interest rates, taxation, the length of the working week, and labour costs). Indeed, even ostensibly domestic decisions by national governments are, and will continue to be, frequently taken with one eye on international reactions, 'while geographical considerations in development and welfare will diminish in importance relative to targets of an aggregate macroeconomic kind'. In short, overall national economic well-being is the issue which will increasingly attract policy-makers' attention, 'not the welfare of particular areas except, perhaps, in the case of regional economic disaster where lobby groups can be effectively organised' (Walmsley and Sorensen, 1988, p. 114).

Rural change has posed fundamental challenges for citizens, business and community leaders, and government officials concerned with the local and national importance of economically strong, environmentally sound and socially vibrant rural areas and communities. One challenge involves gaining a clear, current under-standing of the socio-economic, environmental, and political problems important in rural areas. Another challenge involves identifying and developing feasible policies and programmes for addressing rural problems in ways which provide for greater self reliance, more options, and a healthier environment. A third challenge is in identifying leadership capable of carrying forward policies and programmes. A fourth challenge is posed by the institutional context for formulating and implementing policies and programs for addressing rural problems (e.g., Bouquet and Winter, 1987; Hall and Jenkins, 1995). This latter challenge involves reorganising existing or designing new institutional arrangements to more effectively formulate and implement rural policies and programmes. While not in itself a guarantee of improvements in rural development, effective institutional arrange-ments are an important prerequisite for effective rural policies and programmes (OECD, 1990, p. 12), and they cannot be developed without the appropriate quantity and quality of human skills and commitment.

For those communities struggling to adapt to the globalisation of world economies, and/or who experience downturns in their economic viability and quality of life, tourism development may not necessarily benefit those in most economic need, and the changes that occur from tourism development may serve to reduce their access to social services as they are displaced by increased rents and land, transport and food prices. In short, tourism development may take place in such a way that few tangible (and intangible) rewards flow to local residents in most need. Therefore, the effectiveness and efficacy of rural tourism development must not only be carefully evaluated but also integrated within the wider rural context. Indeed, depending on regional economic, social and environmental characteristics, the most effective tourism development strategy may provide for very little or no tourism development!

Tourism and regional restructuring and development in the European Union

Issues of regional development and social cohesion have been a major focal point of European Union (EU) policy since the 1970s. As the EU has enlarged so the extent of regional disparities has also grown. According to the European Commission (1996a, np), 'the 10 most prosperous regions in the EU are three times as rich, and invest three times as much in their economic fabrics, as the 10 poorest'. In response to problems of regional disparity the EU has established a series of 'structural' funds. One of the main structural funds is the European Regional Development Fund (ERDF) which was established in 1975 following the accession of Britain, Denmark and Ireland to the then European Community. However, the development of single market and the establishment of economic and monetary union in 1999 has provided greater impetus to encourage regional development, with a new fund, the Cohesion Fund, being established to channel financial assistance to the four poorest member states: Spain, Portugal, Greece and Ireland.

Regional policy is regarded as a collaborative effort between the union and national, regional and local authorities. Areas qualifying for EU regional aid programmes are defined according to the nature of their economic problems. Four categories are identified which have regional emphasis:

- Objective 1: promoting the development and structural adjustment of the regions whose development is lagging behind;
- Objective 2: converting regions or areas seriously affected by industrial decline;
- Objective 5b: facilitating the development and structural adjustment of rural areas; and
- Objective 6: promoting the development and structural adjustment of regions with an extremely low population density (European Commission, 1996a).

Top priority has been given to Objective 1 which between 1994 and 1999 will receive ECU96.346 billion, or about 70 per cent of available structural funding. The four regional objectives in total account for almost 85 per cent of the global structural fund budget with the remaining 15 per cent being divided amongst non-regional objectives. In the period 1994–1999, structural fund resources amount to ECU144.5 billion at 1994 prices. This is approximately one-third of the EU budget, or 1.2 per cent of EU Gross National Product. In 1994, about half of the population of the Union was covered by Structural Funds (European Commission, 1996b). The Structural Fund breakdown for each country by objective is shown in Table 3.1.

Table 3.1 European Union structural funding 1994–99 (million of ECU at 1994 prices)

Country	Obj.1	Obj.2	Obj.3&4	Obj.5a	Obj.5b	Obj.6	CI	Total
Austria	162	99	387	380	403	–	143	1,574
Belgium	730	342	465	195	77	–	287	2,096
Denmark	–	119	301	267	54	–	102	843
Finland	–	179	336	347	190	450	150	1,652
France	2,190	3,774	3,203	1,933	2,238	–	1,601	14,938
Germany	13,640	1,566	1,942	1,143	1,227	–	2,206	21,724
Greece	13,980	–	–	–	–	–	1,151	15,131
Ireland	5,620	–	–	–	–	–	483	6,103
Italy	14,860	1,463	1,715	814	901	–	1,893	21,646
Luxembourg	–	15	23	40	6	–	20	104
Netherlands	150	650	1,079	165	150	–	421	2,615
Portugal	13,980	–	–	–	–	–	1,058	15,038
Spain	26,300	2,416	1,843	446	664	–	2,774	34,443
Sweden	–	157	509	204	135	247	125	1,377
U.K.	2,360	4,581	3,377	450	817	–	1,570	13,155
EU Total	93,972	15,360	15,180	6,916	6,862	697	14,051	153,038

CI = Community Initiatives
Source: European Commission, 1996b

Despite regional development long being a significant factor in EU policies, tourism has only recently received serious attention as a mechanism for economic development. Tourism was only being cited for the first time in broad framework legislation in the Treaty of the European Union signed in Maastricht in 1992. In the case of the European Community, Kearney (1992, p. 35) noted that 'European tourism has long suffered from the benign neglect of governments which have still to recognise its economic and social importance in modern economies increasingly dominated by the services sector'. Indeed, Lickorish (1991, p. 179) argued that 'there has never been an explicit European tourism policy'. Nevertheless, it is interesting to note that Airey (1983) observed that regional development was the most frequently mentioned factor in European government tourism policies.

Tourism has become a part of EU planning and policies in the 1990s for a number of reasons. First, tourism is now recognised as an important economic activity. According to the European Commission in 1992, tourism generated 5.5 per cent of the then European Community's national income, accounted for 8 per cent of end-user consumption, and employed 7.5 million full-time workers and 10 million if secondary activities were taken into account (Barnes and Barnes, 1993). Second, the transnational character of some tourism businesses has necessitated the development of a European-wide policy framework. Third, the cultural impacts of tourism have raised concerns over the retention of cultural identity while at the same time attempting to promote the concept of Europe. Fourth, the movement of pollution across national boundaries and the possible movement of capital to locate where environmental standards and costs are lowest. Indeed, the environmental dimensions of tourism have developed as a major EU concern in the tourism area with the need to set sustainable tourism within the context of sustainable development being recognised in the green paper on Tourism from DGXXIII of the European Commission (1995). The paper argues that the attractiveness of a tourist destination, and indeed the economic basis of tourism, depends on the conservation and appropriate management of cultural and natural resources (Bramwell, *et al.*, 1996). Finally, concerns over the social dimensions of poverty and unemployment, particularly in disadvantaged regions, have given impetus to the use of tourism as a tool for employment generation and economic development at a regional level.

One of the most significant European strategies for rural development is LEADER (*liason entre actions de développement de l'économie rurale*). LEADER is a 'Community initiative' launched in 1991 as part of the major 'cohesion' policies of the EU, by the Directorate General for Agriculture of the European Commission. The first phase (LEADER I) ended in December 1994. The second phase (LEADER II) covers the period 1995-1999 (LEADER II, 1995a). LEADER is regarded as a 'bottom up' approach to problems of rural development.

> Apart from the structural problems that are recognisable in the countryside in many parts of the world, the weakening of many rural European areas is marked by the profound changes in which rural Europe has been engaged for several decades.
> Traditional agriculture plays a role which is of less and less importance, significant imbalances have appeared (exodus of young people, depopulation of certain areas, insecurity and unemployment)...(LEADER II, 1995a).

However, new opportunities, including rural tourism, increased demand for 'local' products, demands for improved quality of life by retirees, and the 'greening' of the general population are regarded as being available to rural Europe. Yet, as LEADER acknowledges, the 'drive among government administrations and the various... operators to promote rural tourism... is undoubtedly a response – in some cases prompted by a guilty conscience – to economic crisis and the need to find solutions to it, to the negative effects of reforms of farm structures and to the eradication of basic structures in many rural areas' (LEADER II, 1995b).

LEADER principally funds local action groups which are a combination of public and private partners who have jointly devised a strategy and a set of public and private innovations for the development of a rural area at a community scale, which is defined as being less than 100,000 people. Other rural collective bodies, public or private, e.g., local authorities, business associations or chambers of commerce, can also be funded provided that their activities are related to a local rural development plan (LEADER II, 1995c). However, overall responsibility for the management of the LEADER programme lies with national and/or regional authorities. Leader I received ECU 1,154,697,000 worth of funding (Zarza, 1996, p. 108). The 217 Leader I action groups consisted of 127 rural areas identified as Objective 1 regions ('least developed' regions of Europe) and 90 rural areas identified as Objective 5b areas ('rural zones with difficulties'). Of the 217 LEADER I areas, 71 had a tourism component, which was the dominant activity of the business plans of the local action groups.

LEADER II applies to Objective 6 (areas with very low population density, as well as Objectives I and 5b. The EU's participation has been set at ECU 1.5 billion of which ECU900 million has been allocated to the regions of Objective 1. LEADER II money may be matched with private and public sector funding. The goals of LEADER II are:

- to ensure that support for exemplary local initiatives involving local development continues from LEADER I;
- to support operations that are innovative, suitable as a model and transferable, and that illustrate the new directions that rural development may take;
- to step up exchanges of experiences and the transfer of know-how through a European rural development network; and
- to back transnational cooperation projects developed by local bodies in rural areas which reflect their solidarity (LEADER II, 1995c).

Four types of measures are eligible to meet the goals of LEADER II:

- skills acquisition, e.g., local rural needs analysis, training programmes, and strategies;
- rural innovation programmes – model and transferable programmes which are usually promoted by local action groups that can include: technical support for rural development, vocational training, support for rural tourism, support for small businesses, local exploitation and marketing of agricultural, forestry and fisheries products, and preservation and improvement of the environment and living conditions;

- transnational cooperation, e.g., joint projects between groups from member states; and
- contributions to the European network for regional development (LEADER II, 1995c).

As noted above, rural tourism is a major component of the LEADER programme's regional development initiatives. Yet the first round of the programme has already indicated that the pace of rural tourism product development has been slow, particularly in southern Europe, while substantial problems have been encountered with product marketing. In addition, it has been recognised that 'rural tourism tends to be a low value added product' (LEADER II, 1995b). In France, for example, rural tourism accounts for 25 per cent of all domestic tourism but only 10 per cent of expenditure. In addition, the seasonal nature of rural tourism is problematic. The *Fédération Nationale des Gîtes Ruraux* registers an occupancy average of 15 weeks per year, with an average of 70 per cent capacity in this period, giving an annual occupancy rate of approximately 20 per cent (LEADER II, 1995b) (see Chapter Thirteen).

The projects developed under the LEADER project are extremely diverse ranging from the development of a communications strategy for 'Cathar Country' in Toulouse, France, to the development of 'Via Mediterranea' (a Mediterranean cultural tourism network comprising tourist trails, the construction of numerous visitor interpretation centres, resource centres, museums and walkways), to direct assistance for small business development. An example of LEADER expenditure is provided in Table 3.2 which shows the spending of LEADER I funds on tourism by the South Mayo LEADER Company in Ireland. Under LEADER II, South Mayo will be drawing up area tourism plans with a view to develop a number of activities including:

- training for tourism;
- upgrading of accommodation and renovation of old buildings for self-catering accommodation;
- establishment of hostels;
- activity centres and bed and breakfast businesses where a need is identified;
- development and improvement of leisure amenities for tourists;
- exploitation of the area's heritage and culture;
- development and promotion of local festivals outside the core season;
- marketing of both group and individual projects;
- centralised reservation and booking facilities; and
- possible development of a rural tourism cooperative (Mayo Ireland, 1996b).

However, the LEADER process illustrates some of the major issues that are raised with respect to state intervention in regional development. First, how likely is it that developments established under the programme can be self-sustaining once the programme is finished? In other words, for how long should the state support economically unviable areas and/or tourism developments? Second, what should the long-term role be for the institutions which are established to implement such programmes? As noted above, the design of appropriate institutional arrangements is critical in the coordination of rural development programmes, yet at what point

Table 3.2   Allocation of LEADER 2, 1995–9 funds for rural tourism in South Mayo, Ireland

Allocation	Ir£
Angling facilities	42,953
Bread and breakfast accommodation	27,506
Golf facilities	117,892
Hostel facilities	69,123
Marketing	49,736
Outdoor pursuits	97,667
Other tourist facilities	137,530
Restaurants	45,068
Self catering accommodation	54,078
Water sports	27,272
Total	669,825

Source: Mayo Ireland, 1996a

should the action groups transform themselves into formal regional development organisations or should that role be undertaken by existing local authorities? Third, how can representativeness be assured given that action groups are meant to be part of a bottom-up development process. As the LEADER II (1996) development methodology recognises, 'if people feel that consultation is not genuine, or not offered in terms which are meaningful to them, they are unlikely to take part'. Yet, the document goes on to note that:

> Experience has shown that it is extremely difficult to involve the general public fully and successfully in local development projects. The scale of such involvement is too massive and the public is in any case made up of many different people with different interests, priorities and resources. Moreover only relatively few individuals have the time, resources and inclination to commit themselves to the lengthy and demanding processes of involvement in such projects.
>
> In practice, a better approach is to identify and encourage as wide a range as possible of interest groups covering all aspects of political, economic, social and cultural life, and to focus their interest and attention on the elements and stages of the project which have the most significance and importance to them (LEADER II, 1996).

Although the LEADER II approach may be the most 'practical' to the issue of public participation it may not be the most participatory method of development. The focus on interest groups may well mean that pre-existing interest group conflicts are just dragged into a new policy arena created by the availability of new resources. The trust building which is essential to the creation of effective partnerships may well need to occur at the level of individuals rather than through groups, otherwise networks may dissolve in the absence of the 'carrot' of access to financial resources. Finally, if so many regions are focussing on rural tourism as a development opportunity, to what extent will regions be able to effectively compete in a finite market which is facing a rapidly increasing range of products from which to choose, many of which are similar in orientation. Indeed, by placing so much emphasis on rural tourism development, the LEADER programme may well be creating a situation in which many regions will have to continue to invest in tourism infrastructure, facilities and promotion not so much to gain a competitive advantage, but just to survive. The whole process may become nothing more than a vicious cycle where strong regions prevail and weak regions fall.

The EU, as with many other national and regional authorities, have not learned the lessons of selling places in the global economy. In tourism, as in other regional industries, the active production of places with special qualities, places that can hold the interest of tourists and the tourism industry, has become an important element in competition between areas at all spatial scales (Kearns and Philo, 1993; Marsden, Lowe and Whatmore, 1993; Hall, 1997). As Hudson and Townsend (1992, p. 65) observed:

> As the market has become more differentiated, places have been forced to develop coherent strategies to sell themselves. It is reasonable to suppose that, initially at least, heightened competition will lead to a production of more variegated places within a global economy. But in practice what seems to be happening is the production of 'recursive' and 'serial' monotony, as places are cast in existing moulds to produce virtually identical attractions in different locations. The issue this development raises is the extent to which places will be able to sell themselves, if not as unique, then at least within a not too crowded segment of the market. Will imitative behaviour undercut every place's competitive positions as the initial edge conferred by 'uniqueness' is replaced by serial monotony?

Hudson and Townsend's comment and the discussion of the LEADER programme point to some major tensions in rural tourism development. There is a limited and discerning tourist market, but also a potentially enlarged supply married to a complex web of institutional arrangements. Competition between places is therefore intense and becoming increasingly so. Those with (1) the most effective public and private sector initiatives and (2) well developed inherent natural and human capabilities (both of which may be managed and developed in a sustainable way through such initiatives) will most likely succeed. A genuine commitment from communities is needed. A well defined market niche must be defined. Finally, an understanding of not only local, but wider national and global trends and issues must be integrated into any rural tourism plans and policies.

Conclusion: restructured to what and what role for tourism?

> Given that most economic and social trends are beyond the control of democratically elected governments operating in a mixed economy, governments have two interrelated and inseparable responsibilities. The first, and forward looking or efficiency role, is to facilitate economic change and social change to reflect the emerging order. The second, and more backward looking and caring function, is to ensure the well-being of the weakest members of society who are disadvantaged by the changes taking place and/or unable to adapt to them. Effective government requires sensitive and pro-active treatment of both. There seems to be little merit in reacting piecemeal to problems as they arise, since prevention is generally regarded as better than cure. No successful government or business survives without a well considered corporate philosophy and strategy; both government and business function most efficiently where they can secure stable operating environments (Sorensen, 1993, pp. 278–279).

This chapter has presented a brief overview of the economic, political and social restructuring of western rural areas since the Second World War, thereby providing the context in which (1) rural tourism and recreation are being actively encouraged by the public and private sectors, and (2) the remaining chapters of this book are presented. It charted broad national and international public policy concerns and presented a case study of LEADER, a 'Community initiative' launched in 1991 as part of the major 'cohesion' and restructuring policies of the European Union.

Clearly, rural areas are very different from what they were only a generation ago, as are people's and institution's understandings, images and expectations of rural areas. Some rural communities are reaping the benefits of restructuring programmes, most are susceptible to swings and roundabouts in the markets for agricultural products, others have staple products or services which ameliorate or counterbalance economic cycles. Given that it is likely that development processes in rural areas will exhibit a 'Darwinian flavour', we should critically consider the extent to which economic growth, social cohesion, and, ultimately, the sustainability of rural areas, among other things, will be affected by government policy because so little policy is long term, and so much of it is poorly coordinated. One likely scenario for rural areas is that growth and development processes will be driven by the survival of the fittest in a substantially deregulated marketplace of competing towns, cities and regions (Sorensen, 1990, p. 59). As rural areas change, competition between places will necessarily continue. In this highly competitive and deregulated global marketplace where central government intervention is declining, some regions will be better suited to global and national development, new areas will rise and others will struggle on or wither and die. Rural areas, generally, face not so much a poor future as an uncertain one.

The diversity of rural areas means that there are many potential means of achieving economic and social sustainability. Formulating and implementing rural/ regional development public policy generally and rural tourism policy specifically are onerous tasks, but it seems certain that most will, for better or worse and on different criteria, seek to diversify their economic base from one which is predominantly goods-producing to one which focuses more on high technology or services oriented industries such as tourism. Other areas will change without any necessarily explicit plans as people move to a region for lifestyle or other reasons related to the inherent features and promises of an area.

Tourism and recreation offer great prospects and challenges for rural areas, but there is some way to go before the potentials are realised as the LEADER case study demonstrates. Of particular importance to rural community development are the notions of who participates and who benefits. Ultimately, the formulation and implementation of rural development policies, and therefore tourism public policies, are political activities. At the moment, various tiers of government, government departments, different participants in the industry, interest groups, rural communities, and researchers are struggling with the uncertainties of tourism, rural life and government. Moreover, there are few proven concepts and theories to guide rural development generally, and rural tourism and recreation development specifically (see Chapters One and Two) with rural tourism data availability a major problem (Oppermann, 1996). The chapters which follow clearly demonstrate the contentious nature of rural tourism and recreation policy, planning and development and the fact that tourism is better suited to, and will produce greater net benefits for, some rural communities more than others.

References

Airey, D., 1983, European government approaches to tourism, *Tourism Management*, 4 (4): 234–244

Barnes, I. and Barnes, P., 1993, Tourism policy in the European Community. In *Tourism in Europe: structures and developments*, W. Pompl and P. Lavery, eds., pp. 36–54, CAB International, Wallingford

Beresford.T., 1975, *We plough the fields: British farming today*, Penguin, Harmondsworth

Bouquet, M. and Winter, M., 1987, *Who from their labours rest? conflict and practice in rural tourism*, Avebury, Aldershot

Bowler, I.R., 1979, *Government and agriculture: a spatial perspective*, Longman, London

Bowler, I.R., Bryant, C.R. and Nellis, M.D., eds., 1992, *Contemporary rural systems in transition: economy and society*, Vol. 1 *Agriculture and environment*, CAB International, Wallingford

Bramwell, B., Henry, I., Jackson, G. and van der Straaten, J., 1996, A framework for understanding sustainable tourism management. In *Sustainable tourism management: principles and practice*, B. Bramwell, I. Henry, G. Jackson, A.G. Prat, G. Richards and J. van der Straaten, eds., pp. 23–71, Tilburg University Press, Tilburg

Bramwell, B. and Lane, B., eds., 1994, *Rural tourism and sustainable rural development*. Channel View, Clevedon

Bryant, C.R. and Johnston, T., 1994, *Farming in the city's countryside*, University of Toronto Press, Toronto

Bryant, C.R., Russwurm, L.H. and McClelland, A.G., 1982, *The city's countryside*, Longmans, London

Buckley, H. and Tihanyi, E., 1967, *Canadian policies for rural adjustment*, Special Study 7, Economic Council of Canada, Ottawa

Bull, A., 1995, *The economics of travel and tourism*, Longman, Melbourne

Champion, A., 1987, *Changing places: Britain's demographic, economic and social complexion*, Edward Arnold, London

Clark, G.L. *et al.*, 1992, Objections to economic restructuring and strategies of coercion, *Economic Geography*, **68**: 43–59

Cloke, P. and Goodwin, M., 1992, Conceptualising countryside change: from post-Fordism to rural structured coherence, *Transactions of Institute of British Geographers*, **17**: 321–336

Cloke, P. and Goodwin, M., 1993, Rural change: structured coherence or unstructured coherence, *Terra*, **105**: 166–174

Cloke, P. and Thrift, N., 1987, Intra-class conflict in rural areas. In *Rural restructuring: global processes and their response*, T. Marsden, P. Lowe and S. Whatmore, eds., pp. 165–181, David Fulton Publishers, London

Cloke, P., Goodwin, M. and Milbourne, P., 1995, Regulation theory and rural research: theorising the rural transition, *Environment and Planning A*, **27**: 1245–1261

Day, G., Rees, M. and Murdoch, J., 1989, Social change, rural localities and the state: the restructuring of rural Wales, *Journal of Rural Studies*, **5**: 227–244

Dykeman, F.W., ed., 1990, *Entrepreneurial and sustainable rural communities*, Rural and Small Town Research and Studies, Department of Geography, Mount Allison University, Sackville, N.B.

European Commission, 1995, *Green paper on tourism*, DGXXIII European Commission, Brussels

European Commission, 1996a, *The European Union's policies for regional development and cohesion*, European Commission, Directorate-General XVI, Brussels

European Commission, 1996b, *European Union: regional policy and cohesion ERDF guide*, European Commission, Directorate-General XVI, Brussels

Fagan, R.H. and Webber, M., 1994, *Global restructuring: the Australian experience*, Oxford University Press, Melbourne

Fowke, V.C., 1957, *The national policy and the wheat economy*, University of Toronto Press, Toronto

Fuller, A.M., 1985, The development of farming and farm life in Ontario. In *Farming and the rural community in Ontario*, A.M. Fuller, ed., pp. 1–46, Foundation for Rural Living, Toronto

Gregor, H.F., 1982, *Industrialization of U.S. Agriculture: an interpretive atlas*, Westview, Boulder

Grigg, D., 1992, *The transformation of agriculture in the West*, Blackwell, Oxford

Hall, C.M. and Jenkins, J.M., 1995, *Tourism and public policy*, Routledge, London

Hall, C.M., 1994, *Tourism in the Pacific rim: development, impacts and markets*, Longman Australia, South Melbourne

Hall, C.M., 1997, Geography, marketing and the selling of places, *Journal of Travel and Tourism Marketing*, **6** (3/4): in press

Hudson, R. and Townsend, A., 1992, Tourism employment and policy choices for local government, *Perspectives on tourism policy*, P. Johnson and B. Thomas, eds., pp. 49–68, Mansell, London

Jenkins, J.M., 1995, *Crown land policy-making in New South Wales: a study of the public policy process leading to the development and demise of the Heritage Lands Project*, unpublished, Ph.D. thesis, Department of Geography and Planning, University of New England, Armidale

Johnson, G.L. and Quance, C.L., eds., 1972, *The overproduction trap in U.S. agriculture*, Resources for the Future, Johns Hopkins Press, Baltimore

Kearney, E.P., 1992, Redrawing the political map of tourism: the European view, *Tourism Management*, March: 34–36

Kearns, G. and Philo, C., eds., 1993, *Selling places: the city as cultural capital, past and present*, Pergamon Press, Oxford

Lane, B., 1994, What is rural tourism? *Journal of Sustainable Tourism* **2** (1/2): 7–21

Lawrence, G. Vanclay, F. and Furze, B., 1992, *Agriculture, environment and society: contemporary issues for Australia*, Macmillan, Melbourne

Lawrence, G., 1987, *Capitalism and the countryside*. Pluto Press, Sydney

LEADER II, 1995a, *Welcome to the rural Europe site*, LEADER II Background Note, Rural Europe

LEADER II, 1995b, *Marketing quality rural tourism*, LEADER technical dossier, LEADER II Library, Rural Europe

LEADER II, 1995c, LEADER II, *Development of disadvantaged rural areas of the European Union*, LEADER II Community Measures, Rural Europe

LEADER II, 1996, *Involving people in local development: a necessity*, LEADER dosier, LEADER II local project, Rural Europe

Lickorish, L.J., 1991, Developing a single European tourism policy, *Tourism Management*, **12** (3): 178–184

Marsden, T., Lowe, P. and Whatmore, S., eds., 1993, *Rural restructuring: global processes and their response*, David Fulton Publishers, London

Marsden, T., Murdoch, J., Lowe, P., Munton, R. and Flynn, A., 1993, *Constructing the countryside*, UCL Press, London

Mather, A. S., 1986, *Land use*, Longman, Harlow

Mayo Ireland, 1996a, *South Mayo LEADER Company*, LEADER 1 1992–1994, Mayo Ireland, Mayo

Mayo Ireland, 1996b, *South Mayo LEADER Company*, LEADER 2 1995–1999, Mayo Ireland, Mayo

Middleton, V.T.C., 1982, Tourism in rural areas, *Tourism Management*, **3** (1): 85–99

Mitchell, D., 1975, *The politics of food*, Lorimer, Toronto

OECD, 1990, *Partnerships for rural development*, OECD, Paris

Opperman, M., 1996, Rural tourism in southern Germany, *Annals of Tourism Research*, **23** (1): 86–102

Pacione, M., 1984, *Rural geography*, Harper & Row, Cambridge

Paul, A.H., 1992, The Popper proposals for the Great Plains: a view from the Canadian Prairies, *Great Plains Research*, **2** (2): 199–222

Pawson, E. and Le Heron, R., 1995, *Changing places: a geography of restructuring in New Zealand*, 2nd ed., Longman Paul, Auckland

Pawson, E. and Scott, G., 1992, The regional consequences of economic restructuring: the West Coast, New Zealand (1984–1991), *Journal of Rural Studies*, **8** (4): 373–386

Rural Development Commission, 1996, *Rural issues and facts*, Rural Development Commission, Salisbury

Russwurm, L.H., 1977, *The surroundings of our cities*, Community Planning Press, Ottawa

Sorensen, A. D. and Epps, R., eds., 1993, *Prospects and policies for rural Australia*, Longman Cheshire, Melbourne

Sorensen, A.D., 1990, Virtuous cycles of growth and vicious cycles of decline: regional economic decline in northern New South Wales, In *Change and adjustment in Northern New South Wales.* D.J. Walmsley, ed., Department of Geography and Planning, University of New England, Armidale

Sorensen, A.D., 1993, Approaches to policy, In *Prospects and policies for rural Australia*, Sorensen, A. D. and Epps, R., eds., Longman Cheshire, Melbourne

Stabler, J., 1993, Rural community rationalization. In *Towards a whole rural policy for Canada*, A.R.R.G. Working Paper series 7, Rural Development Institute, Brandon

Troughton, M.J., 1982, *Canadian agriculture*, Akademia Kiado, Budapest

Troughton, M.J., 1983, The failure of agricultural settlement in Northern Ontario, *Nordia*, **17**: 141–151

Troughton, M.J., 1985, The Industrialization of U.S. and Canadian agriculture, *Journal of Geography*, **84**: 255–263

Troughton, M.J., 1990, Decline to development: towards a framework for sustainable rural development. In *Entrepreneurial and sustainable rural communities*, F.W. Dykeman, ed., Rural and Small Town Research and Studies, Department of Geography, Mount Allison University, Sackville

Troughton, M.J., 1991, Canadian agriculture and the Canada-U.S. Free Trade Agreement: a critical appraisal, *Progress in Rural Policy and Planning*, **1**: 179–196

Troughton, M.J., 1997, Social change, discontinuity and polarization in Canadian farm-based rural systems. In *Agricultural restructuring and sustainability*, B. Ilberry, Q. Chiotti and T. Rickard, eds., pp. 279–291, CAB International, Wallingford

Vogeler, I., 1981, *The myth of the family farm: agribusiness dominance in U.S. agriculture*, Westview, Boulder

Walker, G.E., 1987, *Invaded countryside: structures of life in the Toronto fringe*, Geographical Monograph 17, Atkinson College, York University, Toronto

Wallace, I., 1985, Towards a geography of agribusiness, *Progress in Human Geography*, **9**: 491–514

Walmsley, D.J. and Sorensen, A.D., 1988, *Contemporary Australia: explorations in economy, society and geography*, Longman Cheshire, Melbourne

Walmsley, D.J., 1990, Adaptation to change and uncertainty: the social implications for Australia. In *Industrial transformation and challenges in Australia and Canada.* R. Hayter and P. Wilde, eds., Carleton University Press, Ottawa

Yarwood, R., 1996, Rurality, locality and industrial change: a micro-scale investigation of manufacturing growth in the district of Leominster, *Geoforum*, **27** (1): 23–37

Zarza, A.E., 1996, The LEADER programme in the La Rioja Mountains: an example of integral tourist development. In *Sustainable tourism management: principles and practice*, B. Bramwell, I. Henry, G. Jackson, A.G. Prat, G. Richards and J. van der Straaten, eds., pp. 103–120, Tilburg University Press, Tilburg

Zimmermann, C.C. and Moneo, G.W., 1971, *The prairie community system*, Agricultural Economics Research Council of Canada, Ottawa

4 Rural tourism development: Canadian provincial issues

DONALD G. REID

Provincial tourism development

Canada has a federal system of government which embraces three levels of governance, a national government, provinces, and at the local level, municipal governments. Each has a distinct role to play in the development of tourism. National governments often provide the general infrastructure and diplomatic function at the macro scale, which encourages and facilitates tourism development. Logistics, with regard to visa requirements and travel regulations, ongoing research, analysis, and monitoring are prime examples of their involvement (Hall and Jenkins, 1995).

On the other end of the continuum, municipalities, in cooperation with the private sector, are concerned with developing, regulating and coordinating the unique product which defines the destination. Municipalities often provide the developmental superstructure in terms of zoning and other regulatory requirements which shape the construction of facilities and regulate such things as traffic flows and specific site designs. In many cases, they also provide the support services which encourage the tourism function to flourish. Such functions as information centres and grants to business umbrella groups are examples of support services which many municipalities provide to their tourism sector. Municipalities often directly provide, or assist other groups in the community to provide, tourism facilities like museums and non facilitied attractions such as festivals from which many private sector businesses benefit, including hotels and restaurants.

Provincial governments play an important, perhaps pivotal role, in tourism development in their respective jurisdictions. While each level of government provides a distinct role which is unique to its own circumstances, there seems to be a core service offered by this level of government.

Each province in Canada implements tourism strategies and actively promotes tourism which has been growing in importance over the last decade (see Figure 4.1). The provinces in Figure 4.1 were selected because of their coast-to-coast representation and for their diversification. Nova Scotia and Newfoundland are maritime provinces, Ontario is the largest province and located centrally, Manitoba is a prairie province, and British Colombia, the Yukon and North Western Territories represent west coast and the northern regions of Canada.

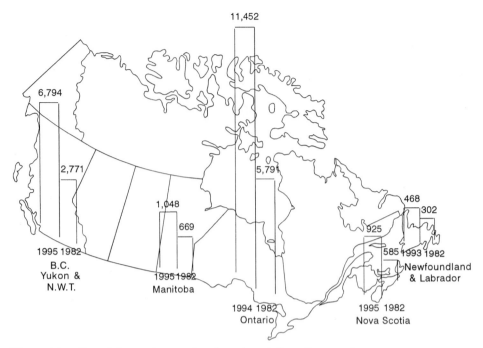

Figure 4.1.   Growth in tourism receipts for selected Canadian provinces

For Ontario, the largest province in Canada, 1994 data (see Figure 4.1) shows total tourism expenditures in the province at Can.$11,452 million. This represents slightly less than a 200% growth rate in just over 10 years. In 1982, Can.$5,791 million was generated in receipts and 172,000 tourism jobs constituted the tourism industry in the province (Ministry of State). This demonstrates the growing importance of tourism to provincial economies in just over a decade.

As traditional manufacturing and heavy industries decline in Canada, the tourism sector receives even more attention as a player in the provincial economy. This is particularly the case for resource-based economies which are endowed with significant natural areas that lend themselves particularly well to outdoor recreation and, therefore, to tourism development. While the expectations for the role that tourism can play in regional economic development may be over-stated, provincial governments, nevertheless, see potential for some economic relief through tourism for many of these failing areas and, therefore, promote the growth of tourism as a tool for economic development (Reid, Fuller and Haywood, 1995).

For example, Ontario is divided into 12 tourism regions. These regions are based on their homogeneity as tourism destination zones. As the location quotient portrayed in Figure 4.2 suggests, some areas lend themselves better than others to sustainable tourism development (Reid *et al.*, 1993). The *location quotients* calculated in Figure 4.2 project the extent to which each region generates more or fewer tourism expenditures or jobs, given their population size in proportion to the province's population. The two areas, Georgian Lakelands (GL) area and Ontario Near North (ONN), produce more tourism expenditures and jobs as a proportion of the province's population than any of the other regions, including the metropolitan

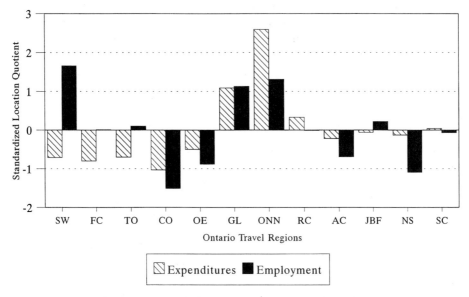

Figure 4.2. Ontario's travel association areas: Location quotients for tourism expenditures and employment
Source: Reid, D.G., A.M. Fuller, K.M. Haywood and J. Bryden, 1993. Reproduced by permission of the Ontario Ministry of Culture, Tourism and Recreation

city of Toronto (TO). Their success may depend on their geographic relationship to the large metropolitan area of Toronto and the southern part of the province, and the landscape which produces an extended outdoor recreation area to adjacent urbanities.

The South Western region (SW), which is a mixture of rural and urban, produces a better-than-average number of tourism jobs but generates expenditures slightly below the mid-line. The other predominantly rural areas in Ontario (Rainbow Country (RC), Algoma Country (AC), James Bay Frontier (JBF), North of Superior (NS), and Sunset Country (SC)), all generate expenditures at about the mid-line which suggests that their tourism industry is making an average contribution to their economies even though they may not yet be producing enough jobs through this sector. These are regions where the tourism attractions are clearly in non-urban centres, even when the region contains an urban area. The regions below the mid-line in terms of generating expenditures and producing jobs through tourism are predominantly urban areas (Festival Country (FC), Central Ontario (CO) and Ontario East (OE)). While these regions are significant tourism destinations they are not as dependent on tourism as are some of the other regions noted above.

Figure 4.2 demonstrates the importance of tourism to the rural economies in the province of Ontario. Of the Can.$11.5 billion generated in total tourism receipts as shown in Figure 4.1, Can.$70.8 million were generated in the predominantly rural regions. While this represents a small fraction of the total tourism receipts for the province, the population of these regions is also a fraction of the total provincial population. Therefore, the revenue comparison may not truly represent the significance of tourism to the province's rural areas, given the lack of potential

economic diversification of these regions. It should also be pointed out that the
Can.$70.8 million designated to come from rural regions does not include the rural
tourism receipts which come from within predominantly urban regions. Some of the
so-called urban regions (e.g., Festival Country) contain significant rural tourism
areas and attractions as well as city events and facilities.

Leadership

Tourism makes a significant contribution to the economic well-being of each of the
provinces. As a result, Provincial governments spend considerable energy in
providing leadership for the development of tourism strategies in their jurisdiction.
Most of these strategies outline in conceptual terms the vision, goals and objectives
for development. Many also lay out the responsibility of the government and suggest
roles for municipalities, NGOs and the private sector umbrella associations which
have an interest in tourism development. Often they will also provide incentives in
the form of grants and low interest loans to encourage development in certain
geographic or thematic areas. Their role is largely to stimulate tourism development.
However, there are exceptions. For instance, in Ontario, the Provincial government
provides such attractions as the Ontario North Science Centre and the Royal
Ontario Museum.

Coordination

Provincial governments provide a coordinating function as well as working with
province-wide organizations. Essentially, most provinces divide their jurisdictions
into regional associations for both administration and product theme development.
Manitoba identifies six regions which provide very different products. The regional
differences are significant with regard to theme and product. The North West
Territories (NWT) also has six regional areas. In this case, the culture and geography
are vastly different across the territory resulting in extremely distinctive cultural and
outdoor tourism experiences between regions. Other provinces in Canada between
the regions differentiate their regions by scenic travel routes. For example, Nova
Scotia is divided into six regions with Cape Breton Island providing a separate
number of scenic sub-trails.

  Whatever the distinguishing characteristic or scheme in each province, it would
seem that all of the Provincial governments find it useful to organize their tourism
products through regional associations. It is generally at this level where the day-to-
day organization and interface between the government and the private sector seems
most predominant. In the larger provinces, regions usually employ an executive
director to carry out the day-to-day business of the association and the provincial
government maintains some form of regional presence, usually in the form of a
consultation service. This does not preclude, however, the various travel and
accommodation associations lobbying provincial and state governments directly
around policy and planning issues at the provincial or state level. Implementation of
these policies, once established and agreed upon, occurs at both the horizontal and

vertical level. That is, top down (vertically) through the various industry organizations (e.g., the bed and breakfast association) and horizontally across individual businesses who belong to the regional associations.

Policy development

Perhaps the most distinguishing feature of mid-level government policy is the lack of any specific policies which focus solely on rural tourism development. Virtually, no Provincial government in Canada has a direct policy which deals exclusively with rural tourism development or even an exclusive section focusing on rural issues in its overarching policy statement or strategy.

Most of the provinces in Canada have policy documents which set out the direction of development for tourism in their jurisdictions. While Ontario does not have a written tourism strategy at present, it has assisted and funded the provincial tourism advisory committee in the development of such a document that was submitted to the Minister of Culture, Recreation and Tourism in February of 1994 (Ministry of Culture, Tourism and Recreation, 1994). As of yet, the ministry has not adopted this strategy as government policy, nor has it developed a policy of its own. This submission, however, provides the direction for tourism development in the province in lieu of, and until such time as, the ministry develops its own statement. Among the major thrusts, the 'Events' section discusses issues related to sports, culture and heritage, some of which are found in rural areas, although such distinctly rural activities as farm vacations are not dealt with at all. In addition, the 'Niches' section fails to identify rural attractions as a special product. While it does refer to outdoor and adventure recreation, it suggests 'that many of these products and others can be found in a single Ontario city'. The same section of the document emphasizes the area of cultural tourism but fails to identify rural Ontario as a large provider of cultural events (Reid *et al.*, 1993).

This should not be surprising given that many government ministries and departments at the senior level also do not have a distinct policy dealing with rural development. Given that rural industries are primarily seen as agricultural, or in some cases engaged in some form of extraction of the natural resource, the closest that one can get to rural policy at the mid-level is agricultural regulation (foodland guidelines in Ontario's case) or legislation dealing with mining or forestry.

Provincial governments develop generic policies which focus on the major urban areas and by default these policies are expected to cover the issues and nuances that facilitate or constrain growth in the countryside. Most of these governments view the rural countryside as abundantly endowed with natural resources which provide a playground for others and which does not require special protective attention. The Ontario Ministry of Natural Resources, which establishes the mandate for provincial parks, is also responsible for promotion and regulation of extractive industries, including forestry and mining. This perhaps explains why both of these activities are being carried out in Ontario's provincial parks.

Rural areas and communities are best represented in the tourism policy and plans in provinces and states where the basic character of the region is of a rural nature.

The NWT in Canada may be the best example of rural jurisdictions where the overall policy for the mid-level government has a rural flavour.

Even in this Province, assistance beyond marketing has been limited, as observed in the following passage from the tourism statement of the tourism industry in the NWT:

> To date the government of the NWT has done little to direct or assist the development of a healthy, growing travel sector... government support for tourism has to date been concentrated in the marketing field. (Government of the North West Territories Tourism Industry, 1983, p. 8).

Stumbling over jurisdictions

Often jurisdictions stumble over each other in an attempt to provide service, or, in some cases, not to provide service as in the case of mid-level ministries or departments. In the case of tourism in Ontario, it may be more accurately stated that ministries attempt to stay out of each other's policy areas, so that some potential developments which could be beneficial to rural tourism development are not generated. Because Ontario has both a ministry responsible for tourism and a Ministry of Agriculture, Food and Rural Affairs, each wants the other to provide service to the rural areas when it comes to tourism development. The tourism ministry suggests that it is the prerogative of the Ministry of Agriculture, Food and Rural Affairs to administer to rural areas (a geographic/spatial approach) and the OMAFRA wants the Ministry of Tourism to administer to rural needs in the area of tourism (a subject/sectoral approach). As a result of this reluctance to take the initiative, few policies and programmes are formulated and implemented because each ministry is waiting for the other to act.

Marketing is a major function of provincial governments

A quick review of the many planning and core policy documents of provincial ministries responsible for, or influential in, tourism development reveals that they have placed a large part of their effort on marketing. The mandate statement for Ontario, the largest province in Canada, states, 'The mandate of the Ministry of Economic Development, Trade and Tourism is to lead and promote Ontario's economic development and market the province as a place for business and jobs growth' (Ontario Ministry of Economic Development Trade and Tourism, 1996). The marketing function is clearly the focus of the mandate guiding the ministry. Those providing advice to the ministry are giving the same message. For example, the strategy submitted to the Ontario Ministry of Culture, Tourism and Recreation by the Tourism Advisory Committee, *Ontario's Tourism Industry* (Ministry of Culture, Tourism and Recreation, 1994, pp. 33–37) provides a section on 'New Directions For Growth' which deals with such issues as:

- branding and imaging;
- niches;

- events;
- demand generators;
- gateway market;
- information; and
- grading and classification.

Notably, all but two of these functions focus on marketing.

A review of an earlier document titled *Ontario – Yours to Discover* (Mill and Morrison, 1985), demonstrates the same orientation. Thus, the focus on marketing is not just a matter of reflecting the needs of the industry at a given point in time. This latter document emphasizes issues including advertising media, slogans to be used in advertising, promotion and publicity, specific strategies for advertising in neighbouring provinces, general features for a USA campaign, and overseas consumer campaigns.

The emphasis of provinces on marketing puts this level of government in the role of supporting the private sector tourism industry rather than on direct involvement in product development or provision, except in the case of public goods provision such as provincial parks and other notable exceptions such as large anchor facilities which are difficult, if not impossible, for the private sector to construct or operate at a profit. In Ontario, for example, such facilities include the Ontario Science Centre, Ontario Place and the Sky Dome, although, in the case of the Sky Dome it was sold to the private sector a few years after construction. It must be pointed out again, that these examples are all located in a metropolitan centre, and it is generally parks which are the provincially owned facilities in rural areas. It would seem that the rural areas receive assistance in the form of anchor facilities by senior level government that is disproportionate to that received by urban centres.

On the surface, it can be argued that the focus on marketing keeps mid-level governments out of meddling in, and without control of, tourism product development and operation, and leaves these crucial matters in the hands of the private sector where it belongs. It does, however, leave rural areas of the provinces at a disadvantage given their level of development, spaciousness and operational separateness, and without the critical mass and necessary resources to construct needed anchor facilities. The particular concern here is with fragmentation of the industry due to the spatial distance separating many local rural jurisdictions which could collectively have an interest in tourism development. This fragmentation and problem of space places constraints on the construction of a regional tourism product which can spawn growth in the regional economy. So, while the marketing of tourism may be an appropriate role for provinces in the urban setting, rural areas may need more direct assistance in matters of coordination, product identification, human resource training and product development.

The need for coordination in rural areas, which may be best provided by the province or state, may go beyond the establishment of regional associations. The coordination focus appears not to be needed as much in the more self-contained urban centres which have a critical mass that allows them to act concertedly and independently because of a single legislative body at the local level. Rural areas, however, are constructed of many local jurisdictions and neighbouring munici-palities which are often not as homogeneous as their urban counterparts. Distance and lack of homogeneity lead to a need for coordination of effort, perhaps, leading to the construction of a regional plan or product. In Ontario, this problem has been addressed by the establishment of twelve regional tourism associations, which unfortunately do not have the financial resources or legislative clout that a provincial government could bring to bear on a problem of this magnitude and importance.

Provincial governments are often criticised for the substantial use of resources and effort put towards marketing a province's tourism product. However, this is a very important role for this level of government to provide. In fact, there is no other entity at this level which has the position or resources to provide this service while, simultaneously, being close enough to the industry to understand its needs and problems. While regional and other tourism associations and the private sector may have sufficient skill and resources to put toward the marketing function, it is the provincial government that has a direct relationship with both federal and local governments to better coordinate advertising and marketing activities between the local and national levels. The provincial ministers responsible for tourism meet regularly to discuss the differences in functions and role among the provinces and the federal government. Through this process each province can gain some benefit by coordinating and piggy backing on each other's marketing schemes.

It is argued that the mid-level government role should be extended beyond that of marketing to include the issues raised in the discussion above. While marketing is important to the success of the tourism industry, product creation and maintenance, in the long-term, will be pivotal to the success or failure of provincial tourism development in rural areas. An attractive marketing scheme will not succeed if the product is not equally as appealing.

Some progress, however, is being made on this front. Perhaps, Nova Scotia provides the best example of this shift in direction. A new *Tourism Strategy* (Tourism Nova Scotia, 1996) outlines the province's direction as it moves toward the next millenium and sets out the goals, strategies and actions which include:

- To have the right products for the right markets;
- To provide customers with quality experiences of good value;
- To market our products effectively;
- To develop effective leadership and partnerships among industry stakeholders;
- To foster a supportive business environment and an entrepreneurial, customer-oriented business culture within the tourism sector;
- To improve transportation access from key markets and to enhance transportation infrastructure within the province; and
- To nurture and protect our tourism assets (Tourism Nova Scotia, 1996, pp. 14–31).

Manitoba also recently engaged in a consultation process leading to a strategic plan for tourism (Ministry of Industry, Trade and Tourism, 1995). In a weighting of important issues, marketing represents the biggest line item in the budget and thus is still the highest priority but not outstandingly so. Other issues of almost equal importance to marketing in the consultation process were research and regulation, product development, regional and community development, infrastructure, human resource development, financing and investment.

This seeming change in direction by the latter strategies may be a result of the overall reduction in government resources and expenditures which has occurred since Ontario developed its document, and the subsequent recognition for the need for provinces to enter into a comprehensive partnership with the other stakeholders in the industry in order to maintain or enhance the tourism product. The difference in focus also may be a result of the fundamental character of the provinces under review. While Ontario is the most urban and largest province in Canada, Nova Scotia and Manitoba are much more rural.

Changes in the future role of the provinces

The changing world economy is producing changes in the role and function of all levels of government. Both the private and government sectors in the developed world have been in the process of reorganization and downsizing since the middle of the 1980s. This phenomenon has not escaped the tourism sector. Many local economies are looking to tourism to provide jobs and income for other industries. Simultaneously, provincial governments are facing reductions in resources with which to stimulate and support the development of the economic activity. The changing role of government at the mid level has not been lost on the Nova Scotia provincial government. Shrinking government resources are resulting in changes in the traditional government/tourism industry partnership and creating increasing need for self-reliance within the tourism industry (Tourism Nova Scotia, 1996, p. 8).

Ontario may be altering completely the function of government services in areas such as tourism. In their newly created mandate statement for the Ministry of Economic Development Trade and Tourism, the pattern of downsizing is clearly recognisable. Essentially, the philosophy suggests that government programs are impeding the development of industry, including tourism. The four core business areas stated in the mandate are:

- marketing the province's favourable business climate and high quality of life;
- working with business to remove barriers (removing barriers means removing subsidies and programs to the business sector and communities);
- equipping entrepreneurs and others with the capabilities for self-reliance; and
- supporting government privatisation.

All this adds up to the dismantling of Ontario's active and supportive role in promoting a viable and sustainable tourism industry. The mandate document points out that this newly configured ministry will save Ontario tax payers Can.$287 million over two years. If Ontario is setting the trend of government restructuring then we are witness to a total alteration of the tourism industry given the prominent role Provincial governments have historically played in tourism development.

Major changes are also occurring at the federal/provincial level which could also dramatically affect the provincial role in tourism development. At a recent Canadian First Ministers' Conference, the federal government offered to completely hand over to the provinces the jurisdiction for a number of presently shared programs, including tourism. Whether or not this becomes a reality in the future is yet to be determined, but it does indicate that the traditional role governments played in stimulating tourism development in the past is changing. It may seem attractive to provincial governments to receive sole control for tourism developments. However, it must be pointed out that the federal government did not offer to pass along their tax expenditures or provide tourism tax credits to the provinces along with the associated responsibilities.

Provincial and national government cost sharing agreements are also likely to soon become a thing of the past. For example, the Canadian Federal Government previously entered into cost sharing agreements with all the provinces (see Murphy 1985, p. 158). With the exceptions of the NWT and the Yukon, which are not provinces but territories with a special relationship to the Government of Canada, the last remaining federal/provincial agreement is with the Province of Manitoba representing about $1.5 billion allocated for tourism development in the province. The recent announcement that the Canadian Government is likely to get out of the tourism business puts renewal of that agreement into question. In order to come to grips with spiralling government deficits the tourism industry is likely to soon see reduced funding support by both senior levels of government. These economic and political changes are cause for considerable concern.

Research, analysis and monitoring

With possible imminent withdrawal of the federal government's role in tourism, and the reduced resources available to the provinces, perhaps the greatest function which may be in jeopardy to the tourism enterprise is the research initiative. Both the federal government and the provinces have put great effort and resources into collecting and analysing tourism data in order to monitor the progress and changes in the tourism sector. Several provinces, including Ontario, have produced important publications such as the Travel Monitor (which was discontinued in 1994) on a regular basis. These publications have provided a ready database and analysis to decision-makers at all levels in both the public and private sectors in the past. Given that the marketing thrust of the provincial government seems to be of priority, even in this time of downsizing, it is conceivable that the research function may be reduced further in favour of continuing the marketing focus, unless a re-evaluation of the province's role is undertaken. This re-evaluation would need to give special recognition to the significant changes taking place in government expenditures. Provincial, in this case territorial, governments who recognise the concern may pick up the challenge. For instance, a recent North West Territories Economic Development and Tourism Strategy statement addressed the issue of research and evaluation (Department of Economic Development and Tourism, 1990, p. 20):

> Changing trends, such as the recent preoccupation with 'educational' holidays, can affect vacation choices. The tourism industry in the North West Territories needs to have up-to-date information to adapt to changing markets, but also to assess the health of the industry at any given time.
>
> The research and evaluation requirements are beyond the capacity of individual entrepreneurs, and the industry itself. Providing this kind of service is a key element of the support the Government of the North West Territories will offer to tourist operators.

Protecting the resource base

Perhaps a second consequence of decentralizing power away from the centre to provincial governments is the province's increasing jurisdiction over the land base. This shift will necessitate a greater concentration of effort in regulating and protecting this resource if a viable and sustainable rural tourism enterprise is to be maintained. In spite of the growing and diversifying tourism sector in rural areas which includes cultural and historic enterprises, the rural tourism product is still heavily weighted in favour of outdoor recreation activities based on the natural environment.

Although provincial and state governments have always paid lip service to tourism as the rising sector of the economy, they have been unable to grasp the implications of making decisions with regard to competing interests. All too often protecting the natural areas on which a sustainable and vital tourism industry depends is given up in favour of the extraction or construction of industries. This may be due in part, to the pressure that multi-national corporations, who own large portions of the extractive industries, can bring to bear on provincial and state governments. Workers also tend to support the extractive industries because of the sizeable wages in those industries compared to the tourism sector which is often seasonal and lower paying.

The need for leadership in training

Regardless of the resource protection issues outlined above, technology is taking its toll on employment in the timber and mining sector. More is being produced today in these industries with fewer people employed than just a decade ago. Tourism, on the other hand, is a labour intensive industry, albeit poorly paying and seasonal. Great effort will need to be put into training many rural people who find themselves displaced from the traditional industries and faced with entering the tourism labour market. The jurisdiction best positioned to respond to large scale training needs are the provincial/state governments. Given their history of working and consulting with the wide range of groups in the tourism sector, Provincial governments are already positioned in a leadership role to coordinate training efforts in partnership with organisations like the regional travel associations. The program of training may need stronger implementation in the countryside than in urban areas given the lack of expertise and the multiplicity of jurisdictions which exist and are in need of assistance.

The need to assist with realistic and rational decision-making

Local jurisdictions are also in need of assistance in assessing their capacity to competitively join the tourism industry. The age of economic globalisation and technological proliferation is necessitating the need to restructure rural communities, particularly those economies lacking economic diversity, and more specifically single industry, resource based communities. As a result of this restructuring, large members of rural communities are turning to tourism first and foremost, for economic survival. Many of them have not accurately assessed their potential to develop and compete successfully in the tourism market place and may, in fact, have an overblown estimation of their potentials.

Tourism is often able to contribute to the restructuring process, but perhaps is receiving too much attention in this regard. Many rural communities have a vast array of natural waters and lands conducive to the development of many outdoor recreation opportunities. However, there is simply too much of these resources for everyone to exploit successfully. Rural communities will have to develop their special niche if they expect to be successful in tourism development. This means they need to expand their product beyond reliance on the natural environment. Provincial governments who possess the proper expertise can play a significant role in counselling rural areas and in assisting them to decide who is to play what role in the region. While, no doubt, most communities can actively develop some level of tourism in their area, not all can be as large a player as they may envisage.

References

Department of Tourism, Culture and Recreation, 1994, *A vision for tourism in Newfoundland and Labrador in the 21st Century*, Government of Newfoundland, St. John's
Department of Economic Development and Tourism, 1990, *Tourism: The northern lure, Government of the Northwest Territories*, Yellowknife
Government of the Northwest Territories, 1983, *Summary report, community based tourism: a strategy for the Northwest Territories tourism industry*, Department of Economic Development, Yellowknife
Government of Ontario, 1991, *Background document. The new Ministry of Economic Development Trade and Tourism: mandate and core business*, Ministry of Economic Development, Trade and Tourism, Toronto
Hall, C.M. and Jenkins, J., 1995, *Tourism and public policy*, Routledge, London
Mill, R.C. and Morrison, A., 1985, *The tourism system: an introductory text*, Prentice Hall, Englewood Cliffs
Ministry of Culture, Tourism and Recreation, 1994, *Ontario's tourism industry: opportunity, progress, innovation*, Queen's Printer, Toronto
Ministry of Economic Development Trade and Tourism, 1996, *Background Document*, Government of Ontario, Toronto
Ministry of Industry, Trade and Tourism, 1995, *Manitoba tourism strategy: a framework for development*, Government of Manitoba, Winnipeg
Ministry of State (Tourism), 1985 (nd.), *Tourism tomorrow: towards a Canadian tourism strategy*, Government of Canada, Ottawa
Ministry of Tourism and Recreation, 1982. Yours to discover, Government of Ontario, Toronto
Murphy, P., 1985, *Tourism: a community approach*, Routledge, New York
Reid, D.G., Fuller, A.M., Haywood, K.M. and Bryden, J., 1993, *The integration of tourism, culture and recreation in rural Ontario: a rural visitation program*, Queen's Printer, Ministry of Culture, Tourism and Recreation, Toronto
Reid, D., Fuller, A.M., Haywood, K.M., 1995, Tourism: Saviour or false hope for the rural economy? *Plan Canada*, **35** (3): 18–25
Tourism Nova Scotia, 1996, *Strategy for tourism*, Government of Nova Scotia, Halifax

5   Rural tourism in Otago and Southland, New Zealand

GEOFFREY KEARSLEY

Southern New Zealand is the country's most important tourist region, offering a diversity of landscapes and cultural and natural heritage experiences in both urban and rural contexts. Otago and Southland are the principal provinces of the southern part of the South Island, a region sometimes referred to as the 'Deep South'. At present, New Zealand attracts around 1.5 million overseas visitors; of these, some 516,000 visit Otago, generating 2.9 million visitor nights, and 241,000 visit Southland, yielding 800,000 visitor nights (New Zealand Tourism Board, 1996). The undisputed focus of tourist activity is Queenstown, New Zealand's premier resort, which attracts 448,000 visitors for 1.6 million nights. However, Dunedin, the principal city has begun to emerge as New Zealand's top secondary destination and currently attracts 184,000 visitors for around 750,000 bednights.

Together, Queenstown and Dunedin form the two foci of an Alpine region based upon adventure and winter sports as well as domestic holiday making and a coastal region that is based upon wildlife, such as penguins and albatross, and upon a rich cultural heritage. The extent of the overall Southern Tourist Region is set out in Figure 5.1, where it can be seen that the Alpine region stretches from Fiordland and the small townships of Manapouri and Te Anau through to Mount Cook and the open country of the Mackenzie Basin. The coastal strip begins with the small town of Oamaru and includes Dunedin and the Catlins Forest Park as well as Stewart Island. The country between the coast and the Alps is sparsely populated save along the principal communication corridors; most of it is medium to high altitude tussock grassland, the New Zealand High Country (Fitzharris and Kearsley, 1988). There are only three land gateways to the region, namely the Haast Pass from the remote West Coast, the Lindis Pass from Mount Cook, and the main coastal highway from Christchurch, State Highway 1. Christchurch is the principal airport, but international flights across the Tasman have begun to use Dunedin as a secondary point of access, while a limited number of ski charters have arrived directly at Queenstown. In spite of this, patterns of movement through the region are complex (Gray, 1992; Kearsley, 1993; Higham, 1996).

Figure 5.1.   The Southern Tourist Region

The context for tourism development

Tourism has emerged as a major part of the New Zealand economy in the past fifteen years. In 1975, there were barely 250,000 international arrivals; there are six times as many today, and tourism has become one of the country's most significant export earners. In 1995/6, tourism earned the country some NZ$ 4.8 billion, a figure that exceeds the receipts from all meat, dairying or from wool (New Zealand Tourism Board, 1996). Of course, agriculture in general is still the basis of the New Zealand economy, but tourism has grown to become a highly significant and economically reliable sector, especially since the progressive deregulation of the national economy since 1984.

Economic deregulation became inevitable in the late 1970s, when the twin impacts of the global oil shocks and Britain's entry into the European Community introduced massive inflation and a loss of previously guaranteed British markets for agricultural products. In the South Island, the impacts of agricultural change were severe, although heavy Government subsidies protected farmers to some extent in the short term (Britton, Le Heron and Pawson 1992). Nonetheless, tourism gradually became an attractive proposition for rural communities, especially those close to the Alpine resorts, where significant growth was taking place, partly under the impetus of substantial ski-field investment.

The initial Government response to economic adversity and perceived dependence on imported energy was to initiate a major public works programme focused upon the development of indigenous energy resources. Oil and gas fields in Taranaki provided a North Island focus; in the South, massive hydro electricity schemes were under way on the Waitaki River. These were to be augmented by yet larger schemes on the Clutha, which is the principal river of Otago. Extensive lignite fields, mostly in remote rural areas, were explored with a view to synthetic fuel production. Popularly known as the 'Think Big' programme, the plan brought significant development to some parts of Central Otago, especially the town of Cromwell, and eased the consequences of agricultural retrenchment. Had energy prices remained at a very high level, 'Think Big' might have succeeded. In the event, energy prices declined, and by 1984, it was clear that the national economy was in dire straits (Crocombe, Enright and Porter, 1991; Everett, 1996).

In Otago, hydro developments were scaled back because of associated costs, engineering difficulties and pressures to conserve some scenic rivers. In particular, the Kawarau River, close to Queenstown, was saved from damming and the nascent white water rafting industry based upon the River thus survived (Kearsley, 1992). Elsewhere in the region, plans to mine lignite and plans for a major aluminium smelter at Dunedin were abandoned as uneconomic and the only project to survive, the Clyde Dam near Cromwell, continued after special empowering legislation and massive cost over-runs (Memon and Kearsley, 1990). The consequences for Dunedin were considerable (Kearsley, 1997b), but were not fully felt in rural areas until a change of Government in 1984 introduced free market policies to what had become a hopelessly protected and seriously ineffective economy (Everett, 1996).

For rural areas, by far the most powerful consequence was the removal of agricultural subsidies. Payments for fertiliser, fencing and stock numbers were just some of the many that were removed; some farms became unprofitable, others were crippled by high interest rates and the inflated prices that had been paid for land in the early 1980s. As farms went into survival mode, expenditure in small rural service centres all but dried up, causing a crisis among service industries, such as contractors, fencers, shearers and the like. At the same time, many farm wives and other family members sought work off the farm or endeavoured to find new diversifications on the farm. A further impact was the privatisation and rationalisation of what had been widely available Government services, such as the railways, Post Office, hospitals and banks. It seemed to many small communities that only tourism was left as a viable source of jobs and community income (Kearsley, 1987). Consequently, many farms attempted to set up tourist ventures, local authorities tried to encourage local festivals and events and many individuals attempted to set up small enterprises such as fishing, guiding or local tours.

There were many examples to follow. Large scale resorts such as Queenstown and Wanaka expanded rapidly, first under the impetus of ski field development and then with the explosion of adventure activities. A.J. Hackett introduced bungy jumping on the Kawarau River, jet boating and white water rafting developed rapidly, and a series of airborne activities was introduced, including parapenting, tandem parachuting, heli-bungying and parasailing. Dunedin consciously introduced tourism into its economic development strategy, and, through a high profile promotional campaign that was a first for New Zealand (Kearsley, 1996, 1997b), provided a clear example of how heritage and wildlife tourism could be engineered and used as a catalyst for economic revival.

The tourism product

The Southern tourist region possesses a vast range of landscape and cultural products that rank among the premier icons of New Zealand tourism (Kearsley, 1996). In the West, the Alpine fold mountains provide spectacular wilderness scenery that is the core of the country's premier World Heritage Area, including the Fiordland and Mount Aspiring National Parks. The Fiordland coast provides unparalleled scenery at the popular destinations of Milford Sound and Doubtful Sound and in a host of wild and remote fiords that are barely visited. This part of the region is one of the greatest temperate wilderness areas in the world and contains famous walking tracks such as the Milford track, the Routeburn and Kepler tracks and a wide range of other, less famous walking opportunities. This region is fringed by a chain of vast glacial lakes; Manapouri and Te Anau in the south and Wakatipu and Wanaka to the north are but the largest among many. Since the National Parks may not contain permanent settlements or, indeed, any habitation, a chain of resorts has grown up along the lake shores.

Inland from the lakes lies a belt of rain shadow alpine foreland and a chain of block mountains; these are the tussock grasslands of the High Country, and it is here that gold was discovered in the 1860s, providing a rich cultural heritage for modern tourism. Massive faulting of the brittle schist rock has led to spectacular barren horst and graben landforms interspersed with small agricultural basins. The east coast is a region of agricultural downlands and sedimentary basins; Dunedin is sited on the caldera of an extinct volcano whose relict landforms provide the harbour and peninsula that are home to a rich wildlife of sea mammals and sea birds.

A hugely variable climate sees Milford Sound receive over 5000 mm of rain and Alexandra less than 25 mm; the continental climate of the interior sees extensive sunshine with winter temperatures falling as low as minus 25°C in the extreme and rising to nearly 40°C in the hottest part of summer. These extremes and the wide altitudinal range have produced a diverse vegetational pattern ranging from alpine herb fields through rain forests and dry grasslands to lowland podocarp forests and agricultural and horticultural landscapes.

The cultural product is based upon European settlement from the early nineteenth century onward. Although an early Polynesian society evolved and adapted over many hundreds of years, few physical traces beyond archaeological sites are left and even the early European settlers, sealers and whalers, left little behind save new names on the land. Permanent settlement on the coast was confirmed with the establishment of Dunedin in 1848, while substantive inland development had to await the discovery of gold in 1861 (Olssen, 1984). Extensive sheep ranching opened up much of the interior as gold production faded. The establishment of a recently diversified agriculture has brought a rapidly growing wine industry and the regular appearance of exotic stock, such as llamas, ostriches and deer.

Resort development

Rural tourism revolves around the nuclei of a series of small resorts that have evolved according to a fairly structured and regular pattern (Kearsley, 1990). Most began in one of two ways (see Table 5.1). Mount Cook and Milford Sound have been resorts of a kind from the earliest days of New Zealand's exploration, and catered for a rich overseas market from the very beginning. Both are located in the hearts of

Table 5.1. A typology of resort development

Stage	Type	Markets	Facilities	Example
1	Summer resort Cribs Retirement	Local Domestic	Limited accommodation A few basic shops Limited activities	Naseby Queenstown (to mid 1950s) Wanaka (to mid 1970s)
	Outpost	Adventures Domestic and international	Quality hotel Specialised facilities	Mount Cook (to mid 1970s) Milford Sound
2	Staging post and stopover	Coach tours Domestic and international Rental cars Campervans	Range of accommodation One or two specialised shops, etc Limited range special attractions More cribs and retirement homes	Te Anau Queenstown (to 1960s) Omarama Tekapo
3	All season destination	Domestic and international	Ski facilities Wide range specialist shops and accommodation Range of activities and theme sites	Wanaka Queenstown (to mid 1970s)
4	International destination resort	International and domestic	Chain hotels; tourism the dominant activity Extensive night life Very wide range activities, facilities	Queenstown

Source: Kearsley 1990. Reproduced with permission.

Figure 5.2. The former goldmining settlement of Arrowtown, now a major tourist destination (G. Kearsley). Reproduced with permission.

National Parks and have little room for expansion; accordingly, they are day destinations with limited facilities or overnight accommodation. The more accessible resorts began either as small gold fields settlements (e.g., Queenstown, Arrowtown (Figure 5.2) and Naseby) or remote service centres for agricultural regions (e.g., Te Anau). Typically, they began as holiday centres for the regional domestic population who preferred their Alpine scenery and continental summers to the more temperate coastline, where most urban people resided. Holiday homes, known locally as cribs, often became retirement homes; many other visitors simply used the extensive municipal camping grounds or 'motor camps' where rudimentary cabins, ablutions and tent or caravan sites were provided.

As international visitors began to arrive and as New Zealanders began to travel more widely, some resorts became overnight or short stay stopovers for scheduled or informal tours and a range of accommodation in the form of motels and motor lodges was developed. Queenstown took this form up to the early 1960s, and this is still the nature of some resorts today (e.g., Omarama, Te Anau). A limited number of places have been able to benefit from ski field development. The first major field was developed at Coronet Peak near Queenstown in the 1950s; the establishment of a winter season made Queenstown an all-year resort and provided the basis for a range of accommodation and ancillary services and facilities. Later developments in the 1970s and 1980s added to Queenstown's choice of ski fields, while the late 1970s

Figure 5.3. Lakeshore tourism developments at Queenstown (G. Kearsley). Reproduced with permission.

developments of the Treble Cone and later the Cardrona ski areas gave Wanaka a similar impetus, so that now these are the premier resorts of the region.

Queenstown's earlier start has enabled it to become a central growth pole for the region and it has outstripped all other resorts to become a truly international destination. Indeed, some New Zealanders now feel that Queenstown is too expensive or is too commercialised for their tastes (Winchester, 1995). Certainly, with a wide range of international hotels, restaurants, shops and activities, and the possibility of a casino, Queenstown has become the hub of the whole region (Figure 5.3).

In recent years, other small settlements have become resorts of a kind. One group is made up of a series of former hydro construction villages, such as Omarama and Twizel on the Waitaki and Cromwell on the Clutha (Memon and Kearsley, 1990). Omarama was bought up by local people desiring cheap holiday homes in the early 1970s, and has proved to be a successful local resort; Twizel was scheduled for total removal (indeed, it was designed to be a temporary town), but local people were able to persuade the Government to allow it to remain and the township is now well on the way to becoming a thriving resort, thanks, in part, to its relatively close proximity to Mount Cook. Cromwell was an old established gold fields town long before its expansion into a construction centre and it was always the formal intention that it should evolve as a domestic resort. This it has been able to do as a result of the newly created hydro lake, Lake Dunstan, that surrounds Cromwell, and massive investment by the Government in facilities such as a swimming pool and shopping centre that would be the envy of much larger townships. Elsewhere, small country towns, suffering still from the long term effects of the late 1980s rural downturn, would like nothing more than to gain a tourist role; their efforts are discussed below.

One notable landscape feature arising from tourist promotion has been the development of tourist oriented promotional icons, often cast from fibreglass on the grand scale. Thus, the small town of Gore boasts a giant brown trout, its neighbour, Clinton, has a team of lifesize Clydesdale horses, and Cromwell, in the heart of an orcharding region, has a huge bowl of fruit. The small settlement of Tuatapere has declared itself to be the sausage capital of the world, for no apparent or particular reason, and the tiny settlement of Tekapo has erected a bronze statue of the sheepdogs that opened up the Mackenzie country.

Changing access and institutional arrangements

In the past, access to rural tourist facilities has depended upon the extent of the road network. Access to the National Parks and other reserves that make up the Conservation Estate has always been guaranteed, because such lands are held by the Crown on behalf of the public; much farmland was extensive grazing and this, too, was traditionally open to recreationists. Indeed, many High Country runholders were prominent in espousing outdoor recreation and it was rare for access permission to be denied. Much of this land was held as pastoral lease from the Crown and, while leaseholders enjoyed most of the privileges of *de facto* private ownership, the public still regarded such country as essentially 'theirs'.

Access, especially to the National Parks, has largely been by foot, although float planes and helicopters have helped to open up much remote country, often to the disgust of wilderness seekers and back country anglers (Booth, 1996; Rogers, 1996). Few roads were available until quite recent times. The Homer Tunnel which links Milford Sound with the road to Te Anau was only opened in the early 1950s; it was not until the mid 1960s that the Haast Pass link with the West Coast was completed and an alternative route via the remote and beautiful Hollyford Valley, which was first attempted in the Depression years has never been completed, despite its 'obvious' value as a further link in completing a major potential circuit between Milford Sound and the West Coast (Kane, 1991; Kearsley, 1993). There are many pressures for a direct link between Milford Sound and Queenstown (the present day trip takes a total of 14 hours), but this would also involve the sacrifice of one of the last unroaded alpine wilderness valleys, the Greenstone.

Many roads still have an unsealed, gravel surface. The Haast Pass road was only completely sealed in 1996, the Southern Scenic Route through the Catlins still has many kilometres of rough gravel as do the important direct links between Queenstown and Wanaka and the Routeburn track, via Glenorchy. Local tourist interests believe that such difficult roads deter overseas visitors who are quite unused to driving in such conditions. As a result, there is often strong political pressure for sealing to be undertaken. On the other hand, locals who are less directly involved in tourism argue that road improvements simply attract a flood of traffic. Certainly, the tourist industry in Te Anau was not helped by recent vast improvements to the

Milford Sound road. With much faster travel, many visitors no longer need to stay over in Te Anau, and its role as the gateway to Milford has diminished.

The ongoing review of the *Land Act 1948* sets out the terms of tenure of the High Country pastoral leases (South Island High Country Working Party, 1994). Agricultural interests are pushing for the ability to purchase the freehold of such country and there has been sympathy for this in Government circles, because the revenue derived from such leases barely covers the cost of administration. At the same time, much of the higher land is marginal, even for the low density grazing that is carried out, but possesses significant conservation values. Thus, it is proposed that individual deals should be struck on a farm by farm basis in which such land should be surrendered to the Conservation Estate with its value set against the cost of freeholding often much smaller areas of better land. Some such deals have already been struck in Otago to the satisfaction of all parties, but their extent is small and very large areas have still to be considered.

Some High Country properties are already involved in tourist ventures, such as four wheel drive trips, and the provision of accommodation and farm experiences (Ibell, 1992). The provisions of pastoral leases forbid any other activity than grazing, so that freeholding will open up many potential opportunities. On the other hand, freeholding will make it easier to enforce trespass notices and to charge for access – to river banks, for example – and it is feared that many traditional routes to the back country and the Conservation Estate may be blocked. Organisations such as Federated Mountain Clubs, Public Access New Zealand, and the Fish and Game Councils have strenuously opposed widespread freeholding on these grounds. In short, the issue is far from an amicable solution.

Other legislative changes have also had an impact on access. The *Occupational Safety and Health Act* makes employers more responsible for workplace accidents and, following the collapse of a small bridge on a North Island farm, some landholders have denied access on the grounds of unacceptable liability. While some progress has been made in clarifying landholder responsibilities so that they are not held responsible for recreationists' safety, some land is still closed and it seems probable that this has proved a welcome excuse in some cases. The *Conservation Act* includes provision for a 20 metre marginal strip along the banks of most streams and significant water bodies; known as the 'Queen's Chain', such riparian strips have been an important source of access to fishing waters and the wider back country (Kearsley, 1997a). A proposal that they could be closed for some part of the year for ostensibly agricultural practices to be carried out has led to concerns that such a provision would make it possible for access to be limited to fee paying commercial guides at some parts of the season. Since the purchase of a modestly priced licence makes almost all waters available to the ordinary angler, such changes are again strongly resisted.

Finally, much of the South Island has been involved in negotiations between the Crown and local Maori. Under New Zealand's founding document, the Treaty of Waitangi, Maori are entitled to certain rights and privileges as the *tangata whenua*, the people of the land or first inhabitants. Resolution of grievances brought by the *Ngai Tahu* people has all but concluded; this involves, in part, transferral of much of the spectacular High Country at the head of Lake Wakatipu to Maori ownership, following its purchase by the Crown. Again, despite Ngai Tahu reassurances, there are concerns that land of high conservation value in the Greenstone and at the start of the Routeburn track might be inappropriately developed through farming or the development of transportation facilities (e.g., a monorail to Milford Sound), and this situation, too, remains to be resolved.

Simultaneously, new opportunities for recreational access have arisen, in particular through the use of redundant railway corridors. The scenically spectacular rail link between Dunedin and Clyde (originally Cromwell) was closed in 1990 following the completion of the Clyde Dam (Graham, 1996). Dunedin City Council bought the first 30 kilometres or so, so as to protect the spectacular Taieri Gorge Railway. The Department of Conservation acquired the remainder for conversion into a long distance walkway, now almost complete and known as the Central Otago Rail Trail. Small townships along the route hope that small scale accommodation and servicing opportunities will arise as use develops. This is the first such use of a redundant rail corridor, but many others exist, albeit in a fragmented state. Opportunities exist for walking and cycle routes in the Catlins (Green, 1992) and beside the main routes from Dunedin to Roxburgh, and from Gore to Mossburn. These would provide cycle access away from heavy traffic to Central Otago and Fiordland, respectively.

Local authority involvement

Since the early 1990s local government has operated on an essentially two tier structure of Regions and Districts, although there is a discontinuous lower tier of Community Boards. Regions have the responsibility of operating the policy level requirements of the *Resource Management Act 1991*, and with dealing with a range of air, land and water management processes. Territorial Local Authorities (TLAs), which are Districts and Cities operate Resource Consents which are essentially permits for development (Coughlan and Kearsley, 1990; Kearsley, 1997b).

The bulk of local authority involvement has come at the District level (Dymond 1996); Otago Regional Council, in particular, has done little for tourism explicitly. This is, in part, because of a limitation within the legislation that only permits promotional activity with the consent of all constituent TLAs, but also because of a preoccupation with rabbit and opossum control. The presence of strong pre-existing local promotional groups and an unwillingness to trespass on the perceived affairs of Queenstown are further disincentives. Southland Regional Council has taken a more proactive tourism development line, although Southland District can lay claim to a number of local development issues, such as the establishment of coordinated farm stay enterprises on the way to Te Anau and in rural Southland (Kearsley, 1987). Nonetheless, one must travel outside the Southern Tourist Region to find really effective tourism strategies at the regional level (e.g., Canterbury, Taranaki and Northland).

Two Districts in particular, Dunedin City and Queenstown Lakes (which includes both Wanaka and Arrowtown), have for long had strong promotion organisations. *Tourism Dunedin* is a truly regional body, with involvement throughout coastal Otago, from Oamaru to the Catlins. Other TLAs have supported Regional or Local Tourist Offices (RTOs and LTOs) to a greater or lesser extent. *Destination*

Queenstown and *Fiordland Promotions* are largely industry led and financed, but *Tourism Dunedin* is largely TLA funded, while strong District support has seen the rise of *Tourism Waitaki* from a series of small promotional groups to a fully fledged RTO. Other Districts have lagged, and Clutha is only in the early stages of developing a tourism strategy (Parker, 1996). In all cases, though, Queenstown and Dunedin have acted as mentors and, sometimes, competitors; they have been both catalyst and example.

Local authority and community initiatives and joint ventures

Local bodies have a long tradition of product development and promotion, from the early days of simple brochures to the sophisticated Visitor Centres and promotional campaigns of today. An early vehicle for TLA involvement has been through joint ventures with local communities to develop festivals and other events. Based upon the traditional 'A & P' shows (Agricultural and Pastoral events) and community fetes, a series of specialised festivals has arisen. Among the more notable are the Alexandra Blossom Festival, which celebrates the orchard industry and Rhododendron Week in Dunedin. A rapidly developing heritage event is the annual Goldfields Cavalcade, which involves a series of cross country horseback treks that converge upon a different location each year. Driven by a small committee of riding enthusiasts, this has become a specialised quality event, which won a national Tourism Award in 1995, but has now left the door open for a more general Goldfields celebration.

Winter Festivals are to be found in the major ski centres, while others have been developed from no particular base. Thus, the 'Golden Guitar', which is a Country and Western event held annually in Gore, is based simply on local enthusiasm. The success of such an event, which does not require a specific resource has inspired several communities to find an event that they can call their own. Generally, though, there is a product base. Two communities have persuaded the electrical generation company ECNZ to support endurance events – 'That Dam Run' on the Waitaki and the 'Kepler Challenge' in Fiordland – while Alexandra has used an ongoing plague of rabbits to organise a particularly gruesome 'Easter Bunny Shoot', the promotional benefits of which are dubious.

Heritage development has proceeded from a strong TLA base. Much of the initiative for the preservation and enhancement of Dunedin's extraordinary architectural heritage has come from Dunedin City Council, while Waitaki District has sponsored and developed the lovely Whitestone precinct, a spectacular rehabilitation of the elegant Victorian white limestone port of Oamaru. This latter is the venue for a week long Heritage Festival that has a strong Chinese and Victorian flavour (Kearsley, 1997b). Local authorities run the many galleries and museums, large and small, that are a distinctive feature of the area, while the Department of Conservation is responsible for the Otago Goldfields Park, a disparate collection of scattered goldfields sites. Craft trails and heritage trails have been developed in some areas; one of the few involvements of the Otago Regional Council in a tourist facility was the establishment and signing of the Otago Goldfields Trail. Local bodies have also lent support to the Mainstreet Programme

Figure 5.4. Lanach Castle, Dunedin. A major tourism attraction on the Otago Peninsula (G. Kearsley). Reproduced with permission.

which aims to bring economic revival and tourism through the tidying and enhancement of small town main streets, many of which have declined as the service function has faded. Here, it is essential that individuality and authenticity should be retained and that look alike, off the peg solutions do not reduce individual character.

Community groups have led to the development of many facilities. The world famous albatross colony at Taiaroa Head on the Otago Peninsula, for example, was initiated and developed by the Otago Peninsula Trust, a voluntary organisation who also run gardens and other venues, and who has taken a lead in providing access to many Peninsula sites (Figure 5.4). Various groups have worked together to make penguins – the rare Yellow-eyed Penguin in particular – virtual icons of Otago wildlife.

Private sector involvement

There are few major companies operating in the region outside the core Queenstown axis, where companies such as *Fiordland Travel, Mount Cook* and *The Helicopter Line* are among the largest. Often, companies are one or two person ventures, especially outside the accommodation area. Consequently, there is a great deal of co-operation with TLAs and RTOs as small minibus tours and adventure or wildlife packages are developed. Inevitably, too, conflicts arise under competitive pressures as too many small companies concentrate on a limited market or when competing operators believe that the RTO is favouring one above another.

While various activities, such as guided fishing or hunting trips, have been developed in small rural towns, few have been sufficiently viable as to provide a comfortable living. The emphasis has therefore been on providing accommodation, both on farms and in townships, as a second income, with other activities available as required. Only around the major resorts has this proved to be any more than a supplement to household earnings, although a fair proportion of such operators are content to accept a lower income in order to enjoy a preferred rural lifestyle or to remain on the land (McKenzie, 1995).

Conclusions

The Southern Tourist Region is New Zealand's premier tourist destination region and Queenstown its principal resort; there are no indications that this will change. The industry is well established in the urban areas and major resorts of the region and it is unlikely that anything but a promising future can be expected. Wilderness and natural area regions are likely also to grow in national significance, especially when the new markets that have come to prominence in recent years (e.g., Korea and Taiwan) comprise many visitors interested in back country experiences. Rural areas, the traditional agricultural regions of Otago and Southland, are likely to be more or less involved in tourism as agricultural and forestry fortunes vary. Currently, a dairying boom in Southland, in particular, has reduced the urgency to diversify into non-agricultural areas such as tourism.

Rural tourism patterns will evolve according to the evolution of the overall tourist region. However, there is no regional strategy for tourism, nor any spatial and structural strategy at the national level, to guide and inform development patterns. Nonetheless, clear choices for development are emerging. The most important of these revolves around the extent to which development is focused upon Queenstown and the extent to which it becomes dispersed throughout the region in a series of resort nodes. Important in this is the location of the region's gateway airport. Currently, most international arrivals are via Christchurch; they then arrive in Queenstown directly or via Mount Cook. Lesser numbers drive down via State Highway 1. This situation, however, is changing.

Queenstown takes some trans-Tasman flights, mostly as ski charters, but topography and length of runway limit the size of aircraft and take-off loadings. Invercargill has developed a small international facility, but has received few flights and it seems as though that development was ill advised. On the other hand, Dunedin has experienced some success with a rapid growth in flights to and from Australia based upon the now defunct *Kiwi Air* and the more enduring *Freedom* subsidiary of Air New Zealand (Bailey, 1994). More importantly, Dunedin plans to expand the runway capacity of the airport to take Boeing 767s and make Singapore accessible by direct flight. More ambitious plans to make Dunedin a major 747 gateway are in the discussion stage. Elsewhere, plans exist for a wholly new facility at Castle Rock midway between Queenstown and Te Anau, while a site close to either Wanaka or Cromwell has also been discussed.

The gateway airport's location will determine to a large extent whether a dispersed or concentrated development will take place. Concentration around Queenstown will restrict rural development away from the core region; dispersal will enhance it. Concentration runs the risk of overdevelopment and a destruction of the very values that attract visitors in the first place, and there is some slight evidence that this is already beginning to happen; it is a problem that requires investigation. On the other hand, a structured policy of partial dispersal could have the result of spreading the tourism benefit more widely and retaining the visitor for longer, effectively growing the cake and sharing it out more widely.

It is clear, in other words, that a regional tourism strategy is required. There have been various attempts to create a 'Southern Macro Region' that would act as a joint marketing and promotion body and this has been successful on a number of occasions, although Queenstown has tended to go its own way more often than not. Whereas a strategic plan for the whole region is lacking, the New Zealand Tourism Board is presently developing just such a plan for the core Queenstown Lakes area. Such a plan is no substitute for a wider plan; this requires the active involvement of both the Otago and the Southland Regional Councils, as well as such agencies as TLAs, industry organisations and Government departments (e.g., the Ministry of Agriculture and the Department of Conservation). There is great potential for the advancement of rural tourism in Otago and Southland, but until greater integration and co-operation is achieved, it will operate as it does today, at a piecemeal and local, albeit relatively successful level.

References

Bailey, M., 1994, The feasibility of Dunedin Airport Limited becoming a trans-Tasman facility, Unpublished Diploma in Tourism dissertation, Centre for Tourism, University of Otago, Dunedin

Booth, K., 1996, The effects of aircraft overflights on recreationists in natural settings, Paper presented at the Tourism Down Under II Conference, Centre for Tourism, University of Otago, Dunedin

Britton, S., Le Heron, R. and Pawson, E., 1992, *Changing places in New Zealand : a geography of restructuring*, New Zealand Geographical Society, Christchurch

Crocombe, G.T., Enright M.J. and Porter M.E., 1991, *Upgrading New Zealand's competitive advantage*, Oxford University Press, Auckland.

Coughlan, G. and Kearsley, G.W., 1990, Selling southern landscapes: the role of local and regional government in New Zealand's tourism development. In *Southern landscapes: essays in honour of Bill Brockie and Ray Hargreaves*, G.W. Kearsley and B.B. Fitzharris, eds., University of Otago, Dunedin

Dymond, S.J., 1996, Indicators of sustainable tourism in New Zealand: a local government perspective, Unpublished Diploma in Tourism dissertation, Centre for Tourism, University of Otago, Dunedin

Everett, A.M., 1996, Strategic management of international business for relationships with New Zealand: a primer for executives and investors, *Management Decision*, **34** (9): 82–104

Fitzharris, B.B. and Kearsley, G.W., 1988, Appreciating our high country. In *Southern approaches*, P.G. Holland and W.B. Johnston, eds., pp. 197–218, New Zealand Geographical Society, Christchurch

Graham, O.J., 1996, The Central Otago rail trail: a study of effects on adjoining landowners' attitudes, Unpublished Diploma in Tourism dissertation, Centre for Tourism, University of Otago, Dunedin

Gray, G.J., 1992, The intranational travel patterns of international visitors to New Zealand, Unpublished MA thesis, Centre for Tourism, University of Otago, Dunedin

Green, J., 1992, Cycle tourism in the Catlins, Unpublished Diploma in Tourism dissertation, Centre for Tourism, University of Otago, Dunedin

Higham, E., 1996, The regional structure of tourism in Southern New Zealand, Unpublished M Tour dissertation, Centre for Tourism, University of Otago, Dunedin

Ibell, J., 1992, Tourism on high country sheep stations, Unpublished Diploma in Tourism dissertation, Centre for Tourism, University of Otago, Dunedin

Kane, S.J., 1991, Use values of the Hollyford Track: with specific reference to the Haast – Hollyford tourist road, Unpublished MA thesis, Department of Geography, University of Otago, Dunedin

Kearsley, G.W., 1987, *Northern Southland rural resources survey*, Resource Development Centre, University of Otago, Dunedin

Kearsley, G.W., 1990, Tourist development and wilderness management in Southern New Zealand, *Australian Geographer*, **21** (2): 127–140

Kearsley, G.W., 1992, Tourism and resource development conflicts on the Kawarau and Shotover rivers *Geojournal*, **29** (3): 263–270

Kearsley, G.W., 1993, Changing patterns of international visitor flows through New Zealand, Paper presented at the XIVth New Zealand Geographical Society Conference, Christchurch, New Zealand.

Kearsley, G.W., 1996, Tourism in Dunedin and Otago: introductory address, *Tourism down under II*, ed. G. Kearsley, Centre for Tourism, University of Otago, Dunedin

Kearsley, G.W., 1997a, Tourism planning and policy in New Zealand. In *Tourism planning and policy in Australia and New Zealand: Issues, cases and practice*, C.M. Hall, J. Jenkins and G.W. Kearsley, eds., Irwin Publishers, Sydney

Kearsley, G.W., 1997b, Public acceptance of heritage tourism as an instrument of urban restructuring: the case of Dunedin. In *Tourism planning and policy in Australia and New Zealand: Issues, cases and practice*, C.M. Hall, J. Jenkins and G.W. Kearsley, eds., Irwin Publishers, Sydney

Memon, P.A. and Kearsley, G.W., 1990, Resource based urban development in the peripheral regions of New Zealand. In *Southern landscapes: essays in honour of Bill Brockie and Ray Hargreaves*, G.W. Kearsley and B.B. Fitzharris, eds., pp. 329–346, University of Otago, Dunedin

McKenzie, G.M., 1995, Rural tourism: the farm hosts' perspective, In *Proceedings, Pan Pacific Business Association conference XII*, pp. 53–55, Dunedin and Queenstown

New Zealand Tourism Board, 1996, *International visitor survey*, 1995/6, New Zealand Tourism Board, Wellington

Olssen, E., 1984, *A history of Otago*, McIndoe, Dunedin

Parker, E.E., 1996, Tourism in the Clutha District, Unpublished Diploma in Tourism dissertation, Centre for Tourism, University of Otago, Dunedin.

Rogers, K., 1996, The effects of aircraft overflights on visitors to the Mount Cook National Park, Unpublished Diploma in Tourism dissertation, Centre for Tourism, University of Otago, Dunedin

South Island High Country Working Party, 1994, *South Island high country review*, Ministries of Conservation, Agriculture and the Environment, Wellington

Winchester, M., 1995, The ugly duckling: domestic tourism in New Zealand with specific reference to Dunedin, Unpublished Diploma in Tourism dissertation, Centre for Tourism, University of Otago, Dunedin

6 Local and resort development

ALISON GILL

Introduction

The scale and type of tourism development in rural areas will differ according to variables such as natural and cultural resource endowment, location, competition, entrepreneurial activity, and institutional arrangements. For some rural communities, tourism is one element in a diversified economy. For others, tourism is the primary economic endeavour which dominates community life and upon which the local area is dependent. The focus of this chapter is upon this latter context; that is, situations in which the community is considered to be a resort.

Resorts vary in character from an extreme such as Disneyworld in central Florida where a combination of market-related location and cheap land determined the development site (Murphy, 1994) to small rural communities in Ontario which depend on a seasonal influx of summer residents to 'cottage country' (Dahms, 1988). Resorts range from comprehensively planned enterprises instigated by one or more major developers to catalytic developments which result from a concentration of smaller tourism enterprises associated with a central attraction or theme which evolve over time (Pearce, 1987). The majority of the former, that is planned integrated resorts, are located either in mountain or coastal regions. Such resorts 'seek to internalise visitor expenditures within the resort precinct' (Stanton and Aislabie, 1992, p. 436). The degree to which local institutions and local residents are involved or exercise any control over development will also vary depending on the institutional arrangements concerning the resort. These range from privately-operated enterprises, such as some ski resorts in North America (e.g., Snowbird, Utah), to resorts which operate as municipalities (e.g., Whistler, British Columbia; Vail, Colorado), with democratically elected officials.

Despite this variability, there are common issues that arise from the interaction between the resort and the local region. The most widespread and persistent of these relate to local area residents' ability to control (1) tourism growth (especially the scale and rate of development); and (2) resource allocation and distribution (especially the availability of housing). The manner in which such issues are resolved is very dependent on the institutional context within which the resort is situated. This chapter explores the above issues after elaborating on the reasons for resort development in rural areas and the distinctive set of stakeholders associated with such developments.

Why areas seek rural development

Unlike the situation in urban areas, single developments are often of particular significance in rural areas, and a single major development may be seen as the base for sustaining the viability of a community, rejuvenating a destination area, providing the rationale for the reimaging of an area and for putting a rural area on the map. While the tourism industry consists primarily of small business enterprises and as such offers opportunities for small scale local entrepreneurs with limited capital to enter the industry, some communities interested in local economic development perceive that large scale exogenous enterprises are the appropriate means of tourism development. In the context of Canadian rural communities, Bryant (1991) has suggested that this occurs because of the traditional 'industrial' model of economic development in which communities seek to attract large scale external investment. An alternative community economic development approach in which endogenous opportunities are pursued is a new concept for many small rural communities. From a tourism perspective, there are examples of both approaches. However, resort developments dependent on recreational activities which require major infrastructural investment (e.g., skiing or golfing) are most commonly examples of the former. Whistler, British Columbia, represents an example of the large scale public and private investment required to achieve international destination status as a resort. In this instance, an integrated, comprehensively planned new resort community was constructed with a heavy reliance on public funds which were used to develop infrastructure and ensure a viable economic environment to attract private investment (Figure 6.1).

There are, however, some examples of communities that have become major tourist destinations through community effort and investment. Chemainus, British Columbia, is one such example. In the face of downsizing in the forest industry the Chemainus community sought to reposition itself as a tourist destination by painting murals of the town's history on downtown buildings. With relatively little investment in the art work and by depending on small scale local enterprises to support the tourism industry it has successfully repositioned itself as a tourist town (Barnes and Hayter, 1992). Chemainus is not, however, a resort community as it lacks the necessary accommodation base and is primarily dependent on a day-visitor market. Drumheller, Alberta, in which the Royal Tyrrell Museum of Palaeontology was built, offers another example of the successful development of a tourist destination in a rural area. In this case, the provincial government initiated and developed the museum as a major heritage attraction and effected a revitalization of the local economy based on cultural tourism (Koster, 1994).

Although many local governments wish to attract tourism as a means of enhancing revenues and creating employment, not all communities actively seek tourism development. Developers who seek to develop a resource such as a beach or ski hill may encounter opposition from local residents or agencies who raise objections on the basis of potential environmental or social disruption. In the case of large scale resort developments, the approval processes are often lengthy, complex and competitive. Not only must proposals demonstrate their economic viability, they must also often conform with rigorous standards relating to environmental impact regulations and increasingly must seek public support through citizen involvement

Figure 6.1. Village centre, Whistler, British Columbia (C.M. Hall)

processes. For example, the environmental review process for the Galena resort near Lake Tahoe, Nevada, which was finally approved in 1990, took eight years and involved 45 government agencies (*Snow Country Magazine*, January/February, 1991), and a recent ski development proposal for Lake Catamount area in Colorado, which successfully passed the environmental review process, encountered opposition from local area residents.

Approval processes vary depending on the regulatory context. In Canada, provincial legislation over land use and changing political viewpoints have resulted in both spatial and temporal variations in the levels of development support for such features as golf courses and ski hills (Beaudry, 1994). In an Australian context, Stanton and Aislabie (1992) note similar problems of institutional uncertainty in dealing with local and State governments when appraising resort investments. They conclude that investor underassessment of uncertainty may reduce or postpone the expected returns to the local community.

Who are the stakeholders?

The establishment of tourism as the major economic activity in a rural area results in a variety of changes which make resorts distinctive from other communities. In addition to the more evident effects such as those on employment and demographic structures or changes to the built or visual environment, other more subjective

changes occur. Most importantly for small communities, the community itself
becomes commodified and territorial boundaries marking the sites of tourism
production may be blurred with those of domestic production. There is an essential
dichotomy between residents who view the community as their home and a place to
live and tourists who view the community as a resource that is commodified and
consumed (Urry, 1995). Such territorial intrusion may lead to resentment against
tourists as residents seek their own spaces (Gill, 1994). While new purpose-built
resorts may not have to contend with problems of integrating an existing community
into their development, tensions between the resort and the community emerge over
time as the resident population becomes established (Williamson, 1991).

The distinctive demographic and social characteristics which resorts exhibit reflect
the nature of the tourism industry. While generalisations can be made, it must be
emphasized that each situation is context-specific and contingent factors will vary
spatially. A general differentiation commonly recognised by residents in many resort
communities distinguishes people in the community on the basis of temporal
differences in their relationship to the community. At its most general level this
would include:

- permanent residents;
- second home owners;
- seasonal workers; and
- tourists.

Each group has a different temporal attachment to the community as well as
differing spatial behaviours and patterns of resource use (Gill, 1994). In addition, a
consideration of key stakeholder groups must also include developers and public
agencies, as they represent the two most powerful elements within the resort. While
the suggestion that categorising residents and tourists can be a useful device for
trying to understand the resort community, it is also fraught with problems. The
categories mentioned are not mutually exclusive. Residents may also be business
investors or even developers; the distinction between tourist and resident is blurred in
the case of second-home owners; and on some issues, such as recreational land-use,
even the distinction between permanent resident and tourist may not be meaningful.

Permanent residents

What constitutes a permanent resident in a resort is often a matter of debate. Length
of residence is a common variable identified in research on communities as the basis
for differing attitudes towards development. A housing study in Whistler (a resort
which has been in existence for about 20 years), used a combined scale of time lived
in the community and intended length of stay to identify three categories of resident:

- short-term (lived in community less than two years and plan to leave in less than a year);
- mid-term (lived in community at least two years but not more than five or lived in community less than two years but no plans to leave for at least a year); and
- long-term residents (lived in community for over five years).

In terms of the level of involvement of residents with the resort community a distinction based on more than just length of residence seems justified. Williamson (1991) has proposed a four-level distinction of residents, with successively fewer numbers of residents at each level. Short-term residents, including seasonal and new arrivals, form the largest component of the population of the resort. They are marginal actors and the majority do not become involved in community issues. Next are 'niche seekers' who are attempting to become established in the resort and are dependent on economic growth. As relative newcomers, they are often very active in community affairs as they seek to establish themselves. If they are unsuccessful they leave. 'Stakeholders' are the next level and are those who have invested in the area through home-ownership or business investment; they, too, are active in community affairs. Their stability in the community may depend on property values and service provision. If property values rapidly increase they may 'cash out'. The smallest group are the 'survivors' amongst whom are often the original power base of the community. They tend to either own their own businesses or be senior members of the larger corporations. Even these long term residents may choose to eventually leave the community if growth and change is too great and larger numbers of newcomers gain control (Rademan, 1987).

What draws many residents to resort communities is lifestyle rather than job opportunity (Rowley, 1991). While undoubtedly some are drawn to the resort because of job opportunities, others seek employment on arrival. There are many cases of professional and skilled workers who have traded in city careers for a resort lifestyle and who find alternative forms of employment in the resort context. While resorts offer opportunities for service sector employment in the tourism industry or in community services, there are also entrepreneurial opportunities in tourism-related services such as retailing. Resident entrepreneurs are often the most politically active in the community perhaps due to their vested interests as both residents and business people. Williams *et al.* (1989) also note that, unlike entrepreneurs in other settings, some operate their businesses at sub-optimal levels in order to accommodate their lifestyle choices.

A rapidly growing sector in many resorts is that of 'tele-commuters', who because of technological advances in communications are able to relocate to high level amenity locations such as resorts. Some of these are self-employed and contribute to a distinctive group of residents who identify themselves as 'consultants'. Adding to this body of residents, who are often not dependent on the tourism industry, are retirees. This latter group often play an active role in community affairs. However, like the foot-loose professionals they tend to lobby for increased community facilities such as health care and are less concerned about the well-being of the tourism industry (Rademan, 1987). Indeed, they may form opposition to tourism-related development proposals. The trend towards real estate development as the means of financing tourism facilities, such as golf courses, has stimulated this market as properties are frequently marketed to appeal to an active retirement lifestyle segment.

Second home owners

Second home owners sometimes make up the majority of property tax payers in resorts, but their importance varies according to the location and nature of the resort. For example, absentee property owners represent 82 per cent of the total number of property owners in Whistler (Resort Municipality of Whistler, 1995). While rarely politically or socially involved in community affairs, they could potentially, in places where they have voting rights, be effectively organised to swing votes. In the United States, second-home owners cannot vote in municipal elections in their place of second residence. However, in Canada, a recent British Columbia Provincial government attempt to exclude non-residents from voting in municipal elections was overturned. While often supporting improvements to recreational amenities in the resort, second-home owners may oppose development if it encroaches on their sense of place (Gartner, 1986). In Wisconsin, second home owners' attitudes and perceptions are as important in determining community direction as permanent resident perceptions (Girard and Gartner, 1993).

Defining the resort second home owner is increasingly difficult as various forms of resort property ownership are introduced. Girard and Gartner (1993) further suggest that subgroups or subcultures may exist within second home populations, perhaps delineated by age and income. Traditionally in North America, the second-home owner was a cottager who used a lake, mountain or seaside property for summer family vacations. Such properties still exist and many places, such as the Rideau Lakes area of eastern Ontario and Cultus Lake, British Columbia (Halseth, 1993; Halseth and Rosenberg, 1995), the beach communities of Lake Winnipeg in Manitoba (Lehr *et al.*, 1991) and Wasagaming, in Riding Mountain National Park in Manitoba (Stadel, 1996), are still more traditional summer resort areas. More recently, the construction of second home properties is linked to recreational developments such as ski and golf resorts as developers seek to recoup their capital investment through the sale of real estate. In some instances (e.g., Whistler), ski corporations are granted development rights by the municipality in return for the construction of ski lifts – a 'land for lifts'-policy. Such development has been primarily in the form of condominium or hotel-condominium developments which are sold either individually or as time-share units. Frequently, units are purchased as investment properties which are rented out to tourists instead of being for personal use (Gill and Clark, 1992). The growing demand for second home properties is a key factor in stimulating competition for housing and driving up real estate prices in resort markets.

The more traditional second home owner does exist in resort communities, and there is a growing trend towards relocation or retirement to these properties. In a Whistler survey of second home owners, 28 per cent indicated their intention to move permanently to the resort at some future date (Resort Municipality of Whistler, 1995). Halseth and Rosenberg (1990) have documented the type of conversions that occur in second home properties in Cultus Lake, British Columbia, as individuals prepare their summer homes for full time occupancy. There are many implications for the future of resort areas if such residents form a significant component of the population. These may include pressure on the resort to provide improved medical facilities, as well as resistance to tourism-related development.

Seasonal workers

In most resorts, seasonal peaks in tourist visitation occur in either the summer or winter season. Seasonality contributes to the frequent criticism that tourism creates only low paying, low skilled jobs (Ioannides, 1995) and results in the need for a numerically flexible labour force. It is often not possible to meet peak labour demands locally and thus resorts must draw on more distant labour pools (Hammes, 1994). This group is usually young, receives low pay and is frequently non-unionised. In ski resorts, in particular, many workers are students, including students from abroad who are working on temporary employment exchange visas. In Canadian ski resorts, for example, Australian students make up an identifiable component of this temporary labour market. Temporary workers are generally detached both socially and politically from the community, and, in instances, are not even residents as they cannot afford to live in the resort and some must commute from neighbouring communities.

Tourists

Tourists can be differentiated according to a variety of categories such as place of origin (regional; national; international); length of stay (day, short and long stay visitors); or types of activity (skiing; golfing). Such variables have been identified as affecting tourists–resident interaction, and the nature of the relationship between tourists and residents (e.g., Liu and Var, 1986; Long *et al.*, 1990; Lankford, 1994). The success or otherwise of a resort is determined by the ability of the resort to successfully compete with other tourist destinations for market share. Thus, meeting the needs of the tourist is paramount. These needs go beyond the physical provision of high quality attractions, accommodation and infrastructure. There is growing recognition that hospitality in the form of friendly and welcoming residents is an equally important component of a successful resort. Matching tourist demand to the resort offerings is achieved through marketing efforts which vary in amount and quality depending on the type of resort. While major resorts employ sophisticated marketing strategies based on sound statistical research, effective marketing strategies are often lacking in small towns that have evolved into tourist destinations (Go *et al.*, 1992).

Institutional arrangements

The role of federal and provincial/state governments

All resorts operate within the framework of various forms of government regulation, even those that are privately-owned ventures. At the broadest scale, Provincial/State and, at times, federal agencies support and stimulate resort development to achieve political goals such as regional development. Resort developers rely on government partnerships to provide the infrastructural base for development. Tourism also relies on the state for coordinated marketing and place promotion (Britton, 1991). The provision of access is essential for tourism development and the private sector is heavily dependent on government provision of transportation facilities such as highways and airports. For example, in Hawaii, in order to encourage and support the development of the privately-developed Mauna Lani resort in 1972, the government constructed a coast highway, the Keahole Airport, a regional water system, and made improvements to Kawaihae Harbor (Innskeep, 1991). There are also examples of more direct government support to private developers, as in the case of the Canadian Tourism Industry Development Subsidiary Agreements (TIDSA) during the latter part of the 1970s and early 1980s (Montgomery and Murphy, 1983). This source of federal funding together with matching provincial funds was instrumental in stimulating many tourism initiatives across Canada, including the resort of Whistler.

While tourism falls within the service sector economy, it is nevertheless a resource-dependent industry (Innskeep, 1991). National and regional governments play a major role in environmental regulation and also the administration of public lands upon which, especially in North America, much recreational use is dependent. Resort developers who are dependent on access to these lands generally must negotiate lease or purchase agreements with the government agencies. For example, in the United States, half of all downhill skiing activity in 170 different ski areas occurs on land leased from the US Forest Service. In recent years, growing environmental concerns over the impacts of recreational developments, especially ski hills and golf courses, have resulted in often prolonged negotiation and stalled development proposals. Perhaps, surprisingly, opposition to development in rural and wilderness areas is more strongly expressed by urban residents than rural residents (Saremba and Gill, 1991). This is explained by the greater degree of economic dependency by rural residents on the local area.

Recently, most major ski resorts in North America have expanded their operations to offer year-round recreational opportunities. This reflects not only market demand for high quality resort accommodation and amenities which for reasons of economic viability require year-round use, but also longer term concerns over the future of the ski industry in the face of global warming (McBoyle and Wall, 1991). This has an impact on the spatial patterns of tourist behaviour in such areas with summer tourists exhibiting more spatially disperse patterns of activity. In rural areas where outdoor recreational activities and scenic resources form the basis of the tourism industry, the resources often lie beyond municipal control. For example, in Whistler, use of back-country de facto municipal boundaries has necessitated negotiation with the provincial Ministry of Forests, to designate areas for recreational use in order to reduce conflict. In many situations, however, the multi jurisdictional nature of the recreational lands on which tourism is dependent is a problem for the resort. In particular, tourism landscapes which form such an integral component of most resort products exhibit essential characteristics of common pool resources, notably: the inability to control overuse and the lack of incentive for investment (Healy, 1994). As Keane (1990) notes, problems associated with rights of access and ownership can cause a particular form of market failure which can only be resolved by some form of collective initiative.

Local government and the private sector

Resorts exhibit a variety of organizational structures. Some resorts, including many of the western United States ski resorts (e.g., Keystone, Colorado; Beaver Creek, Colorado; Squaw Valley, California) (Dorward, 1990), or the Disney resorts, are privately-owned corporate entities. Others such as Manchester, Vermont; Vail, Colorado (Dorward, 1990), or Nantucket, Massachusetts (Lewis, 1991), are municipalities. Generally speaking, privately-owned resorts have small permanent populations with limited employee accommodation. The impact of these resorts is felt more on neighbouring communities which serve the resort in terms of provision of housing and community services. In Canada, a few communities, such as Whistler, British Columbia; Cavendish, Prince Edward Island and Banff, Alberta, are designated as 'Resort Municipalities'. Similar models are in place in resorts such as Sanctuary Cove on Australia's Gold Coast. Whistler was the first Canadian resort to be granted such a designation. In addition to establishing a municipally-run land development company and ensuring on-going coordination of planning through regular revisions of the Official Community Plan, this designation also requires that all businesses in the Village and designated 'resort lands' join the Whistler Resort Association (WRA). The primary mandate of the WRA is to market Whistler in a coordinated manner as a year-round international resort area. This addresses a common problem in tourist areas where individual tourism companies have been reluctant to engage in coordinated marketing and place promotion because rival firms, who have not shared in the marketing costs, may also reap the benefits (Britton, 1991). In Whistler, resort status also establishes the financial mechanism to maintain a quality tourism environment by levying a two per cent hotel tax.

The need to control and coordinate the aesthetic and environmental quality of the resort is a critical component in maintaining a successful resort. This requires the establishment of strict by-laws to steer development accordingly. While zoning regulations establish basic land use patterns, the application of design guidelines is also a common feature in planned resorts. Design guidelines regulate such features as height, style and material of allowable buildings with the objective of coordinating the visual image of the resort (Dorward, 1990). In North America, resort design has become a specialized profession for a small number of architects and designers, and their influence is evident in resort design internationally (e.g., new resorts in Australia and Japan). Such designers pay attention not only to the aesthetics of place and an understanding of environmental constraints and opportunities (e.g., snow load on roofs or viewshed), but also to an overall experiential sense of place.

Growth issues

The degree of planning in a resort will depend on the type and age of the resort. Comprehensively planned integrated resorts are a relatively recent phenomenon whereas older resorts that have evolved over time have often lacked such coordinated approaches. Inskeep (1991) notes that post-development planning of older resorts for improvement or expansion has become common in recent years so that they can maintain their economic viability and compete effectively with newer planned resorts. In resort settings, the challenge for managers is how to balance the needs of tourists and residents in an environment of constant change. The need to remain competitive creates problems for some resorts as it requires considerable public expenditure on such features as high or aesthetic building quality, infrastructure that can accommodate peak demands (e.g., water, transport and sewers); or aesthetic considerations such as landscaping, underground parking and appropriate building design. While these costs can be recouped from commercial developments, the cost of developing community facilities places a heavy financial burden on the local government. In new resorts in the early stages of development, the primary goal is to achieve a level of development which will ensure the desired market position. Priority is placed on attracting investment to develop infrastructure and facilities serving tourists' needs in order to achieve a 'critical mass' of tourism development. During this stage, the needs of the resident population become secondary as all efforts are placed on revenue-generating construction which will guarantee investors a return on their capital. This explains the lack of employee housing and community facilities in many planned resorts. Capital is fluid and if too many requirements reduce potential profits, investors will go elsewhere. In new resorts, investment risks are already high as resorts must compete with other destinations to establish their markets (Stanton and Aislabie, 1992). Once the resort has established itself as a tourist destination then the challenge of addressing the needs of residents is considered. While clearly this post-hoc consideration of residents' needs seems inappropriate, economic considerations in developer-driven resort projects seem, at least in the past, to have dictated such an approach. Emerging longer-term visions of resort viability linked to the recognition that good resorts are good communities may, however, lead to more integrated approaches in which residents' needs as well as those of the tourist are considered to be of equal importance (Minger, 1991).

As notions of sustainable development increasingly enter the policy arena, the role of residents in the planning process is enhanced (Simmons, 1994). To date, most community-based efforts to incorporate residents in tourism planning relates to specific development projects or to sporadic endeavours associated with up-dating community plans. However, programs such as the Community Tourism Action Plan (CTAP) process, which has been widely applied in Alberta and British Columbia, is an example of more broadly-based involvement of residents in tourism planning (Go et al., 1992). With direction and facilitation support from the Provincial government, communities have engaged in strategic tourism planning. While this process mainly represents community efforts in areas of emergent tourism development rather than in a resort context, it does provide a model for citizen involvement in tourism planning.

On-going collaborative planning with all stakeholders in tourist communities is rare (Jamal and Getz, 1995). However, some resort communities in North America (e.g., Aspen, Colorado; Lake Tahoe, Nevada; Whistler, British Columbia) are turning to growth management practices as a guide to more integrated approaches (Gill and Williams, 1994). In essence, growth management is a systematic impact management strategy which calls for an integrated sharing of ideas between citizens and managers (Innes, 1993). The greatest challenge to growth management planning is to reconcile different value systems concerning desired conditions. The stakeholder groups identified earlier represent the key groups who hold differing visions of how they perceive the future of the resort. A key element in managing growth is the establishment of a monitoring system to provide the data for tracking change. Some resort communities in North America have begun to collect a variety of environmental, social and economic indicators. However, none have as yet developed as comprehensive a monitoring system as the one introduced in Whistler in 1994. This system is still in the process of evolving, aided by annual community meetings, which provide stakeholders the opportunity to offer comments and recommendations.

Affordable housing

In a recent study of growth in Colorado resort areas (Rademan *et al.*, 1995), lack of affordable housing was identified by 80 per cent of the 210 respondents as the most important growth problem. Congestion and traffic were cited as a problem by 76 per cent and environmental degradation by 64 per cent. A 1990 study of Whistler residents ranked environmental quality, and provision of community facilities, and affordable housing as the three main concerns of residents (Gill, 1991). Of these issues, the problem of providing affordable housing is the most difficult to resolve. Whereas issues of environmental quality or traffic congestion are problems shared by both residents and tourists, and can justifiably be dealt with as components of resort quality, the issue of affordable housing, at least in the short term, seems to run at odds with the profit motive which drives resort development.

The housing market is largely driven by the external demands of the tourism industry, especially the demand for second home properties. As resorts become successful, the availability of accommodation within the price range of workers is reduced. In North America, until recently, the housing needs of employees were generally ignored. Many resorts, such as the ski resorts of Colorado, have matured and so, too, has the pemanent labour force. This has resulted in an increasing demand for family housing rather than that suited to the young single worker (Culbertson and Kolberg, 1991). The lack of affordable housing affects not only those engaged in the tourism industry, but also workers engaged in low-to-moderate income jobs in community services such as schools, hospitals or municipal offices. The lack of housing has led to some residents leaving the resort and others being displaced to adjacent communities, thus creating a ripple effect in housing demand spreading out from the resort. In Aspen, for example, only one-third of the workforce can afford to live in the community; the rest commute. In Nantucket, Massachusetts, even many long term employees must move every six months because leases run from May to October to allow landlords to charge high summer rents (Lewis, 1991). Such displacement seriously undermines the sense of community and associated community functions. Seasonal workers who are not provided accommodation by their employer are often forced either to live in overcrowded conditions or to commute.

Various solutions to the employee housing problem have been attempted. For seasonal workers, larger resort employers such as hotels or ski corporations often provide staff accommodation in the form of dormitories or apartments. This type of housing is often not popular with other community residents who sometimes adopt a NIMBY (not in my back yard) approach (Rademan, 1987). Concerns over rowdiness, crime and noise are often cited as objections to such proposals in residential resort neighbourhoods. It is not uncommon for established home owners to raise objections to any form of employee housing in their neighbourhood as they fear a decline in property values. Mixed deed-restricted and market-rate condominium projects in Aspen were unsuccessful, in part because of this concern (Culbertson and Kolberg, 1991).

Resorts are seeking a variety of solutions to the problem of providing affordable housing to employees. The regulation of rental accommodation in auxiliary suites in single family homes provides one source of affordable rental housing. In many resorts, such units cannot legally be rented out as they are in single family zoned neighbourhoods. By-laws have, however, been amended in places like Aspen and Whistler to make these suites legal for rental if the occupants are employees. This approach is common in resorts in Switzerland where it is a requirement of single family home construction to include an employee suite. Employee-owned units are also increasingly being made available as many resort communities now force residential developers to include employee units as a requirement of development approval. In Whistler, as elsewhere, charges are also levied on developers of new non-residential properties. The money goes to a resort housing society which is responsible for constructing and managing affordable housing. Density bonuses and other benefits are also used in some resorts, with incentives including affordable units (Culbertson and Kolberg, 1991). In many cases, affordable housing falls far short of demand and allocation of available housing relies on such mechanisms as lotteries. A further problem which challenges resort managers is the regulation and control of employee designated units to ensure that they remain strictly as affordable units and do not re-enter the market as market-rate housing stock or become rented out as tourism accommodation. The nature of deed-restrictions in Aspen/Pitkin County, Colorado, has, for example, had to be reduced, limiting resale prices to a 3 per cent annual increase over the original purchase price (Culbertson and Kolberg, 1991).

Summary and conclusions

Resort developments impact on local areas both positively and negatively. While on the one hand they stimulate regional development by creating jobs and offering opportunities for entrepreneurial activities, these jobs may be seasonal and, especially in areas where tourism is replacing resource-based industry, may be perceived as low paid. High labour market demands frequently create an influx of new and sometimes temporary residents to the local area. This can have an impact on the social environment of the resort and neighbouring communities. Resorts and the recreational amenities associated with them attract not only tourists but also permanent and second-home residents who are drawn to the area for life-style reasons. This has the effect of driving up real estate prices and creating a ripple effect out from the resort. In particular, resort employees often seek more affordable housing in neighbouring communities to the resort, which, in turn, increases demand and subsequently housing prices in these communities.

To remain competitive, resorts must respond to changing market demand. This requires sound, on-going (strategic) planning. There is increasing acknowledgment of the need for resort residents to be an integral part of this process as, for example, in growth management approaches. The greatest challenge for resort managers is how to balance the needs of residents and tourist, especially with regard to such issues as affordable housing, environmental quality and overall growth demands. As many resorts broaden their recreational amenities to offer year-round opportunities, resorts are increasingly being perceived as desirable places of permanent residence by footloose professionals, retirees and others. This may, in turn, affect the direction of future growth in resorts as new residents assert their influence.

References

Barnes, T. and Hayter, R., 1992, 'The little town that did': flexible accumulation and community response in Chemainus, B. C. *Regional Studies*, **26**: 647–663.

Beaudry, M., 1994, BC government flip flops on ski resort proposal, *Ski Canada*, December: 20

Britton, S., 1991, Tourism, capital and place: towards a critical geography of tourism, *Environment and Planning D: Society and Space*, **9**: 451–478

Bryant, C.R., 1991, Community development and restructuring of rural employment in Canada, paper presented at the Contemporary Social and Economic Restructuring of Rural Areas International Seminar UK, August 12–17

Culbertson, K. and Kolberg, J., 1991, Worker housing in resorts: Aspen's experience, *Urban LAM*, **50**(4): 12–12

Dahms, F., 1988, *The heart of the country*, Deneau, Toronto

Dorward, S., 1990, *Design for mountain communities: a landscape and architectural guide*, Van Nostrand Reinhold, New York

Gartner, W., 1986, Environmental impacts of recreational home developments, *Annals of Tourism Research*, **13** :38–57

Gill, A., 1991, Issues and problems of community development in Whistler, British Columbia. In *Mountain resort development: proceedings of the Vail conference*, A. Gill and R. Hartmann, eds., pp. 27–32, Centre for Tourism Policy and Research, Simon Fraser University, Burnaby

Gill, A., 1994, Competing for community needs in the resort environment In *Quality management in urban tourism: balancing business and the environment conference proceedings*, P. Murphy, ed., pp. 412–423, University of Victoria, Victoria

Gill, A. and Clark, P. , 1992, Second-home development in the resort municipality of Whistler, British Columbia, In *British Columbia: Geographical essays in honour of A. MacPherson*, P. M. Koroscil, ed., pp. 281–294, Department of Geography, Simon Fraser University, Burnaby

Gill, A. and Williams, P.W., 1994, Managing growth in mountain tourism communities, *Tourism Management*, **15** (3): 212–220

Girard, T.C. and Gartner, W.C., 1993, Second home second view: host community perceptions, *Annals of Tourism Research*, **20** (4): 685–700

Go, F., Milne, D. and Whittles, L., 1992, Communities as destinations: a marketing taxonomy for the effective implementation of the tourism action plan, *Journal of Travel Research*, Spring: 31–37

Halseth, G., 1993, Communities within communities: changing 'residential' areas at Cultus Lake, British Columbia, *Journal of Rural Studies*, **9**: 175–187

Halseth, G. and Rosenberg, M., 1990, Conversion of recreational residences: a case study of its measurement and management, *Canadian Journal of Regional Science*, **13**: 99–115

Halseth, G. and Rosenberg, M., 1995, Cottagers in an urban field, *Professional Geographer*, **47** (2): 148–159

Hammes, D.L., 1994, Resort development impact on labour and land markets, *Annals of Tourism Research*, **21** (4): 729–744

Healy, R.G., 1994, The 'common pool' problem in tourism landscapes, *Annals of Tourism Research*, **21** (3): 596–611

Innes, J., 1993, Implementing state growth management in the United States: strategies for coordination. In J.M. Stein, ed., *Growth management: the planning challenge of the 1990s*, Sage, Newbury Park

Inskeep, E., 1991, *Tourism planning: an integrated and sustainable development approach*, Van Nostrand Reinhold, New York

Ioannides, D., 1995, Strengthening the ties between tourism and economic geography: a theoretical agenda, *Professional Geographer*, **47**: 49–60

Jamal, T.B. and Getz, D., 1995, Collaboration theory and community tourism planning, *Annals of Tourism Reseach*, **22**: 186–204

Keane, M.J., 1990, Economic development capacity amongst small rural communities, *Journal of Rural Studies*, **6**: 291–301

Koster, E., 1994, Culture-tourism partnerships – the role of the modern museum. In *Quality Management in Urban Tourism: Balancing Business and the Environment Conference Proceedings*, P. Murphy, ed., pp. 243–254, University of Victoria, Victoria

Lankford, S.V., 1994, Attitudes and perceptions towards tourism and rural regional development, *Journal of Travel Research*, **32** (3): 35–43

Lehr, J., Selwood, J. and Badiuk, E., 1991, Ethnicity, religion and class as elements in the evolution of Lake Winnipeg resorts, *Canadian Geographer*, **35** (1): 46-58

Lewis, S., 1991, Building affordable housing in unaffordable places, *Planning*, **57** (12): 24–27

Long, P.T., Perdue, R.R. and Allen, L.R., 1990, Rural residents, tourism perceptions and attitudes by community level of tourism, *Journal of Travel Research*, **28** (3): 3–9

Liu, J.C. and Var, T., 1986, Residents' attitudes towards tourism impacts in Hawaii, *Annals of Tourism Research*, **13**: 193–214

McBoyle, G. and Wall, G., 1991, Great Lakes skiing and climate change. In *Mountain resort development: proceedings of the Vail conference*, A. Gill and R. Hartmann, eds., pp. 82–84, Centre for Tourism Policy and Research, Simon Fraser University, Burnaby

Minger, T., 1991, The green resort: environmental stewardship and the resort community. In *Mountain resort development: proceedings of the Vail conference*, A. Gill and R. Hartmann, eds., pp. 66–69, Centre for Tourism Policy and Research, Simon Fraser University, Burnaby

Montgomery, G. and Murphy, P., 1983, Government involvement in tourism development: a case study of TIDSA implementation in British Columbia. In *Tourism in Canada: selected issues and options*, Western Geographical Series Vol. 21, P. Murphy, ed., pp. 183–209, Department of Geography University of Victoria, Victoria

Murphy, P.E., 1994, Attraction management lessons from three Disney theme parks: balancing business and environment. In *Quality Management in Urban Tourism: Balancing Business and the Environment Conference Proceedings*, P. Murphy, ed., pp. 492–502, University of Victoria, Victoria

Pearce, D., 1987, *Tourism today: a geographic analysis*, Longman, London

Rademan, M.C., 1987, Ski town predictions: obstacles ahead, *Planning*, **53** (2): 17–21

Rademan, M., Klusmire, M. and Baker, T., 1995, *Symposium on growth in resort areas*, Colorado Association of Ski Towns, mimeo

Resort Municipality of Whistler, 1995, *1995 community and resort monitoring program*, Planning Department, RMOW, Whistler.

Rowley, B., 1991, Escape to the mountains, *Snow Country Magazine*, July/August: 51–61

Saremba, J. and Gill, A.M., 1991, Value conflicts in mountain park settings, *Annals of Tourism Research*, **18** (3): 455–472

Simmons, D., 1994, Community participation in tourism planning, *Tourism Management*, **15** (2): 98–108

Snow Country Magazine, 1991, Tahoe resort: the future, *Snow Country Magazine*, January/February: 10

Stadel, C., 1996, The seasonal resort of Wasagaming, Riding Mountain National Park. In *The

Geography of Manitoba: Its Land and Its People, J. Welsted, J. Even'tt and C. Stadel, eds., pp. 298–300, University of Manitoba Press, Winnipeg

Stanton, J. and Aislabie, C., 1992, Up-market integrated resorts in Australia, *Annals of Tourism Research*, **19**: 435–49

Urry, J., 1995, *Consuming places*, Routledge, London

Williamson, D., 1991, Which came first, the community or the resort? In *Mountain resort development: proceedings of the Vail conference*, A. Gill and R. Hartmann, eds., pp. 22–26, Centre for Tourism Policy and Research, Simon Fraser University, Burnaby

Williams, A. M., Shaw, G. and Greenwood, J., 1989, From tourist to tourism entrepreneur, from consumption to production: evidence from Cornwall, England, *Environment and Planning* A, **21**: 1639–53

Part Three:
Image and Reimaging of Rural Areas

7 Image and reimaging of rural areas

RICHARD W. BUTLER AND C. MICHAEL HALL

Introduction

This chapter will introduce two basic elements: the changing image of rural areas in the second half of the twentieth century, as the urban population in particular sees such areas as potential locations for a greater variety of activities than simply food production, and the deliberate attempts to change the perception of rural areas or reimage them to meet new policy objectives for different levels of government and the private sector. The way people view rural areas is of fundamental importance for the way they use rural areas. There are an increasingly diverse set of viewpoints or perceptions of rural areas, what they are, what they could be, what they should be, and how they could be brought there. Inevitably such a variety of viewpoints can result in disagreement over goals and objectives, and policies and methods of achieving such goals. Such disagreements can occur at all levels, including within local communities, as well as between different levels of government, and between the public and private sectors.

Tourism images

The notion of 'image' has long been a major interest in the study of tourism. Research on authentic and inauthentic tourist experiences and the manner in which images of attractions, cultures and destinations are used in advertising and promotion has been well-represented in the tourism literature (e.g., see Urry, 1990). Both the nature of the destination image and the manner in which it is created are of utmost importance because the appeal of tourist attractions arises largely from the image conjured up, partly from direct or related experience and partly from external sources and influences (Hunt, 1975). Mental images are the basis for the evaluation and selection of an individual's choice of a destination. As Goodall (1988, p. 3) recognised 'Each individual, given their personal likes and dislikes, has a preferential image of their ideal holiday. This conditions their expectations, setting an aspiration level or evaluative image, against which actual holiday opportunities are compared'. According to Murphy (1985, p. 11), 'This image may be defined as the sum of beliefs, ideas, and impressions that a person has regarding a destination.

It is a personal composite view of a destination's tourism potential, and where prices are comparable it is often the decisive factor in a tourist's selection process'. However, as Murphy (1985, p. 11) went on to note:

> The images are not necessarily the same for each visitor and this makes it difficult to allocate resources and plan for the future land use in destination areas. To overcome this problem many areas attempt to appeal to a specific group through extensive and expensive promotion, presenting themselves as a family-oriented resort, a place for rugged outdoor enthusiasts, or a swinging locale for night people.

Undoubtedly, there are many sources of the images that people hold for places and products. In the nineteenth century, for example, images of the British countryside for many of the new urban middle class, came not only from their own personal experience, but also from their exposure to novels (e.g., Thomas Hardy), poetry (e.g., Wordsworth), and paintings (e.g., Constable). The work of artists and writers and the increased dissemination of their work through improvements in communication technology helped to reinforce the creation of the countryside as a distinct cultural entity. Ironically, the newly idealised British rural landscape was itself a product of the agricultural restructuring begun with the enclosure movement and reinforced by the economy of the late eighteenth and early nineteenth century industrial revolution. It was within this social environment that the countryside was set in opposition to the 'evils' of industrial cities, and the image of a rural idyll established within much of the urban mind (Lansbury, 1970). While this image of a rural arcadia masked the poverty, displacement and poor working conditions of many rural inhabitants, it was an image that was to become part of urban popular culture. The personal experience of the countryside by this middle-class urban population was dramatically increased through greater access to specific regions, which had been the subject of the artist's eye and the writer's pen, and which were now more accessible through the advent of the railways.

In the twentieth century, the media often continue to portray images of a simpler, somehow 'purer' country life to its primarily urban audience, through television (e.g., *All Creatures Great and Small,* the television serialisation of the books of James Herriot on veterinary life in the Yorkshire Dales), radio (*The Archers,* 'An everyday story of country folk'), and lifestyle magazines (e.g., *Country Life, Country Style*). Elements of the countryside, real or imagined, are also transported to urban areas through the growth of shops which specialise in 'cottage' and 'heritage' furniture and household goods, e.g., kitchenware and basketware, by which urbanites are able to bring the country into the city in symbolic and, sometimes, functional forms. However, perhaps most significantly of all in terms of reinforcement or maintenance of rurality is tourism.

Continued accessibility to the countryside was primarily achieved through greater personal access to the automobile, which allowed people to explore to a more personal and intimate level wider areas of the countryside. In twentieth century Britain and other vestiges of empire the accumulated image of the romantic countryside of hedgerows, churchyards and happy labourers was developed further to include the village pub, the cricket green and country fairs and festivals. Similar, but different themes, e.g., the romance of the vineyard and markets in town squares are to be found in many European countries, for example, the idealised Provence of

Peter Mayle's books and subsequent television programme, *A Year in Provence*. As Britton (1991, p. 475) observed, 'As a major, yet typically unappreciated and unacknowledged, avenue of accumulation in the late twentieth century, tourism is one of the most important elements in the shaping of popular consciousness of places and in determining the creation of social images of those places'.

Tourism and the shaping of place

Although rural areas have long served to attract visitors through their inherent appeal, it is only in recent years that regions have explicitly sought to develop, image and promote themselves in an integrated fashion in order to make themselves more attractive to tourists, investors and employees. Within the geography, tourism and marketing literature, the concepts of 'place marketing' (e.g., Madsen, 1992) also described as 'selling places' (e.g., Burgess, 1982; Kearns and Philo 1993), 'geographical marketing' (e.g., Ashworth and Voogd, 1988) or 'reimaging strategies' (Roche, 1992; Hall, 1994), has come to receive significant attention over the past decade. Urban areas have been the subject of the vast majority of research into place promotion (e.g., Bramham, *et al.* 1989; Watson, 1991; Roche, 1992). Following the deindustrialisation of many industrial and waterfront areas in the 1970s and 1980s, tourism was perceived as a mechanism to regenerate urban areas through the creation of urban leisure and tourism space. This process appears almost universal in industrialised nations. Such a situation led Harvey (1988, in Urry, 1990, p. 128) to ask 'How many museums, cultural centres, convention and exhibition halls, hotels, marinas, shopping malls, waterfront developments can we stand?'. Countryside change reflects the same national and international transitions in economic, political and social structures as do urban areas (Cloke, 1989, 1993). Tourism is also a major policy response to the changing base of agricultural industries in a global economy. A rural counterpart of Harvey's question of redevelopment of the inner city is 'How many heritage trails, pioneer museums and villages, historic houses, roadside produce stalls, authentic country cooking, festivals, country shoppes, and Devonshire teas can we stand?'

Rural imaging processes are characterised by some or all of the following:

- the development of a critical mass of visitor attractions and facilities (e.g., the development of heritage sites);
- the hosting of events and festivals (e.g., Highland Games or produce-based events, such as wine and food festivals);
- the development of rural tourism strategies and policies often associated with new or renewed regional tourism organisations and the related development of regional marketing and promotional campaigns (e.g., 'Hardy Country' or 'Herriot Country' in England) (Figure 7.1); and
- the development of leisure and cultural services and projects to support the regional marketing and tourism effort (e.g., the creation and renewal of regional museums and support for local arts and crafts).

In line with the themes of rural regional and economic development discussed in Chapters Two and Three, the principal aims of imaging strategies are to attract

Figure 7.1. 'Herriot Country', the Yorkshire Dales (C.M. Hall)

tourism expenditure, generate employment in tourism and related industries, foster positive images for potential investors and local inhabitants, and provide an environment which will attract and retain the interest of professionals who now constitute the core work force in the new service industries (Hall, 1994), whether it be for second homes, early retirement, commuter housing or the electronic cottage.

The ramifications of imaging strategies as an approach to dealing with the consequences of deindustrialisation and the new global economy are far reaching, particularly in the way in which places are now perceived as products to be promoted and sold. 'The primary goal of the place marketer is to construct a new image of the place to replace either vague or negative images previously held by current or potential residents, investors and visitors' (Holcomb, 1993, p. 133), in order to effectively compete with other places within the constraints of a global economy. 'This marketing operation involved the construction or selective tailoring of particular images of place, which enmeshed with the dynamics of the global economy and legitimised particular conceptions of what were 'appropriate' state policy responses' (Sadler, 1993, p. 175).

Kotler *et al.* (1993, p. 18) refer to the need for places to adopt a process of 'strategic place marketing' for regional revitalization in order to design a community 'to satisfy the needs of its key constituencies'. That process embraces four core activities:

- Designing the right mix of community features and services;
- Setting attractive incentives for the current and potential buyers and users of its goods and services;

- Delivering a place's products and services in an efficient, accessible way; and
- Promoting the place's values and image so that the potential users are fully aware of the place's distinctive advantages (1993, p. 18).

'Place marketing means designing a place to satisfy the needs of its target markets. It succeeds when citizens and businesses are pleased with their communities, and meet the expectations of visitors and investors' (Kotler *et al.*, 1993, p. 99). Various investments can be made to a place to 'improve livability, investibility, and visitability', a process comprised of the four components of place:

- place as character;
- place as a fixed environment;
- place as a service provider; and
- place as entertainment and recreation (Kotler *et al.*, 1993, p. 100).

The identification of character as being significant for place promotion is of critical importance for rural areas and notions of rurality. Places are increasingly being packaged around a series of real or imagined cultural traditions and representations, often focussing on a particular interpretation of the enterprise history of a place, e.g., industrial history (agricultural or otherwise) or a romanticised vision of heritage (Figure 7.2). Kotler *et al.* see this as an appropriate means of forging new images in the marketplace. However, other commentators argue that this may be an inappropriate form of political socialisation whereby images of places are manipulated in order to manufacture an apparent cultural and political consensus, 'designed to convince people, many of whom will be disadvantaged and potentially disaffected, that they are important cogs in a successful community and that all sorts of 'good things' are really being done on their behalf' (Philo and Kearns, 1993, p. 3). Indeed, Yarwood (1996) notes that particular social and cultural constructions of rurality may act as a kind of cultural 'glue' between new rounds of investment in the process of industrial change. Yet constructions of rurality are significant for both people within a place and those who are drawn by such constructions. According to Norkunas (1993, p. 2):

> The postindustrial world engenders feelings of alienation and soul... the tourist seeks to see life as it really is, to get in touch with the natives, to enter the intimate space of the other in order to have an experience of real life, an authentic experience. Yet tourism ends up by promoting the preservation of fictional re-creations of ethnicity as ethnicity becomes commodities to be bought and sold. Village life becomes something to see in the recreational repertoire of the tourist rather than a complex of real social activity.

Tourism may therefore reinforce those aspects of rurality and, hence, identity which have become commodified through the process of place marketing. In commodifying place as a product that can be revitalised, advertised and marketed, rural places are presented not so much 'as foci of attachment and concern, but as bundles of social and economic opportunity *competing* against one another in the open (and unregulated) *market* for a share of the capital investment cake (whether this be the investment of enterprises, tourists, local consumers or whatever)' (Philo and Kearns, 1993, p. 18). The 'terrain of thinking' about regional development which emphasises the significance of market forces in the global economy has, therefore,

Figure 7.2. The extremely popular National Trust attraction of Sissinghurst, Kent (C.M. Hall)

contributed not only to an economic restructuring of rural areas but substantial cultural restructuring as well.

While both urban and rural areas are being intensively imaged and marketed as tourism destinations the underlying necessity for such imaging and reimaging is somewhat different. In industrial and urban areas the abandoned structures that remain are often converted and modified to serve new purposes, often tourism, heritage and leisure services related, but also including plantation forestry on former farmlands and agribusiness, based on increasingly larger landholdings. In the countryside, however, the processes related to new industrial forms such as agribusiness and plantation forestry, serve to simplify the appearance of the countryside. In so doing they remove much of the traditional appeal of the landscape on which the tourism and recreation industry has been based and the complex set of economic and socio-cultural relationships which served to define traditional ways of rural life and the very sustainability of the countryside (see Chapter Three).

The relationship between the development of the modern agricultural industrial economy and the emergence of rural heritage tourism is explored in Chapter Eight by Jean-Michel Dewailly. With particular reference to the European experience, Dewailly argues that heritage tourism needs to be seen as a reaction to the simplification of the countryside through industrialisation and modernisation, which has led to a corresponding decline in 'traditional' rural lifestyles. Issues of authenticity and identity associated with rural heritage therefore need to be seen in the context of a dialectical relationship between rural and urban places. The challenge for rural areas is to ensure that the commodification of rural heritage for economic gain does not lead to a lessening of the cultural value of such heritage for local communities and visitor alike.

Issues of commodification are also taken up in Chapter Nine by Hopkins. Through a review of rural images used in tourism advertising in Southern Ontario, Canada, Hopkins identifies the various rural myths which are used by operators to sell their product. Although writing from the North American experience, Hopkins reinforces the concerns of Dewailly with respect to the images that are sold of rural places and the reality behind them, and asks the fundamental question of 'how to keep the place-myths alive?'

Perhaps some answers to this question can be seen in Chapter Ten by Janiskee and Drews with respect to rural festivals and community reimaging in the United States. The chapter provides a review and a series of case studies of some of the ways in which communities have used festivals as a means of both community celebration and as a mechanism to attract tourists and associated spending. However, while festivals are generally seen in a positive light it is salutory to note that, as in Chapters Eight and Nine, Janiskee and Drews caution the reader with respect to the sustainability of some festivals and ask whether market saturation is being reached in some quarters and as to whether the 'novelty aspect of rural festivals is wearing thin with many urbanites'. Interestingly, in relation to the discussions on the importance of regional linkages raised earlier in this book, the authors conclude that better strategies for new product development and marketing, greater market awareness, and improved coordination and planning between various festivals in a given region, may greatly improve the longevity and returns from such festivals.

Images and myths are powerful things and it is these that advertisers sell. Myth(s) of the rural are extremely influential. Place-myths are constructed via images of place promotion. The chapters in this section play close attention to the role of these myths and images not only in terms of attracting visitors and investment but also how they affect the way rural places look at themselves. Therefore, it is vital that issues surrounding rural tourism and recreation go beyond conventional economic analysis to investigate the ways in which rural tourism development is integrated into the social, political and environmental dimensions of rurality.

References

Ashworth, G.J. and Voogd, H., 1988, Marketing the city: concepts, processes and Dutch applications, *Town Planning Review*, **59** (1): 65–80

Bramham, P., Henry, I., Mommaas, H. & van der Poel, H., eds., 1989, *Leisure and urban processes: critical studies of leisure policy in Western European cities*, Routledge, London and New York

Britton, S.G., 1991, Tourism, capital and place: towards a critical geography of tourism, *Environment and Planning D: Society and Space*, **9** (4): 451–478

Burgess, J., 1982, Selling places: environmental images for the executive, *Regional Studies*, **16**: 1–17

Cloke, P., 1989, Rural geography and political economy. In *New models in geography*, vol.1, R. Peet and N. Thrift, eds., pp. 164–197, Unwin Hyman, London

Cloke, P., 1993, On problems and solutions: the reproduction of problems for rural communities in Britain during the 1980s, *Journal of Rural Studies* 9: 113–121

Goodall, B., 1988, How tourists choose their holidays: an analytical framework. In *Marketing in the tourism industry the promotion of destination regions*, B. Goodall and G. Ashworth, eds., pp. 1–17, Routledge, London

Hall, C.M., 1994, *Tourism and politics: policy, power and place*, John Wiley, Chichester

Holcomb, B., 1993. Revisioning place: de- and re-constructing the image of the industrial city. In *Selling places: the city as cultural capital, past and present*, G. Kearns and C. Philo, eds., pp. 133–143, Pergamon Press, Oxford

Hunt, J.D., 1975, Image as a factor in tourist development, *Journal of Travel Research*, **13** (3): 1–7

Kearns, G. and Philo, C., 1993, Preface, In *Selling places: the city as cultural capital, past and present*, G. Kearns and C. Philo, eds., pp. ix–x, Pergamon Press, Oxford

Kotler, P., Haider, D.H. and Rein, I., 1993, *Marketing places: attracting investment, industry, and tourism to cities, states, and nations*. The Free Press, New York

Lansbury, C., 1970, *Arcady in Australia: the evocation of Australia in nineteenth-century English literature*, Melbourne University Press, Carlton

Madsen, H., 1992, Place-marketing in Liverpool: a review, *International Journal of Urban and Regional Research*, **16** (4): 633–640

Murphy, P.E. 1985, *Tourism: a community approach*, Methuen, New York

Norkunas, M.K., 1993, *The politics of memory: tourism, History, and ethnicity in Monterey, California*, State University of New York Press, Albany

Philo, C. and Kearns, C., 1993, Culture, history, capital: a crucial introduction to the selling of places. In selling places: the city as cultural capital, past and present, G. Kearne and C. Philo, eds., pp. 1–32, Pergamon Press, Oxford.

Roche, M., 1992, Mega-events and micro-modernization: on the sociology of the new urban tourism, *British Journal of Sociology*, **43** (4): 563–600

Sadler, D., 1993, Place-marketing, competitive places and the construction of hegemony in Britain in the 1980s. In *Selling places: the city as cultural capital, past and present*, G. Kearns and C. Philo, eds., pp. 175–192, Pergamon Press, Oxford

Urry, J., 1990, *The tourist gaze: leisure and travel in contemporary societies*, Sage Publications, London

Watson, S., 1991, Gilding the smokestacks: the new symbolic representation of deindustrialised regions, *Environment and Planning D: Society and Space*, **9**: 59–70

Yarwood, R., 1996, Rurality, locality and industrial change: a micro-scale investigation of manufacturing growth in the district of Leominster, *Geoforum*, **27** (1): 23–37

8   Images of heritage in rural regions

JEAN-MICHEL DEWAILLY

Rural tourism[1] is expanding. As rural tourism has increased, so the rural landscape itself, along with the images and perceptions associated with it, has necessarily changed. That the rural landscape is changing is not new, it has been occurring since the Industrial Revolution (Bétaille, 1976). However, to varying degrees between countries and regions, the rate of change has dramatically accelerated in the last few decades following the impact of increasing mechanisation and the intensification of agriculture. A rural exodus was evident almost everywhere, even if it has now ceased in some regions. In most of the developed countries, where much tourism impact has occurred, a reduced farming population now exists in rural regions. Nevertheless, the countryside has come to attract new rural investors and indeed people, often townspeople, who are attracted by the prospect of a rural lifestyle.

Following these changes, which are broadly outlined below, agricultural 'improvements' have served to substantially change the countryside, through, among other things, increases in property size, the cutting down of hedgerows and banks of trees, the levelling of embankments, and the flattening of terraces. This simplification of the countryside has occurred in all countries where intensive agricultural activities exist, and perhaps most notably in Europe, where the oldest and very varied agrarian landscapes bring together both agriculture and tourism. The London Basin, the Parisian Basin, Brittany, the Benelux countries, and various regions in America, Canada, Argentina, Australia and Germany have all experienced similar change. With respect to England and Wales, Patmore (1983, p. 166) notes that between 1946 and 1974, a quarter of all the hedgerows in those countries 'were removed – about 190,000 kilometres in all, or 7,250km a year – and there is every sign that the process is continuing…The direct impact on the landscape is immediate and obvious: equally serious, and even more insidious, has been the concomitant reduction of habitats for both flora and fauna'.

The rapid transformation of the countryside since the nineteenth century has given rise to various heritage conservation movements. Indeed, the forms that these movements have assumed have grown in much the same way as their motivations and their opponents. Most notably, they have grown substantially since the end of the Second World War, at the same time that mass tourism and leisure were developing. The countryside no longer provided only tranquillity, extensive horizons, and rural walks. Instead, it increasingly provided opportunities to:

discover a previously ignored heritage, participate in certain types of cultural tourism, and directly experience rural communities and learn about their lifestyles. Such developments come under the category of 'durable' or 'sustainable' tourism that is respectful of destination communities (Bramwell and Lane, 1994) and which is gaining the support of increasing numbers of townspeople who see in this movement not only the opportunity to conserve their increasingly threatened heritage but also to profit from it. The latter, in particular, is important to the local host population who hope for new, and often much needed, economic activity. As Gaudriault (1995) noted, manifestations of the 'rural crisis' have exposed a conscience for heritage. For example, in northern Portugal, the 'rooms with character' and the 'traditional lifestyles' are what tourists attach importance to in their choice of rural accommodation (Edwards, 1991, p. 153), thereby demonstrating the importance of certain aspects of heritage in tourist attitudes, motivations and perceptions.

The simultaneous movement of town and rural people in favour of heritage leads to the commodification of the 'rural' as it is incorporated into the tourist product. This process rests primarily on the heritage dimension, which stimulates the interest of townsfolk, and the economic dimension, which motivates the townsfolk.

This chapter aims to outline the various aspects of rural heritage tourism and, in turn, discusses the concepts of authenticity and identity which underly rural heritage tourism. The chapter then examines the forms and processes by which rural heritage has come to be regarded as significant, identifying key factors and policies determining rural heritage. The chapter concludes with a critical appraisal of the cultural tourist setting of rural heritage. Although few studies have been undertaken on rural heritage tourism, the potential scope for discussion of such a subject is a large and onerous task. Consequently, this chapter is designed to present a few areas of thought rather than to attempt an exhaustive review of developments around the world.

The nature and concept of rural heritage

A great diversity

Two observations are fundamental to understanding heritage in rural regions: first, rural heritage is much larger than purely agricultural heritage; and, second, 'rural business no longer depends solely on farmers' (Gaudriault, 1995, p. 36). Heritage touches all spheres of traditional rural life. It is interconnected with everything which is concerned with the existence of a productive society, linked first and foremost to the land, and which has progressively altered under the growth of urbanisation and its associated impacts.

A general overview of rural heritage demonstrates the wide variety of its constituent elements, but suggests also some problems which are bound up with its commodification as a tourist product. A major element of rural heritage is the landscape, where the countryside stands in opposition to the town (although such a distinction may rest uneasily with inhabitants of the rural-urban fringe). This countryside incorporates natural and human elements (e.g., relief, watercourses, meadows, forest, and marshes), whose division and balance are often the result of a long history of human-environment interaction. An almost infinite combination of rural landscapes are available in terms of their:

- *form*, e.g., wheat fields in the Canadian Prairies or massive tracts of the American Middle West;
- *shape*, e.g., the tiny crofts of the Hebrides or the vast tracts of land of the Ukraine;
- *enclosures*, e.g., the Norman copse, the stone walls of the Peak District or the bare open field; and
- *transport networks*, e.g., canals (as in The Netherlands), or rural lanes and footpaths (as in Britain) which may traverse the land in a checkered pattern.

Added to this is the built heritage, including isolated farms, hamlets, and villages, and also little farms relatively untouched by modernisation and recent urban expansion. Many people appreciate the forms, colours and atmosphere of such places, where vernacular architecture (e.g., stone, brick, wooden or loam farm houses, houses and workshops of business people and artisans, small-scale factories, market places, wash-houses, bridges, windmills, schools and restored stations, old cafes and gardens); religious architecture (e.g., churches, bell towers [which are often the 'hallmark' of villages, as in Brittany, Ireland and Poland], chapels, graveyards and holy crosses); and, sometimes, elements of military architecture (e.g., fortified castles, ramparts, and fortified gates and moats), combine in a particular location, often for many hundreds of years, in such a way that they have now become an attractive heritage attraction if accompanied by relevant product development.

However, all these built and preserved elements of heritage, which are often the most tangible element of a society, are not the only ones of interest to the tourist. In addition, everything which can be conveniently called 'art' and 'folk' traditions have potential to attract tourists, including:

- agriculture and artisan machines, tools, and vehicles (from hearses to fire engines and carts);
- the traditional business, domestic and recreational life of families and business people;
- significant civil and religious events;
- story-telling, e.g., legends, folk-tales, evenings by the fire-side, stories which refer to famous local personalities, real and mythical.
- colloquial language and dialect;
- local music;
- trades which are in the process of disappearing (thatchers, carpenters, timber framers, mud wall builders, and blacksmiths); and
- local cuisine.

Clearly, the list is potentially almost endless. It can also easily be observed that 'heritage' is not necessarily just an object which is threatened with disappearance or only has a limited distribution. For example, typical villages and chalets which form part of the basis of Austrian rural tourism are not threatened at all, even if it is appropriate to pay close attention to architectural and urban trends which could be destructive. Similarly, in France, the Association of the Finest French Villages formed a group of 139 'characteristic' villages in 1993, having received 28.3 million visitors (Duez and Valeix, 1995, p. 121).

Given these rather large number of heritage elements, it is necessary to ask, 'can everything be heritage?' Elevating places or objects to the status of 'heritage' can involve costly conservation or revitalisation measures. While such measures may add value to, and help define, the heritage product, they may also be ongoing and costly. Therefore, it is important for product development decisions to be made which will not only identify certain elements as 'heritage', but which also make them understandable to the tourist and capable of attracting tourist expenditure.

The development of heritage products may create increased desire for access from both the local population and from visitors. Both groups may have the same goal in terms of visiting heritage, but their experiences and interpretation can be substantially different, at times generating conflict. Therefore, the commodification of heritage poses important questions of 'authenticity' and 'identity'. The next section briefly examines these issues.

Authenticity and identity

According to Ashworth (1992, pp. 96–97), 'it could be argued that any resource remains latent until activated by a use for it but in this case resources are in a real sense created as much as activated'. Perceived authenticity on the part of the visitor, rather than simply conservation, is therefore necessary to transform history into heritage and complete the process of commodification. As Jeudy (1994, p. 65) stated, 'the value of heritage exceeds tourist valorisation more than scientific and aesthetic values which are not minimised to any great extent'.

The question of the criteria for heritage conservation are therefore significant. The first criterion is that of rarity. The speed at which conservation measures are adopted is often a function of its rarity. In this case, the uniqueness of an object appears as a guarantee of its value. The measures undertaken are varied, including classification as a monument or historic site, restoration, demolition and rebuilding. The criterion of authenticity can also be linked to that of rarity. However, the idea of authenticity can lead to much debate, as it is not only an historical criterion, given to an object or a monument of a certain age, and therefore requiring specific conservation measures with due respect to the past. It is also an ethnological criteria, according to which this object has had a meaning, has indeed had a utility in its society of origin. Gaugue (1995, p. 363) reports that in Africa, 'authentic' is defined as 'having known no evolution, and the least European influence must not be detected in an exhibit'. According to Gaugue, 'the "traditional" African object is the most often valued by those responsible for heritage as an ethnographic object proof of material culture' (1995, 63), whereas historical objects concern power, wars, old towns, and commerce. But it could also be argued that a non-genuine object also has its function because from the moment it has been created a function is attributed to it. An *autochtone* could then speak of the authenticity of a non-genuine piece.

For a tourist, ignorant of the culture or history of a destination, imitation objects can provide all the characteristics associated with authenticity. How many souvenirs brought from one country pass for products of that country, when they have been imported from elsewhere? If the idea of authenticity is, in principle, objective, the actual experience that individuals have can mask a very different relationship to reality. The object of their experience can be more or less authentic, and they will not judge it less so, wrongly or rightly, that their own experience is authentically real or otherwise. Commodification of heritage poses serious questions with respect to authenticity and the tourist experience. For example, is it better, to protect at great expense an old, poorly positioned but truly authentic country house which is not very accessible to the public, or to construct an 'artificial' (for the local 'purist' inhabitant) one which is attractive and well positioned and which offers all the characteristics of authenticity for the visitor?

De Kadt, for example, recognises that authenticity is a major element in the visitor experience: 'authenticity as a characteristic of alternative tourism is wholly focused on the tourist . . . it concerns his or her perceptions of the reality encountered in the tourist experience' (1992, p. 51). Yet, the issue of authenticity does not only apply to the tourist. All consumers of heritage will have different perceptions of authenticity. There are 'different versions of authenticity as defined by different customers' (Ashworth, 1992, p. 98). As Meyer and Richard somewhat ironically remarked:

> when a town dweller nowadays, often sprung from the depths of the countryside, becomes . . . 'a rural tourist', he is looking for a return to his roots, to authenticity and often to childhood . . . He dreams . . . of jam jars, hot apple tarts, walls nostalgically nibbled by the wild-grape, standing watch by the fire-side . . .
> The local administrator . . . deciphers the PDZR, the PIM, the FIDAR, and the FRILE, in a classified zone in Objective 1, 2, or 5 B according to the last European directive passed by DATAR, The Préfecture, consular offices and local authorities (1991–1992, pp. 11–12).

From a tourist perspective, it is often difficult to know, then, what is appropriate to preserve and to offer for the curiosity of the visitor. Jeudy (1994, p. 68) even emphasises 'the necessary paradox of creating authentic crafts'. Indeed, to satisfy the tourist and sometimes to rejuvenate imitations of lost crafts, there has been a tendency to recreate objects that are displayed for economic profit, e.g., pseudo 'old pubs' or 'old houses', traditional games, local costumes and music and dance groups.

The maintenance (in fact the notion) of authenticity, dubious and debatable though it is, indeed touches on the essential question of identity. In fact, more and more often, authenticity is the basis for a local or regional identity to be contrasted with neighbouring ones, a means of reactivating an ancient heritage, even if not really authentic, and exposing tourists to it in order to assert difference, cultural richness, identity, and perhaps even prominence or change. As Gaugue (1995, p. 34) notes, 'in former communist countries, the museum must become the place for national exhibitions of culture, which had stopped existing under the previous regime'. In Romania, for example, where thousands of traditional villages were 'restructured' by the state communist regime (that is demolished and replaced by large collective tenements in the name of progress), one is witnessing, with the appearance of rural tourism and homestay accommodation in areas such as Moldavia, Bucovina, and Maramures, the revival of traditional individual rural lifestyles and housing because of the value attached to it by both to the local people and the tourists. Similarly, Bauer (1995, p. 159), underscores the importance of identity in producing images of a destination. For the tourist, it is important to identify destinations by a simple, even simplistic, image of a heritage which is often concealed from the tourist, e.g., 'Baroque Bavaria', 'Gothic Picardy', 'Scotland, Land of Castles', 'Holland, country of windmills', and 'Quebec, French America'.

Cultural identity is often accompanied by a geopolitical identity, which is based on certain quasi-nationalistic ideologies. Gaugue (1995, p. 29) underlines that for many in nineteenth century Europe and twentieth century Africa, it was important to 'conserve examples of rural traditions and folklore, symbols of a culture threatened by urbanisation and industrialisation'. However, identity needs to be supported by cultural authenticity. And both can be promoted through reconstructing identical replicas. This action, despite the greatest possible attempts to be true to the original, will not satisfy the ethnologist or the purist, but it will provide a substitute considered as adequate to satisfy the local desire for education, encourage tourist visitation, and convey to the tourist appropriate interpretive messages. At the same time, it will provide welcome economic impacts.

A particular image that is confirmed or reinforced through these unauthentic or authentic cultural artifacts, and which serves to maintain the collective memory and identity of a locality, will simultaneously provide a focal point for the attractiveness of a region in relation to its competitors. In a tourist context, identity serves a double function: inwardly, it assists in providing local cohesion; externally, it assists in providing an opening in the tourist market. This situation gives rise to a dual paradox – the creation of heritage which reinforces local particularisms but also the banalities of tourism, while increasing regional tourism product differentiation when local identity needs to be asserted in a homogenous way in the face of external tourist pressures (Ashworth, 1992). Therefore, tourist destinations find themselves in a situation in which they must unceasingly assert an identity which the tourist flow constantly tends to trivialise and make banal; it becomes from that moment indispensable to 'understand how a heritage doesn't exclude its own metamorphosis' (Jeudy, 1994, p. 63).

In the imaging process, although different groups encounter the same heritage objects and artefacts, they will not share the same values and perceptions in response to those objects. For the local community, memory, attachment, and symbolism are often of primary importance, with authenticity playing an essential role because it 'deals with meaning' (De Kadt, 1992, pp. 51–52). In contrast, visitors attach more to the unfamiliar, the exotic, and the picturesque in their cultural exploration.

The local community often becomes the intermediary, by means of interpretation, explaining heritage, and encouraging the visitor to encounter, participate and contribute to the heritage experience, even although they are not able to actually belong to the local community. However, it is necessary to determine carefully what is being interpreted, who is going to develop interpretation strategies, and for whom and how, because different messages can be conveyed to different groups, and because it is vital that communities convey a political message which is appropriate for encouraging support for heritage conservation (Ashworth, 1992). Inevitably, 'putting heritage into the limelight' is a response both to the excesses of contrived authenticity by a local population and the need to maintain attractiveness to the visitor in order 'to prove that revenue from heritage is possible in the medium and long term' (Tiard, 1987, p. 30). Indeed, it is interesting to note that the preoccupation of visitors with heritage can raise the consciousness of local communities about its value and, consequently, may stir up defensive actions, such as conservation, restoration, and revitalisation. In many rural regions facing depopulation, abandoned traditional farms are being converted by townspeople into second or first homes before the local rural inhabitants, but also certain 'foreigners' or 'outsiders', take them over again and establish rural homesteads, country inns, workshops and small handicraft shops which are sensitive to the local heritage qualities which had almost been lost (Dewailly and Flament, 1993).

There is therefore a permanent dialectical movement between rural people and visitors in the search for authenticity and identity. Although ideas of authenticity and identity will not be the same thing for each group, heritage provides the focal point for the dialectic between the countryside and the town; heritage attracts the majority of visitors who are curious about the past.

The form and process of recognising rural heritage

Although the attraction of rural heritage to tourists is stronger than ever, rural heritage is an old phenomenon, which has been supported by numerous political actors with more or less convergent interests. The next section looks at the emergence of recognition for rural tourism and some of the policy aspects which surround it.

The emergence of recognition for rural tourism

The rural heritage conservation movement has been primarily European based. Several phases can be distinguished in its development, although there is, of course, considerable overlap between these phases depending on the place and the context within which rural heritage is located. The origins of the movement lie in the European regions where traditional rural lifestyles had been most profoundly affected by the Industrial Revolution and its effects, most notably the rural exodus to nearby and attractive industrial towns. The abandonment of traditional lifestyles by rural communities aroused a corresponding attention and increased attachment to the artefacts and objects which characterised the former lifestyles.

The formal beginnings of the rural heritage conservation movement can be traced to the establishment of folk museums in Scandinavia and, in particular, to the creation of the Nordic Museum in Stockholm by Hazelius in 1873. A follower of the pan-Scandinavian movement, Hazelius sought to collect in this museum objects from all the regions where Scandinavian was spoken and was seen to be gradually disappearing. His collection grew so large that by 1891 he was able to open the first open-air museum in the world at Skansen, consisting of houses, farms, rural buildings, and representative artefacts of all the regions of Scandinavia. Around the same period, the Danish Folk museum opened near Copenhagen, where its founder, B. Olsen, wanted 'to teach young people everything which belonged to Denmark's past, to consolidate the memory of lost provinces and open the way to a spiritual and intellectual reconquest' (De Jong and Skougaard, 1992, in Gaugue, 1995, p. 29).

In 1895, the Norwegian Folk Museum was established in Oslo, reaffirming Norwegian identity at a time when Norway was strongly trying to gain its independence from Sweden (obtained in 1905). Similarly, the Open Air Museum in Arnhem, first established in The Netherlands in 1912, also wanted to demonstrate 'the cultural unity of the nations . . . the immovable solidarity of its eleven provinces' (Van den Ven, 1920, in Gaugue, 1995, p. 30). This type of rural heritage attraction has since spread rapidly throughout Europe. In 1974, 183 folk museum were recorded of which 70 per cent were in Northern Europe (Zippelius, 1974). By 1987, the number of folk museums had grown to 396 for all of Europe (Dewailly, 1990, p. 90). The development of folk museums has gathered pace outside of Europe, including Africa, where, according to Gaugue (1995), museums of a similar type are found at Niamey (Niger), Parakou (Benin), Dar es Salaam, (Tanzania), Bobo-Dioulasso (Burkina-Faso), Nairobi (Kenya), and Bujumbura (Burundi). All of these museums were established since these countries gained independence and indicate the role of heritage in helping reinforce newly acquired national unity and identity.

Ethnological and geopolitical considerations may be integrated in the creation phase of conserving rural heritage places through the establishment of folk museums (e.g., in Western Europe in the late nineteenth and early twentieth century or in post-independence Africa or, more recently, in the former state communist nations of Eastern Europe). The conservation of houses, farms, furniture, traditional objects, and other items serves both considerations, to varying degrees, according to place and time, as:

- a reminder of declining ways of rural life;
- a claim of identity (sometimes even nationalist identity); and
- as an economic activity which is induced by tourism.

This economic dimension has become increasingly important in the second half of the twentieth century. After the Second World War, the growing intensification of agriculture and the increased modernisation of the countryside brought about a rapid decline in the use of traditional rural heritage components: tractors replaced horses; farms became mechanised; rural lands were rezoned, thereby radically modifying thousand year old rural landscapes; and running water, electricity and central heating became available in the countryside therefore making many of the utensils which had been a part of daily life obsolete or at the very least less popular. Water was no longer drawn from the wells; the bread oven and the individual wine press were no longer used; cooking at the large chimney place largely ceased. Similarly, the communal washing place and, soon, the church, in many cases, were no longer focal points of community life. At the same time, old houses, barns, castles and chapels were dismantled and then transported, when they did not go to the United States or Japan, to rich suburbs in large towns. Rural business people found it increasingly difficult to make a living. Some, from that period, diversified their businesses by providing opportunities to consumers to experience various aspects of rural life, e.g., homestays, farmstays, accommodation with host families, guest-houses, rental of rural cottages or unoccupied rooms, equestrian centres or artisan's studios in old empty farm buildings. France (e.g., rural cottages), the British Isles (e.g., bed and breakfast), Germany and Austria (e.g., rooms available for rent in farmhouses) offer the better known types of this approach to economic diversification, but such economic utilisation of the rural built heritage is now used throughout Europe as well in many other developed countries.

In the 1970s, an ecological dimension was added to this form of 'green tourism'. Tourism in rural areas is often thought as a form of 'soft' tourism in which the economic value of place heritage appears as an effective means of promoting forms of development which resist the 'invasion' of holiday village ghettos. Moreover, in terms of built heritage, there is now an even greater interest in the quality of the surrounding countryside and the promotion of activities which harmonise with the local environment (e.g. rural walks, hiking). Through these developments, there has been a natural progression towards the appearance of 'eco-tourism' – a form of tourism which is respectful of the natural and socio-cultural environment in which it occurs. Therefore, in the last two decades significant new forms of tourism have begun to appear, including:

- collections of small tourist houses in Casamance, Senegal (Ciaccio, 1985);
- rural cottages for walkers in the Moroccan Atlas (Fassi Fihri, 1991);
- tourism in local dwellings in Portugal (Cavaco, 1985; Edwards, 1991);
- nature-based tourism in Central America (Place, 1991) and Brazil (Ruschman, 1992); and
- various forms of special interest tourism (Weiler and Hall, 1992).

To this ecological and then eco-tourism movement was added a more substantial cultural dimension which gained momentum towards the end of the 1980s. Cultural heritage tourism products were developed in which economic value was ascribed through both the attraction of built heritage to visitors and the consumption of wider forms of local cultural expressions, such as those described earlier in the chapter (Bergeron, 1992). Therefore, there is a proliferation of (1) rural festivals founded on particular events (which are often the reconstruction of historical events) (see Chapter Ten); (2) cultural tours and itineraries which link small museums, and workshops and factories which are still in use; and (3) the promotion of the working and social life of specific country regions as a tourist attraction. These products have been developed by tour operators, government tourist organisations, and tourism associations at various levels. For example, the

- 'Silk and Spice Routes' that UNESCO has assisted in developing and coordinating between Western Europe and the Far East;
- various textile routes of northwestern Europe, such as the 'Scottish Woollen Border Trail' to the south of Edinburgh or the 'Textile Route' in the west of Belgian Hainault (Delbaere, 1994, 1995);
- 'Hop Route', in the West of Belgian Flanders; and
- 'Franco-Swiss Clock Route' through the Jura.

Such tourist routes and trails can link and assist the development of a host of large and small museums, many of which contribute to the protection and economic value of rural heritage tourism and contribute to the revitalisation of their region (Maier et al., 1994, Dewailly, 1996).

For over a century, many motivations have underpinned recognition of the significance of rural tourism. These motivations can be traced according to the place in which rural tourism occurs, and its general stage of tourism development and wider economic, social and political development. However, regardless of specific motivations, the economic dimensions of heritage and the consequent development of heritage attractions are now extremely significant to rural communities.

Actors and politics

The exploitation of rural heritage by tourism involves an extraordinary mixture of individuals and groups, and planned and unplanned public and private actions (see Chapter Two on rural policy). While only a brief glimpse of these political processes can be given, it seems that in the process of rural heritage tourism development, cultural and heritage values have given way primarily to commercial values. Although it is very difficult to generalise because of different national and political contexts, the importance of the financial 'bottom-line' certainly has not disappeared, and has undoubtedly even been reinforced during these difficult economic times when general budgetary restrictions have been popular with national and regional governments. But doubtless, too, it has become blurred behind the increasingly respectable and presentable political and promotional image on which tourism is based, and for which heritage can act as an excellent support, rather than the reality of rural heritage tourism development.

In the nineteenth century, enlightened, learned, intellectual individuals – amateur archaeologists – who were interested in protecting heritage and to 'commercialise' it for reasons of tourism, were moved more by a concern with ethnology and/or ideology than tourists or commercial reasons. In recent decades, we continue to see innovative farmers and rural people transform the shell of an old farm homestead or an ancient barn into rural tourist accommodation; or restore old cellars for tasting and selling their cheese, wine, jam and conserves; or transform a former pigeon coop or an old stable to serve rustic meals, often set against a backdrop of rural vernacular architecture, farm tools, and the traditional manufacturing and wine-making processes, in such a way that the tourist can experience something that appears authentic. The targeted tourist is nearly always a person from the city, who is attracted to the apparent simplicity of indigenous local rural lifestyles in contrast to their own, and for whom the experience is commodified by way of some form of financial transaction. However, by doing this, according to the dialectical relationship between rural people and urban visitors described above, tourists inevitably disturb the lifestyle that they hope to discover.

When rural heritage development takes off, the activities of individuals are quite quickly replaced by associations, who have both commercial and lobbying power. For example, since its foundation in 1895, the National Trust in Britain has been widely acknowledged as having substantially contributed to protecting and making available to the public a predominantly rural heritage threatened by ruin or neglect (see Gaze, 1988). In France, since 1971, the Rural Tourism Association (Association Tourism en Espace Rural (TER)) has served to provide a cooperative umbrella organisation for numerous participants in rural tourism, most notably the powerful National Federation of French Rural Cottages, itself an association created in 1955, each of whom are in agreement in recognising the positive functions of the protection of traditional rural places. Edwards (1991) notes a number of similar associations created during the 1980s in Portugal and in South West England. Frequently, public authorities aid such associations through the development of cooperative agreements and the provision of financial subsidies which may assist the contributions that these regional associations make to the development and maintenance of regional infrastructure. Such activities and the establishment of associations help to maintain the population base of rural areas, promote economic diversification, and assist in the preservation of a rich heritage.

The creation of ecomuseums in France highlights the increased significance of private sector associations. Ecomuseums are local heritage conservation structures, brought to life by and for the local population, but with a view to creating new activities to encourage local economic development. With the assistance of such associations, ecomuseums receive aid from the state, regions, and the 'departements', in terms of defined local objectives. For example, the Ecomuseum of Alsace, near Mulhouse, which receives 350,000 visitors annually, combines locally owned built heritage, the founder association as a major stakeholder in the cultural project and a private society which manages the museum (Grodwohl, 1994).

Public authorities have also become directly involved in rural tourism because of the lobbying activities of the associations. For example, in the 1970s, the French government identified 'hospitable country areas' as a major element of rural tourism policy. These 'country areas' – small homogeneous rural tourism regions – had as their primary objective the development of hospitality for tourists, and were selected on the basis of the richness of their heritage and the quality of tourism-related projects which added value to the regional tourism product. Numerous joint associations and committees were established, which combined departments, communes, the Departments of Agriculture, Chambers of Commerce and Industry, and other local partners. This policy initiative made tourism more dynamic in a number of regional areas in France and partly contributed to the protection of their heritage.

Several countries have developed even more ambitious rural policies with respect to more extensive areas of the rural landscape. For example, the national parks of England and Wales, the French 'natural regional parks', and the Germany 'nature parks', where the protection of the countryside and rural heritage is regarded as an agent of development which serve both the local population and the growing number of people from the cities who come to visit these spaces (Cumming and Trustcott, 1995a, b, c). Even in the United States and Canada, the large size of natural parks and the presence of a nature less impacted by humanity than in Europe does not prevent attention being given to the vestiges of human occupation in the countryside, which relate to those of the original inhabitants and to those that are attributed to pioneers and early colonists.

Heritage development and exploitation

Staged attractions are an important element in the achievement of political goals with respect to heritage. Parks or attractions, such as visitor centres, country houses and interpretative centres, add value to heritage and make an effort to make visitors aware of what is necessary for preservation. These attractions create employment and encourage financial investment, but also lead to increased local pride as well as pleasure and discovery for the visitors.

Thanks to their size, the different types of parks can also better protect *in situ* certain buildings or objects, thereby also lending them a greater authenticity. This is opposed to grouping such heritage *en masse* which possibly offers ease of management and tourist attractiveness at the expense of reduction in authenticity. These larger parks or ecomuseums offer a wider tourist product to the visitor through visits to museums or typical localities, practical demonstrations (e.g., wheat threshing, the traditional gathering or the harvesting of agricultural products, horse shoeing, and flour milling in old windmills), folk dancing in traditional costume, games and sometimes reinactments of events with the public, horse riding in Europe or elephant riding in Thailand, videos, souvenirs and gadgets in all forms, exhibitions, publications, 'typical' farm produce, traditional meals, and also short stays which combine visits, meals and evenings 'by the fire', and social gatherings. There is no lack of imagination in providing paid recreational activies which create economic value for local heritage. Small towns are generally linked to this heritage development, for they not only offer complementary structures in terms of heritage (e.g., cattle markets, market-places, and small museums), but also offer accommodation and dining. Obviously, the more commodification is pushed, the more the artificiality and the subsequent loss of authenticity. There are no lack of cases where local dances presented to the public lack meaning, where 'farm produce' has been bought at the neighbouring supermarket, and where 'local' craftspersons have a number of products brought in from other countries.

Conclusion

Unquestionably, rural heritage is now the object of greater attention, as much for its socio-cultural value as its economic significance. There is no lack of ambiguities and conflicts with respect to heritage and its economic value. The general problems of financing heritage were not be discussed in detail here. The principle question lies in understanding if authenticity and local identity are seen primarily from a heritage and cultural perspective or from an economic perspective with respect to their tourist attractiveness. That answer depends on the relationship between the various interests which are present and through the heritage policies which are put in place. As Ashworth (1992) has pointed out, should the latter be considered as an element of identity or as an economic component? The result can only be 'a compromise between the economic demand of producing a profit and the social and cultural demands' (Gaudriault, 1995, p. 36). But that does not completely resolve the problem. If economic logic prevails, how can the tourist product be periodically renewed without affecting even more an already diminished authenticity at the very time that rural heritage enterprises are being encouraged? Such renewal appears increasingly indispensable in a competitive market place. If the new product has been judged authentic, after a time can it be made more than or differently from 'the authentic'? The necessary renewal of the tourist product complicates the question of authenticity in a confined regional area. If the cultural aspect succeeds with the objective of reanimating culture, of rediscovering the identity of a society in crisis, how can society itself, which looked towards the past, be permanently revitalised? Jeudy (1994, p. 66) expressed this difficulty well when he wrote that 'ecomuseums seem to be at a crossroad at present, as if they had accomplished their mission, and they must however, continue to survive. Their originality is being gradually erased in favour of a stagnation of their function'. The question of the coherence of heritage policies is therefore asked in terms of the regions concerned, the actors involved, and the potential for economic disaster. The answers are many. It can only be a matter of a subtle balance, continuously called into question, as much by the weight of local factors as by new research or even the general development of society at large.

Whatever the present success of heritage policies in the rural context, it seems that interest in rural heritage corresponds to a large extent to the discovery of 'innovative' tourism developments, until now unexploited, which offer, for the moment, new market opportunities because they correspond both to public demand and to preoccupations with product diversification, regional development, and concerns over identity. One of the big challenges will be the sustainability of rural heritage tourism. On the one hand, concern over the economic value of this heritage emphasises the need to recognise the problems of competition between products which will have increasing difficulty in differentiating themselves in the marketplace. After the euphoria of the introductory stage, economic viability will not always be guaranteed. What will remain, if public money does not come to the rescue of certain private, interesting but quite fragile projects? How many now protected sites will become neglected? According to Gaudriault (1995, p. 390), 'we need to understand, that many other places will revert to an unmaintained condition'. On the other hand, it is important that stakeholders retain recognition of the significance of their actions and their values, and the foundation of their original commitment. It is probable that it will not always be so. Consequently, if the present heritage policies are evidence of a growing integration of rural tourist areas in the economic cycle of tourism, due to urbanisation and increased mobility, it can be considered that they indicate also a stage in general 'touristification' (Dewailly and Flament, 1993), which, in turn, affects our open space and our societies and tends increasingly to standardise them.

Endnote

1. This chapter encompasses the use of the terms 'agritourism' and 'green tourism' under the umbrella of 'rural tourism'. Although certain differences are recognised, it is not the intention of this chapter to analyse the specific use of these terms.

References

Ashworth, G., 1992, Heritage and tourism: an argument, two problems and three solutions. In *Spatial implications of tourism*, C. Fleischer-van Rooijen, ed., pp. 95–104, Geo Pers, Amsterdam

Bauer, M., 1995, Les territoires et leur interprétation. Un exemple savoyard, *Cahiers d'Espaces*, **42**, p. 154–163.

Bergeron, R., 1992, Tourisme et patrimoine dans les campagnes lyonnaises, *Revue de Geographie de Lyon*, **67**, 1, p. 19–30.

Bramwell, B. and Lane, B., eds., 1994, *Rural development and sustainable development*, Channel View Publications, Clevedon

Cavaco, C., 1985, *Tourisme et milieu rural au Portugal*, Colloque International de Géographie du Tourisme, Université de Liège, 30 Septembre–1 Octobre

Ciaccio, C., 1985, Le tourisme rural au Sénégal. In *Le tourisme et la récréation en milieu rural*, C. Christians, ed., pp. 93–101, Colloque International de Géographie du Tourisme, Université de Liège

Cumming, R. and Truscott, R., 1995a, France: planning and the role of the Parcs Naturels Regionaux, *Report for the natural and built environment professions*, **3**: 8–10

Cumming, R. and Truscott, R., 1995b, Le Boulonnais. A case study, *Report for the natural and built environment professions*, **4**: 6–8

Cumming, R. and Truscott, R., 1995c, L'Espace naturel régional (Région Nord-Pas-de-Calais), *Report for the natural and built environment professions*, **5**: 12–14

De Jong, A. and Skougaard, M., 1992, Les premiers musées de plein air, *Museum* 175

De Kadt, E., 1992, Making the alternative sustainable: lessons from development for tourism. In *Tourism alternatives*, V. Smith and W. Eadington, eds., pp. 47–75, John Wiley, New York

Delbaere, R., 1994, *La route du textile dans le Hainaut Occidental belge*, Paper presented at the Conference on the Geography of Tourism, Oppland College, Lillehammer, Norway, 6–12 August

Delbaere, R., 1995, *Développements récents des itinéraires textiles du Conseil de l'Europe, ou le tourisme dans la voie de la mémoire ouvrière*, Communication au Colloque de la Commission Française de Géographie du Tourisme et des Loisirs, Majorque, Espagne, 16-23 Septembre

Dewailly, J.M., 1990, *Tourisme et aménagement en Europe du Nord*, Masson, coll. Géographie, VIII

Dewailly, J.M., 1996, *Museums and regional reconversion in Northern France*, Centre des Hautes Etudes Touristiques, Aix-en-Provence, Cahiers du Tourisme, série C, no. 195

Dewailly, J.M. and Flament, E., 1993, *Géographie du tourisme et des loisirs*, SEDES, coll. DIEM

Duez, M. and Valeix, J.C., 1995, Les villages de caractère: atout touristique et élément d'aménagement du territoire, *Cahiers d'Espaces*, **42**: 120–124

Edwards, J., 1991, Guest-host perceptions of rural tourism in England and Portugal. In *The tourism industry: an international analysis*, T. Sinclair and M.J. Stabler, eds, pp. 143–164, CAB International, Oxford

Fassi Fihri, E., 1991, *Mountain tourism, survey of experience*, International Geographical Union, Commission of Geography of Leisure and Recreation, Marrakech Conference, Octobre

Gaudriault, M.C., 1995, Paysages: les plus désespérés sont les champs les plus beaux, *Cahiers d'Espaces*, **42**: 35–39

Gaugue, A., 1995, Géopolitique des musées en Afrique tropicale. La mise en scène de la nation, Thèse de doctorat, Université de Paris VIII, Paris

Gaze, J., 1988, *Figures in a landscape: a history of the National Trust*, Barrie & Jenkins in association with the National Trust, London

Grodwohl, M., 1994, Dixième anniversaire de l'écomusée d'Alsace. Identité régionale et économie touristique, *Cahiers d'Espaces*, **37**: 166–169

Jeudy, H.P., 1994, Métamorphose des patrimoines, *Cahiers d'Espaces*, **37**: 63–68

Maier, J., Ludwig, J. and Oergel, L., 1994, *The impacts of museums on the economic and cultural development of a region: examples of different types of museums in Upper Franconia, Bavaria*, Paper presented to Tourism Conference, Oppland College, Lillehammer, Norway, 6–12 August

Meyer, R. and Richard, C., 1991–1992, Tourisme rural et ruralité du tourisme, *Espaces*, **113**: 10–14

Patmore, J.A., 1983, *Recreation and resources*, Basil Blackwell, Oxford

Place, S., 1991, Nature tourism and rural development in Tortuguero (Costa-Rica), *Annals of Tourism Research*, **2**: 186–201

Ruschman, D., 1992, Ecological tourism in Brazil, *Tourism Management*, **1**: 125–128

Tiard, M., 1987, La mise en scène du patrimoine, *Espaces*, **85**: 27–32

Van den Ven, D., 1920, *Neerlands-volksleven*, Zalbommel
Weiler, B. and Hall, C.M., eds., 1992, *Special interest tourism*, Wiley, Chichester
Zippelius, A., 1974, *Handbuch der europischen freilichtmuseen*, Rheinland Verlag, Munich

9 Commodifying the countryside: marketing myths of rurality

JEFFREY HOPKINS

The 'countryside' is a place-image deeply entrenched in the geographical imagination of Canadians, an image that is fundamental to the promotion and consumption of rural tourism. In a nation where the population is overwhelmingly 'urban' (Census Canada, 1991, in Ley and Bourne, 1993), the 'countryside' is some other place, a place spatially, temporally and psychologically distanced from the everyday urban life of most people. Distance enhances differences, be they real or imagined, and it is imagination that both inspires and sustains the construction of place-myths; the connoted, embellished identities attributed to places (Shields, 1991; Urry, 1995). In order to attract urban tourists, the rural tourism industry both promotes and accentuates urban-rural differences by drawing upon country images that evoke and aggrandize myths of rurality (see Chapter Seven). Without such imagery the myths collapse, and with their demise, so falls a 'rustic' place that caters to the desires and imagination of urbanites, and more importantly, an industry that employs and profits. What are the identities and attractions used to promote and commodify the countryside? What myths and values are evoked to idealize a place as rural? And what, if any, are the paradoxes and problems for the long-term marketability and commercial viability of rural tourism?

This chapter presents a critical interpretation of the format, content, and signs used to represent, commodify and promote the rural countryside of Southwestern Ontario. The analysis is grounded in socio-semiotics, a part of the larger field of cultural studies concerned with representation and identity. Using 210 printed pieces of free promotional material[1] gathered at several tourist information booths along the main coastal highway of Lake Huron[2] (Figure 9.1), the production and consumption of the themes, values, myths and identities attributed to the 'rural place' are qualified, their ideological connotations discussed, and their possible consequences for the long-term economic viability of rural tourism in the sample area and beyond are considered. Doing so is in direct response to the recent calls for further investigation into the new meanings currently represented in rural places (Cloke, 1993; Cloke and Thrift, 1994), their emergent 'rural' identities (Halfacre, 1993; Urry, 1995), and the development of cultural studies to place promotion (Gold, 1994). Of the three major research areas on place promotion: public policy, marketing, and image communication, this work falls primarily in the latter category by addressing the place-images of the countryside as communicated to consumers

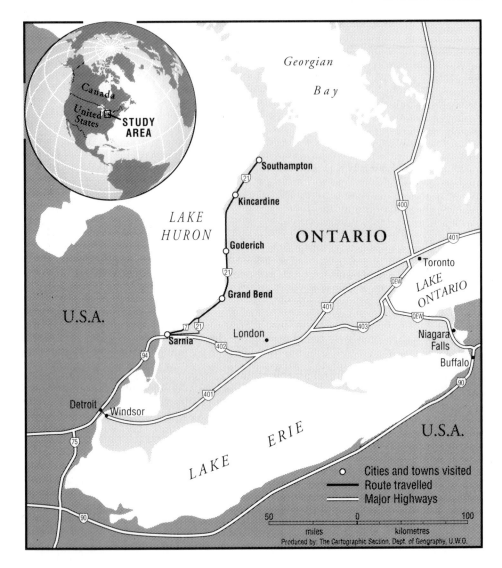

Figure 9.1. Map of Southern Ontario

through marketing advertisements (Ward and Gold, 1994). Before addressing the specific case study along Lake Huron, a brief overview of place promotion and the commodification of the countryside is presented, followed by an explanation of the semiotic approach used to critique the rural place-image.

Place promotion as necessity

Publicly praising the attributes of a place is as ancient as humanity's love for the natural landscape and the desire to share it with others; marketing a place is a more recent venture. Place promotion is defined by Ward and Gold (1994, p. 2) as 'the conscious use of publicity and marketing to communicate selective images of specific geographic localities or areas to a target audience'. It is not simply a public proclamation of hometown pride by local inhabitants; it is an orchestrated and deliberate attempt to communicate specific images about a place to a particular group of consumers with the intention of altering their attitudes and behaviour (Ashworth and Voogd, 1994). On the surface, such 'boosterism' is hardly novel: the 'New World' was promoted as exceptionally fertile to potential settlers during the age of European expansion; 19th-century British residential suburbs were heralded for their natural and secure domestic settings to potential home-buyers (Ward and Gold 1994); and late-19th century and early-20th century Ontario boasted of cheap and plentiful Niagara Falls power to attract industry (Ward 1994). Similarly, competition between regions, cities and sites for resources, business, industry and residents has always existed. But on closer inspection, both place promotion and the nature of the competition between places have changed.

There are various fundamental shifts in Western societies, both hidden and visible, that have heightened both the nature and necessity for place promotion. Ashworth and Voogd (1994) note several economic and political transformations that have contributed to this situation. The rise of the global economy, particularly in the tourism and service sectors, has provided new opportunities for some places to develop and promote their recreational and leisure facilities (Goeldner, 1992). Post-industrial restructuring has compelled others to exploit and promote local tourist attractions, particularly natural amenities, in an attempt to minimise, halt or reverse economic decline induced by collapse or contraction in more conventional, primary and manufacturing based sectors (see Chapter Three). Funding cuts, the lessening of the welfare state, and the prevailing market-driven policy stance of Canada's governing bodies has also encouraged local townships, counties and municipalities to market themselves to investors and consumers alike. Place promotion is now part of economic development, planning and policy at most levels of government, and it has long been an essential part of the tourism industry.

At a deeper level, the prevalence of tourism and place promotion is both the cause and consequence of a spatially liberated, consumeristic, image-driven culture. The automobile has made formerly marginalised locations accessible in two comple-mentary ways: potential 'day visitors' and overnight motortrip tourists have come into being, thus expanding the demand for leisure and tourist destinations, and most places have access to the tourist market. In other words, almost any location is now connected to almost any other location. The tourism market is therefore a highly competitive arena where places must be advertised in order to attract not simply tourists but 'place consumers' (Ashworth and Voogd, 1990). In a consumption-oriented society, places, like virtually all merchandise, services and experiences for sale on the market, are 'commodified'; they are themselves consumable products: place-commodities. Whether at the scale of individual sites with specific amenities and services (e.g., a campground) or at the level of entire region or country (e.g., The Great Lakes), a place is both a context for consumption and a consumable entity in itself (Ashworth and Voogd, 1994). 'Place' is 'a centre of felt value ... a repository of meaning' which has a physical setting, a location, and a sense of identity (Billinge, 1986, p. 346; Burgess and Wood, 1988, p. 95). It is the meanings, values, experiences and identities attributed to a place by the promoter that are marketed in the form of advertisements. These are not designed to sell the place-commodity per se, but 'something else', a packaged, recognisable brand of place: a place-image (Lash and Urry, 1994). Selling images is not unique to the tourism industry; it is ubiquitous in contemporary Western society. Social life is saturated by media and advertising; we are an image-driven culture (Baudrillard, 1981, 1983; Debord, 1983).

The tourism industry is thus indicative of an important cultural shift in our society:

- the increase in leisure services of consumption replacing the agricultural and manufacturing industries of accumulation (King, 1988);
- the growing intrusion of fantasy and spectacle into everyday places (Hopkins, 1990; Urry, 1990; Sorkin, 1992; Francaviglia 1996); and
- the pervasiveness of images transmitted through various media (DeKerckhove 1995: Kellner 1995).

The fact that tourism has come to the countryside, that it is now commodified, promoted and consumed, is to be expected in the context of today's global capitalism, the expansion of information and communication technologies, and rising consumer demands for entertainment, leisure and recreation. But what the 'rural' has come to mean in light of these changes is open to question; a re-interpretation of rural identity is wanting. Using a socio-semiotic approach, this study contributes to the challenge by critiquing the meanings and images of 'rural' as represented and promoted in printed advertisements of country places.

Socio-semiotics, signs and ideology

Semiotics, the study of signs and sign systems, is an established analytical tool of critical theory used to interpret cultural creations, be they advertisements or otherwise. Given its potential for theoretical insight into, and analytical utility in, the production and interpretation of culture, semiotics has become part of the interdisciplinary debate within cultural studies on social theory and interpretive methods. Viewed from a semiotic perspective, culture is 'the constant process of producing meanings' from the perpetual succession of social practices and shared experiences (Fiske, 1989, p. 1). Because culture is both a mediator and medium of social interaction, cultural creations may be interpreted semiotically, that is, as a collection of signs or texts (Gottdiener, 1982; Sebeok, 1986). A 'sign' is most commonly defined as 'something that stands for something else', such as each of these written words standing for or representing an object, idea or meaning (Sebeok, 1986, p. 936). A 'sign system' or 'text' is a systematically related collection of objects, events or phenomena taken as signs, such as the words comprising this sentence and the meanings and ideas it conveys. 'Signification' is the process whereby 'something' (the 'signifier' or 'expression') comes to stand for 'something else' (the 'signified' or 'content'); it is a social process whereby objects, events or phenomena taken as signs or sign systems are given meanings. By focusing on the processes of signification, whereby signs are produced and consumed, semiotics is made applicable to 'the whole of culture': architecture, cities, film, language, literature, and of course place advertisements and rural landscapes, are all potentially subject to semiotic analyses (Eco, 1976).

Socio-semiotics is a specific branch of semiotics that studies both signs and social contexts; the connection between ideologically-charged sign systems and the material culture of everyday life is the focus. More precisely, the junction of the signifiers of the sign – 'the substance of expression' – and the signified ideologies of the sign – 'the form of content' – is the principle concern of a socio-semiotic analysis (Gottdiener, 1995, p. 56). It is used here, albeit in a simplified version, because our interest rests not with the place-promotional signs themselves but with identifying and interpreting the ideologies, values, and myths of rurality that they connote, and the larger political, economic, and cultural contexts in which these meanings are produced and consumed.

In this instance, the object of analysis, the phenomena of material culture examined, are place-promotion advertisements: 'controlled messages and symbols' designed to project images at prospective customers and alter their perceptions, produce connections and stimulate desires away from the point of sale (Middleton, 1988, p. 157). These are quite literally ideologically-charged signs used by promoters to communicate with, and attract, customers (Volosinov, 1930, in Noth, 1995). 'Ideology' is any system of values, beliefs or norms that facilitate the interests and domination of a particular group, class or society (Gregory, 1986; Noth, 1995). It follows that the tourism industry may be said to operate with a sign system that facilitates its own ideology of consumption by attempting to manipulate the leisure and recreational decisions of people for the purposes of selling commodities: tourist places. This practice of consumer manipulation by commodity industries is termed 'logotechniques' (Barthes, 1967, in Gottdiener, 1995); it is realised here by representing the tourist place as a commodified, packaged image by means of various semiotic methods operating through advertisements. By examining these methods of representation and their ideological content (the signified connoted values, belief and norms), the meanings, identities, and myths of the 'rural' become evident, and their inherent paradoxes, contradictions and potential problems for long-term commercial sustainability may be discerned.

Analysis

As with all attempts to interpret the intangible qualities of material culture, analyzing the meanings of advertisments is not an exact science. The range of rational and persuasive interpretations is broad, making no one version definitive. What follows is an interpretation grounded in semiotic analysis, but in no way does this examination exhaust the numerous meanings to be found. Nevertheless, it does identify the sense of place that the promotional literature attempts to convey.

The analysis proceeds in four interrelated and increasingly abstract sections. First, a content analysis of the 210 pieces of advertising material is presented to provide an overview of the signifiers (substance of the expressions) used in the sign system under examination. This quantitative assessment establishes the format, sponsor (message sender), scale and function of the place-commodity promoted in the advertisement. Secondly, all 85 slogans and, thirdly, all 74 logos found in the promotional material are assessed for their signifiers (form of content). Slogans and logos are two common promotional techniques used to establish images and identities in the minds of consumers, hence their importance in this study (Barke and Harrop, 1994). The former attempt to denote 'the essence of a product' through the linguistic code of written words (Middleton, 1988, p. 157), while the latter attempt to convey key themes and identifying symbols through a visual code of icons (Gold, 1994; Noth, 1995). Both of these sign systems, like all sign systems, possess secondary meanings beyond the literal meanings they denote; they connote countless secondary meanings (Bloomfield, 1933, in Noth, 1995). Myths consist of these connotative signs or meanings, and it is myths, these second order signs systems built on connotations (Barthes, 1982), that are especially important in understanding the commodification, marketing and consumption of the rural identity. The fourth and final focus of analysis thus examines the place-myths constructed via the promotional imagery.

Content analysis

As summarized in Table 9.1, the vast bulk of the promotional material was expressed in the form of one- or two-page, multi-coloured pamphlets, which included both written and visual texts. Slightly less than half of the promotional material included slogans[3]: short, catchy phrases highlighted by font size, stylized print or position. Maps were present in four out of five advertisements, making them the most frequently used illustration, followed by photographs, black and white sketches, and logos[4], all of which were on more than half of all advertisements: quick product identification and easy access for consumers appear to be of primary importance to sponsors (message senders). Although government, community and professional agencies participate, the majority of the promotional sponsors are small, independent, private businesses; virtually all sponsors are commercially-driven. This point is further supported by the inclusion of explicitly stated admission costs on the majority of advertised attractions; the remaining attractions, although 'free' in the sense that no charge is levied to enter or gaze, still encourage visitation, where tourists will no doubt consume some commodity or other, if only food, drink or gasoline. Over two-thirds of the literature promote specific sites, rather than larger scale areas, such as a town, county or province; most were accommodation (e.g., bed and breakfasts, motels and campgrounds), followed by shops specialising in arts and crafts, antiques and 'boutiqued' items.

   The place-image that emerges below is thus created by almost 200 primarily small, independent businesses promoting their specific commodities, most of which take the form of an overnight experience or access to allegedly unique sales items. The place-image they create for the Lake Huron shoreline is, however, surprisingly consistent. As the analysis of advertising slogans indicates, there are a relatively few themes or motifs that emerge amidst the rhetoric.

Table 9.1 Content analysis of promotional literature

Medium			*%*
Pamphlet			44
Guide book			18
Glossy brochure			18
Flyer (1 page)			17
News sheet			3
Format			*%*
Number of pages:	1 to 2		70
	3 to 4		8
	5 or >		22
> 50% Text, < 50% Illustration			65
< 50% Text, > 50% Illustration			30
Text only			5
Two tones			47
Three tones			18
Four or more tones			35
Slogans			46
Illustrations			*%*
Map			80
Photographs			69
	Black & White	39	
	Colour	30	
	None	31	
Sketches			56
	Black & White	92	
	Colour	8	
Logo			52
Sponsor			*%*
Private Enterprise			54
Professional/Community Association			14
Provincial Government Agency			11
Regional/County Agency			11
Local Town/Village			10
Promotional Scale			*%*
Specific Site			69
Province/Region/County			20
Local Town/Village			11
Admission Cost			*%*
Cost			56
Free			44
Dominant Area, Activity or Service Promoted			*%*
Province/Region/County			10
Local Town/Village			9

Table 9.1 *cont.*

Specific Site		81
	Accommodations	46	
	Camping	13	
	Arts, Crafts, Antiques, Boutiques	12	
	Museums	9	
	Events, Festivals, Fairs	3	
	Theatre	3	
	Hiking	3	
	Dining & food	2	
	Fishing	2	
	Themed/amusement parks	1	
	Produce	1	
	Miscellaneous Other	7	

($N = 120$)

Slogan analysis

Slogans are loaded with secondary or connotative meanings; they signify more than a superficial glimpse might suggest, and they are intended to operate as such. These short, memorable, uncomplicated phrases are used to capture attention and encourage consumption by evoking strong, positive impressions associated with the commodity (Burgess, 1982; Middleton, 1988). It is these secondary connoted meanings, beyond the literal denoted meanings of the slogans or 'rhetoric,' that reveal both the ideologies and the recurring themes which constitute the mythic identities of rurality. As Table 9.2 illustrates, there are at least four dominant themes or 'codes' apparent in the slogans when they are grouped according to their denotations. Collectively, these evoke at least 25 different myths.

'The environment'   Almost half of the slogans (45 per cent) employ an environmental theme, which can be subdivided into three specialised codes: place experience, nature, and landscape. The rural offers experiences of 'discovery', 'fun', 'pleasure', and 'magic', a place where there is 'so much to explore!' It is a natural setting brimming with 'wholesome' delights, e.g., 'sun, sand, surf and snow', where humans and nature, e.g., 'earth, water, air, fire', are in harmonious 'co-operation.' It is a landscape full of 'beauty,' 'wilderness' and 'treasures,' truly a 'wonderland' worthy of 'a peek'. These slogans not only portray the rural environment as an amusement, a garden, a scenery, they connote numerous myths. The rural is signified as 'unique', 'unexplored', 'magical' and 'memorable'. It is a 'playground', where 'innocence', 'harmony', 'spirituality' and 'life' may be experienced amidst the 'idyllic' and 'great outdoors'.

'Ideal community'   One in four slogans (26 per cent) use the theme or code of the 'ideal community'. Tourists are invited to 'come to the country', to 'visit, relax and enjoy' a 'friendly community' where you 'arrive as a guest and leave as a friend'. The countryside is 'a family place to be', where there is 'clean' and 'quiet' 'fun for everyone', where farmers trust you to 'pick your own' fruits and vegetables, and local

Table 9.2 Promotional slogans: themes and myths of rural places

Place (commodity)	Slogan (denotation/rhetoric)	Myths and themes (connotation/ideology)
		Theme 1: Environment (45%)
		A) 'Place Experience' (23%)
Blyth	'Discover the magic of Blyth'	
Grand Bend	'Grand Bend a great state of mind'	
Huron County	'North Huron: Discover it today!'	
Ontario	'More to explore!'	Magical
Port Elgin	'Experience Port Elgin'	
St. Jacobs	'So much to explore!'	
Amusement Park	'Plan your day on Safari'	
Art Galleries	'Discover the original art of Ontario's West Coast'	Memorable
Campground	'Ontario's best kept secret'	
Campground	'For your leisure pleasure'	Playground
Fishout Pond	'Fishing at its best!'	
Inn	'The place to stay in Grand Bend'	
Inn	'A place to remember'	
Inn	'Lake Huron's finest'	
Inn	'Like always. Like never before'	Unexplored
Nuclear Plant	'Explore the world of nuclear energy'	
Retirement Community	'A special place for you'	
Riding Stable	'A fun recreational facility'	Unique
Theatre	'Discover the magic of summer theatre'	
Theatre	'Summer at the Roxy'	
		B) 'Nature' (12%)
Arkona	'The little apple'	
Exeter	'Home of the White Squirrel'	Harmony
Grand Bend	'Sun, sand, surf and snow'	
Sarnia Area	'Blue Water excitement'	
Bed & Breakfast	'Take time to smell the roses'	Innocence
Drag Race	'Thunder by the beach'	
Festival	'Earth, water, air, fire'	

Table 9.2 cont.

Place (commodity)	Slogan (denotation/rhetoric)	Myths and Themes (connotation/ideology)
Fishing Lodge	'Salmon Heaven is usually in a helluva' place'	Life
Housing Development	'Built in co-operation with nature …'.	Spirituality
Restaurant	'Wholesome, fresh food'	
		C) 'Landscape' (9%)
Goderich	'The prettiest town in Canada'	Idyllic
Southampton	'The vacation wonderland'	Spectacle
Campground	'Great family camping in a beautiful natural setting'	
Campground	'Camp in the beauty of natural surroundings'	Great
Huron Tourism Assoc.	'Ontario's West Coast'	Outdoors
Lake Huron Guide	'Take a peek... Find the treasures'	
Provincial Park	'Discover the fun, discover the wilderness, discover...Point Farms!'	
		Theme 2: Ideal Community (26%)
Theatre	'Theatre in the Country'	
Ontario	'Ontario. Relax. Take a breather'	Family
Amusement Park	'Family fun all day'	
Amusement Farm	'We are waiting for ewe!'	
Antiquer's Guide	'We're glad you're here!'	
Bed & Breakfast	'Arrive as a guest and leave as a friend'	Friendship
Bed & Breakfast	'Share a special, warm, relaxing atmosphere'	
Bed & Breakfast	'Visit, relax and enjoy'	
Boat Tours	'Come on board'	
Boutique	'A gift shop with a personal touch'	
Campground	'A family place to be'	
Campground	'A new family campground'	
Campground	'Clean quiet family camping'	Inclusivity
Campground	'Experience family camping pleasure'	
Campground	'Family camping on the lake'	
Crafts	'A small and friendly place to visit'	
Golf Club	'The friendly 18'	
Lodge	'Come to the country'	

Source	Slogan	Theme/Dimension
Museum	'You'll never know who you'll meet'	Courtesy
Ontario Farmers' Market Guide	'Pick your own'	
Resort	'Family fun for Every one'	
Retirement	'The friendly community for independent	
Community	and active adults'	
Zoo	'Family fun at its best'	Safety
		Theme 3: Advantage (15%)
Forest	'North Lampton's economic centre'	
Owen Sound	'Within Reach...Beyond Belief'	Centrality
Wasaga Beach	'The world's longest freshwater beach'	
Bed & Breakfast	'A perfect summer or winter getaway in the country'	
Bruce Peninsula	'Find yourself in Bruce County'	
Bruce Trail	'The path of discovery'	Entrance
Campground	'Home of country music'	
Campground	'Where the fun begins'	
Children's Camp	'The biggest and best goalie school in North America'	
Children's Camp	'Where it starts'	Exit
Crafts	'The store you won't want to miss!'	
Lodge	'A great country vacation getaway'	
Resorts Ontario Guide	'Great escapes'	Spatial Exotica
		Theme 4: Heritage (14%)
Hay Township	'150 Years of Diversified Progress'	
Southampton	'Historic Southampton - oldest port on the Bruce Coast'	Historical Participation
Antiques	'Come in for a visit & you will find the best of yesterday & today'	
Bed & Breakfast	'Turn of the century bed and breakfast'	Important Identity
Inn	'...innkeeping since 1832'	
Museum	'Share our past'	
Museum	'Start at the heart'	Simplicity
Museum	'Step back in time to childhood days'	
Museum	'The 20th century begins in Waterloo County'	Stability
	'Turn back the clock to the beginning of the 20th century'	
Tannery Outlet	'A tradition of quality since 1894'	
Walking Tour Guide	'Discovering historic Bayfield'	Education

(N = 85)

merchants provide 'a personal touch'. Such rhetoric connotes myths of 'friendship', 'inclusivity', 'courtesy', 'family', and by extension, 'safety'. The rural place-commodity is thus ascribed with family values, e.g., trust, sharing, togetherness, and the status of an ideal community, where safety, courtesy, friendship and civility still prevail.

'Locational advantage'   Going to the countryside has its locational advantages, according to one in seven slogans (15 per cent). Along the shoreline of Lake Huron, one can be in 'the economic centre', at the 'home of country music' or on the very site 'where the fun begins'. A trip to the countryside is itself 'a path of discovery' leading to a 'great escape' where you can 'find yourself'. The 'perfect summer or winter getaway in the country' is not without its share of spatial spectacle; once there tourists may indulge in 'the biggest and best' and visually feast on 'the world's longest freshwater beach'. The rural-place is heralded as both a mythical 'exit' from one's everyday world (and perhaps one's own everyday identity) and an 'entrance' to another place, a 'central' place, where the spatially unusual ('spatial exotica') is to be found, gazed upon and consumed.

'Heritage'   Finally, historical identities are emphasised by one in six mottos (14 per cent). By 'turning back the clock' to the 'turn of the century', tourists may 'step back in time to childhood days'. In the past, they will 'share' in 'tradition' and 'discover' the 'oldest', the 'heart,' and 'the best of yesterday and today'. This rhetoric suggests the commodified countryside signifies several historical myths: the rural past holds 'important identities' about ourselves, hence their designation as historical sites; visitors can actively 'participate' in the past by occupying historical sites; and the rural place is an 'educational' experience, where tourists may learn about and thus continue to value the countryside. The past also connotes 'simplicity' and 'stability'. In an age of intense, rapid and uncertain change, the countryside purports to offer a return to a less hectic, constant, and secure place (see Chapters Seven and Eight).

These motifs and myths associated with the slogans would appear to be among the chief characteristics of the rural identity in this study area. Although these are not the only sign vehicles used to promote rurality, many of the same themes and some of the same myths are emphasised through logos.

Logo analysis

Logos, like slogans, signify more than a cursory glance might reveal, but, compared to the latter, the former are especially rich in secondary or connotative meanings. This complexity is a function of the logo's sign-type; they are iconic symbols that connote a surplus of meanings, and consequently an abundance of myths. Logos are graphic representations intended to impart images in the minds of consumers which will encourage consumption. By creating a recognizable trademark. the commodity and/or its producers or sponsors are given an identity or brand recognition which conveys positive, often multiple and abstract, messages (Barke and Harrop, 1994).

When the logo or sign resembles that which it stands for or represents, it is termed an iconic sign or 'icon'; in other words, the signifer (expression) and the signified (content) resemble one another, such as in the case of a photograph or bust of a person (Peirce, 1955). Icons are compounded with multiple secondary connotations or 'surplus meanings' because, to re-phrase a cliche, a pictoral representation is worth a thousand words; visual images are loaded signs. Where these secondary meanings are numerous and take precedence over the denotative meaning of the sign, they become 'symbols': signs that signify learned, abstract connotations or myths (Noth, 1995). It is these secondary connoted meanings, beyond the literal 'denotated' meanings of the symbolic icons, that reveal the ideologies and mythic identities of rurality.

As Table 9.3 illustrates, there are at least four dominant themes or codes apparent in the icons that comprise and denote the logos, which collectively symbolize numerous connoted myths. These themes emerged as each logo's dominant iconic features were observed and then grouped with other logos sharing similar denotative icons. Most logos contained combinations of various iconic signs, such as wild animals, trees, water, the sun and vegetation, each of which may symbolise any number of things (e.g., 'tree' as symbol for the myths of Christmas, Eden, life, knowledge, nature, paradise, rebirth, redemption). Because of this, not all logos could be analysed here in their entirety. For the sake of brevity, one logo from each code was selected for further analysis on the basis that it was among the best examples of its particular theme. This analysis thus shows the emergent themes or codes of the icons, the major icon types used within each code, and eighteen different myths connoted by four symbols.

Natural environment: 'the squirrel' By far the most recurring logo theme was the 'natural environment'. Two-thirds of all logos (64 per cent) included one or more of nine different icon types: 'forest animals' (bears, birds, deers, fish and squirrels) were the most commonly used icon, followed in descending order of frequency by 'trees', 'water', 'sun', 'flowers and vegetation', 'hills', 'field', 'moon or stars', and finally 'insects', namely butterflies. Collectively, these symbols sustain and reinforce the themes of 'nature' and the 'environment' and the connoted myths associated with them.

For example, the country town of Exeter, Ontario (the place commodity) employs the symbol of a squirrel as its logo. As illustrated in Table 9.3, it is a forest animal portrayed as more 'mild' than 'wild'. The squirrel's chubby, big-eyed face, its plump belly, and fluffy, immense tail connotes 'innocence'. Its closed eyes, outstretched arms, apparent yawn, and seated position signify both 'relaxation' and 'friendliness'. These physical features and human-like qualities make this squirrel a cartoon figure, and cartoons evoke myths of 'childhood'. Nature is presented as docile and 'domesticated'.

Heritage: 'grandma's kitchen' The second most widely used logo theme was 'heritage', evident in one in five logos. 'Historic buildings', 'period clothing', and 'antique artifacts' and 'antique machines' were the icons employed in this motif. Together these produce and reinforce yet another familiar theme prominent in the slogans: the past.

This motif is particularly well-illustrated by the logo adopted by a general store

Table 9.3 Promotional logos—themes, icons and symbolised myths

Theme/code	Icon (denotation)	Logo example (symbol)	Myths (connotation/ideology)
1. Natural Environment (64%)	Forest animal Trees Water Sun Flowers and vegetation Hill Field Moon/stars Insect		Childhood Friendly Innocence Relaxation Nature domesticated
2. Heritage (20%)	Historic buildings Period clothing Antique artifacts Antique machines		Family Goodness Home Nourishment Safety
3. Agriculture (16%)	Crops Farm animals Farm machinery Farm buildings		Family Farm Life Happiness Home Human/nature balance
4. Recreation (12%)	Sports equipment Boat Automobile Campfire		Romance Socialising Summer Time-immortal Wilderness

(the place commodity) that specialises in kitchen wares and specialty foods: a female tending to her stove. The woman's hair is gathered in a bun, her little wire 'granny' glasses, and the frilly, floor-length apron covering her portly body signify 'grandmother'. The warmth of her facial expression is probably equalled only by the warmth of the antique stove, atop which sits a pot of what must most certainly be a home-made dish. This is a powerful symbol evoking myths of 'family', 'home' and, by implication, 'safety'. The food, like grandma herself, epitomises 'nourishment' and 'goodness'.

Agriculture: 'farmstead'   Perhaps most surprising is the low incidence of use of the theme of 'agricultural' exhibits, a point to be addressed in more detail below. One in six logos drew from this code (16 per cent). Four icons dominated these logos: 'crops', usually wheat; 'farm animals', such as cows, sheep, wild boars or horses; 'farm machinery', such as tractors or combines; and 'farm buildings', usually barns and silos. These are among the most potent symbols of the traditional, agrarian-based countryside, which explains why, perhaps, one of these symbols was adopted by the Ontario Farm and Country Accomodations Association (place commodity sponsor), whose logo employs three farm buildings, a barn, a silo and a house, with a tree nestled in between and a radiant sun overhead. These icons are by themselves loaded with symbolism, as the example of 'tree' used above makes clear. Together, they connote numerous myths, but five will suffice. This logo symbolizes myths of a simple 'home' down on the 'family' farm, where the sun or 'happiness' always shines. People here live close to the land in harmonious 'balance' with nature; humans in the house, plants in the field and silo, and animals in the barn. This logo condenses and romaticizes 'farm life' itself.

Recreation: 'campfire bear'   Icons representing 'sports equipment' (e.g., golf clubs), 'boats', 'automobiles' and 'campfires' constituted the logos of this code. Only nine logos (about one in ten advertisements) drew directly from this theme, thereby reinforcing myths observed in many of the above slogans: rurality as 'playground', as the 'great outdoors', as a 'fun' place. Myths found in other logos also surface in this final theme. Take for example the logo used by a family campground (place commodity). Another forest animal, this time a bright-eyed, smiling 'Teddy' bear, is depicted standing upright roasting a hot dog on the end of a stick over a campfire. Myths of 'innocence', 'childhood', 'nourishment' and 'nature domesticated' are symbolised once again, albeit through different icons. Still, there are other myths connoted here by the campfire: 'romance', 'socialising', 'summertime', 'time-immortal' and 'wilderness'. This is a visually simple logo, which effectively captures the simple joys, perhaps the primal pleasures, of camping in the woods.

Place-myths

The codes and myths identified in the slogans and logos convey images that combine to create the place-myths of the rural countryside. What emerges is a place where the 'natural environment' is a central and highly valued characteristic. References to sensational outdoor experiences, spectacular landscapes and idyllic settings are

conveyed many times over. The past is also held in high esteem, with slogans and logos repeatedly stressing 'heritage' sites, historical experiences and crafted goods. The countryside is a place of 'community,' where innocence, safety, friendship and family values still prevail. These three are by far among the most dominant place-myths, but at least two less prominent others are notable. The myth of 'spatial exotica', of a place of transformation where the ordinary ends and adventure, fun and recreation begins, emerges as a prevalent theme, suggesting that the unusual, the extraordinary, the unique are desirable. Lastly, the myth of countryside as a 'pastoral retreat', a place to escape one's own urban world of work, responsibility and routine, and adopt a simpler, more natural, 'rustic' way of life, if only temporarily.

Place-myths such as these are the commodities marketed by the place sponsors and consumed by tourists. The material products and actual sites and experiences available along Lake Huron are not what are being sold or purchased *per se*. In an image-driven culture, they are the signs of rurality – the connoted myths of a place – that are consumed (Baudrillard, 1981; Lash and Urry, 1994; Gottdiener, 1995). 'Rurality' is a brand name for a particular place-commodity found in the countryside.

Conclusions

'Rural culture' is the key commodity exchanged in the tourist landscape of Southwestern Ontario's countryside, whose identity as a place of agriculture and the production of foodstuffs is shifting, or at the very least broadening, to one of rural culture and the consumption of myths. According to the promotional literature, Lake Huron's countryside has taken on mythical qualities of a special place with unique characteristics that distinguish it from the city. The 'rural' is imagined as a spatial and temporal retreat from the urban environs, a place close to nature, rich in community ties, where life is lived at a slower pace in settlements situated amidst pastoral, idyllic settings. Here, one can purchase memorable experiences untouched by commercialism. Therein lies the ideological paradox that poses the greatest threat to the long-term marketability and commercial viability of 'rurality': how to keep the place-myths alive!

Imagination and desire fuel place-myths, but familiarity and dashed expectations will dissolve them. Repetitious themes, tired icons, re-worked symbols and similar place-products, regardless of the rhetoric in which they are wrapped, dampen consumer appetites. The low number and consistency of themes and place-myths found relative to the over 200 promoters examined suggest this might be a potential problem along the shores of Lake Huron. The fact that similar promotional themes have been identified in at least two studies of rural Britain (Cloke, 1993; Urry, 1995), lends further grounds for concern. In short, how many nature/heritage/community themed tourist places does it take before market-saturation occurs in the country-side? And, finally, how does the rural place maintain its rustic identity if overrun with urban tourists who inadvertently help to destroy the very rural retreat they seek to consume in relative peace and quiet? These are among the very real challenges facing 'rural' areas.

Endnotes

1. Because printed material is the most utilised advertising format in the travel and tourism industry, it was an obvious choice for analysis (Middleton 1988, p. 174). All free promotional sales literature – guide books, pamphlets, glossy brochures, flyers and newssheets – displayed at the four tourist information booths encountered on route – Grand Bend, Goderich, Kincardine and Southampton – was collected. A total of 248 different pieces were gathered; 38 were discarded because they were business cards or they pertained to services and attractions in nearby cities or to American destinations. Although by no means exhaustive of rural tourism advertisements throughout Southwestern Ontario, the material sampled is argued to be illustrative of rural tourism in the region. Tourist sites as far north as Tobermory on Georgian Bay, as far south as Blenheim on Lake Brie, as far east as Wasaga Beach, and numerous tourist attractions and destinations therein, were represented in the promotional literature.
2. The 220 kilometre traverse, conducted during June 25–27, 1996, extended from Sarnia to Southampton on Highways #7 and #21. This route was selected for three reasons: it is part of two much larger provincially designated tourist routes – 'The Bluewater Route' and 'The Lake Huron Circle Tour' (Ontario Ministry of Economic Development, Trade and Tourism 1996) and would, presumably, provide a study area rich in tourist activity; it transacts a dominant agricultural region within Ontario and would likely exhibit a 'country landscape', however so manifested; and finally, the distance travelled was both feasible given the temporal and financial constraints of the researcher and of sufficient size to collect a workable data set.
3. As indicated in Table 9.1, 46 per cent of the promotional literature included a slogan. The motto 'Ontario's East Coast' was found on 11 different pieces, but repetitious slogans were only counted once. Nonetheless, 86 different slogans were found on 40 per cent of all the advertised material collected.
4. 109 of the 210 pieces of data exhibited a logo, as indicated by the 52 per cent figure in Table 9.1. Repetitious logos were counted only once, lowering the number of different logos analysed to 74.

References

Ashworth, G. and Voogd, H., 1990, Can places be sold for tourism? In *Marketing tourism places*, G. Ashworth and B. Goodall, eds., pp. 1–16, Routledge, New York

Ashworth, G.J. and Voogd, H., 1994, Marketing and place promotion. In *Place promotion: the use of publicity and marketing to sell towns and regions*, J.R. Gold and S.V. Ward, eds., pp. 39–52, John Wiley and Sons, Chichester

Barke, M. and Harrop, K., 1994, Selling the industrial town: identity, image and illusion. In *Place promotion: the use of publicity and marketing to sell towns and regions*, J.R. Gold and S.V. Ward, eds., pp. 93–114, John Wiley and Sons, Chichester

Barthes, R., 1982, Myth today. In *A Barthes reader*, S. Sontag, ed., pp. 93–149, Hill and Wang, New York

Baudrillard, J. 1981, *For a critique of the political economy of the sign*, Telos, St Louis

Baudrillard, J., 1983, *Simulations*, P. Foss, P. Patton and P. Beitchman (Trans.), Semiotext(e), New York

Billinge, M., 1986, Place. In *The dictionary of human geography*, 2nd ed. R.J. Johnston, D. Gregory and D.M. Smith, eds., p. 346. Basil Blackwell, Oxford

Burgess, J., 1982, Selling places: environmental images for the executive, *Regional Studies*, **16** (1): 1–17

Burgess, J. and Wood, P., 1988, Decoding docklands. In *Qualitative methods in human geography*, J. Eyles and D. Smith, eds., pp. 94–117, Polity, Oxford

Cloke, P. 1993, The countryside as commodity: new rural spaces for leisure, In *Leisure and the environment*, S. Glyptis, ed., pp. 53–67, Belhaven, New York

Cloke, P. and Thrift, N., 1994, Refiguring the 'rural'. In *Writing the rural: five cultural geographies*. Edited by Paul Cloke, ed., pp. 1–5, Paul Chapman, London

Debord, G., 1983, *Society of the spectacle*, Black and Red, Detroit

DeKerckhove, D., 1995, *The skin of culture*, Somerville House, Toronto

Eco, U., 1976, *A theory of semiotics*, Indiana University, Bloomington

Fiske, J., 1989, *Reading the popular*, Unwin Hyman, Boston

Francaviglia, R.V., 1996, *Main street revisited: time, space and image building in small-town America*, Iowa University, Iowa City

Goeldner, C.R., 1992, Trends in North American tourism, *American Behavioral Scientist*, **36** (2): 144–54

Gold, J.R., 1994, Locating the message: place promotion as image communication. In *Place promotion: the use of publicity and marketing to sell towns and regions*, J.R. Gold and S.V. Ward, eds., pp. 19–37, John Wiley, Chichester

Gottdiener, M., 1982, Disneyland: a utopian urban space, *Urban Life*, **11** (2): 139–62

Gottdiener, M., 1995, *Postmodern semiotics: material culture and the forms of postmodern life*, Basil Blackwell, Cambridge

Gregory, D., 1986, Ideology. In *Dictionary of human geography*, 2nd ed., R.J. Johnston, D. Gregory and D.M. Smith, eds., pp. 214–15, Basil Blackwell, Oxford

Halfacre, K.H., 1993, Locality and social representation: space, discourse and alternative definitions of the rural, *Journal of Rural Studies*, **9** (1): 23–37

Hopkins, J., 1990, West Edmonton Mall: landscape of myths and elsewhereness, *The Canadian Geographer*, **34** (1): 2–17

Kellner, D., 1995, *Media culture*, Routledge, New York

King, R.J., 1988, Urban design in capitalist society, Environment and Planning D: *Society and Space*, **6**: 445–74

Lash, S. and Urry, J., 1994, *Economies of signs and space*, Sage, Thousand Oaks

Ley, D.F. and Bourne, L.S., 1993, Introduction: the social context and diversity of urban Canada. In *The changing social geography of Canadian cities*, L. Bourne and D. Ley, eds., p. 5, McGill-Queen's University, Montreal & Kingston

Middleton, V.T.C., 1988, *Marketing in travel and tourism*, Heinemann, London

Noth, W., 1995, *Handbook of semiotics*, Indiana University, Indianapolis

Ontario Ministry of Economic Development, Trade and Tourism, 1996, *Trip planner: South Central Ontario*, Ministry of Culture, Tourism and Recreation, Toronto

Peirce, C.S., 1955, *Philosophical writings of Peirce*, Dover Publications, New York

Sebeok, T.A. (ed.), 1986, *Encyclopedic dictionary of semiotics*, Mouton de Gruyter, New York

Shields, R., 1991, *Places on the margin: alternative geographies of modernity*, Routledge, New York

Sorkin, M., ed., 1992, *Variations on a theme park*, Noonday, New York

Urry, J., 1990, *The tourist gaze*, Sage, London

Urry, J., 1995, *Consuming places*, Routledge, New York

Ward, S.V., 1994, Time and place: key themes in place promotion in the USA, Canada and Britain since 1870. In *Place promotion: the use of publicity and marketing to sell towns and regions*, J.R. Gold and S.V. Ward, eds., pp. 53–74, John Wiley, Chichester

Ward, S.V. and Gold, J.R., 1994, Introduction. In *Place promotion: the use of publicity and marketing to sell towns and regions*, J.R. Gold and S.V. Ward, eds., pp. 1–17, John Wiley, Chichester

10 Rural festivals and community reimaging

ROBERT L. JANISKEE AND PATRICIA L. DREWS

Introduction

Festivals have come to play an important role in the economy and culture of rural America. For most of the nation's history, the community-wide celebrations in a typical small town consisted of little more than the ubiquitous Independence Day celebration, an all-school reunion or homecoming, and perhaps a Founders Day or agricultural fair. By the mid-1960s, however, a new pattern began to emerge (Janiskee, 1994). More and more rural communities began to produce new annual festivals or street fairs designed for family entertainment and oriented to themes such as crop harvests, foods, historical events, folkways, and spring blossoms (Janiskee, 1980, 1991, 1996a). The concept proved immensely popular, and by 1996 at least 10,000 festivals were being produced on a recurring basis in small towns throughout America (Amusement Business, 1996; S.E.N. Inc., 1996).

Festivals can be small or large, simple or complex, and oriented to any theme. Each, however, is a formal period or programme of entertaining activities having a festive character and publicly celebrating some concept, fact, or happening (Getz, 1991; Hall, 1992). The typical small town festival is a family-style event that includes a parade, music, dancing, food, arts and crafts, games, contests, and related activities (Janiskee, 1996a). It is sponsored by a service club or business association, relies heavily on volunteers, uses public venues, and attracts 5,000 to 50,000 people over a one to three-day run on a weekend or holiday. It is considered a success if it provides wholesome fun and returns enough money to the producer to offset expenses, but it is also meant to raise funds for service organisations, put money in the pockets of local vendors, provide a showcase for local talent, create a positive image of the host community, instil community pride, promote clean-ups and fix-ups, and make business sponsors happy (Mayfield and Crompton, 1995; Uysal et al., 1993).

Festival producers can use a variety of tactics to recover their expenses, including soliciting business sponsorships (Ukman, 1993), renting booth spaces, collecting admission fees at entertainment venues, selling food and beverages, and requiring commercial vendors to pay sales commissions (Schmader and Jackson, 1990). Rapidly escalating production costs have forced most festivals to rely more heavily on money, goods, and services supplied by commercial sponsors. Most events receive at least some support from local businesses, and many larger festivals now also receive substantial backing from national corporations who want their names and logos associated with widely publicised events that provide wholesome entertainment.

Comparatively few festivals are intended to make money for their producers, but many play an important role in generating a visitor industry for their host communities. Festivals attract out-of-towners for many reasons (Mohr *et al.*, 1993; Saleh and Ryan, 1993). While forecasting festival attendance and expenditures is an imprecise science (Mules and McDonald, 1994), small towns located in the daytripper zones of urban centres are generally assured of attracting thousands of visitors to their community celebrations. Sharing in the festival spoils are dozens of local merchants, restaurateurs, hoteliers, crafters, entertainers, and other providers of goods or services. The inherent appeal of festivals is a tremendous asset for the many nondescript rural places that would otherwise attract few visitors. It is also a major boon for locales with physical or cultural assets that are attractive to travellers and tourists on a seasonal or year round basis. In such cases, festival production can lure additional media attention, boost visitation, heighten public awareness of local attractions, and strengthen the image of the community as a fun place to visit.

Various processes set in motion by festival production make the host communities more appealing to residents and visitors alike. As festival time approaches, residents invest more time and effort in clean-ups, fix-ups, and other things that make the community more presentable. As the years pass, festival production provides motivation and money for community improvement projects such as redeveloping downtowns, preserving and restoring historic buildings, renovating old theatres, constructing parks and community centres, planting trees, paving streets, and installing holiday decorations (Janiskee, 1996b).

Townscapes or landscapes tend to evolve in ways that reflect the nature of the festivals that take place there. In many small towns, festival logos or slogans are prominently displayed throughout the year on welcome signs, billboards, water tanks, banners, and in other prominent places. Some towns have huge statues of their festival mascots or other festival-related landmarks such as the million-gallon 'Peachoid' water tower in Gaffney, home of the South Carolina Peach Festival. Festival themes influence all sorts of things that people do to demonstrate civic pride and community spirit. Thus, for example, people who live in a town that hosts an annual heritage-themed festival and a cherry blossom festival are inclined to preserve their old buildings and plant more cherry trees on their property. In other cases, a festival's programmed activities may have an enduring effect. A town that hosts a festival with a mural-in-a-day project grows richer in murals every year.

Knowing that festivals are effective tools for promoting desirable growth and change, community leaders routinely incorporate festival production into long term plans for visitor industry development. Most festival producers instinctively know or quickly learn that their events should be based on the community's existing cultural and physical resources so as to provide a strong foundation for marketing (Chacko and Schaffer, 1993). For example, a rural community that attracts visitors primarily because it has vineyards and wineries might reasonably host a Winefest with winery tours, tastings, a grape stomping contest, and related activities (see Chapter Twelve by Hall and Macionis).

Reinforcing existing appeals

Comparatively few rural festivals are part of any conscious effort to reposition tourist destinations (tourism products) for targeted markets. Rather, they simply highlight local attractions and reinforce the prevailing image of rural communities as attractive environments in which to live, work, and play (see Chapter Nine by Hopkins). Thus, for example, one rural community might use festival production to reinforce the public perception that it is a quaint fishing village, while others might produce events that reinforce the image of an historic town, a centre of apple production, an artists' colony, a gateway to a national park, or a great place to hunt waterfowl. Whatever they may do, however, they are capitalizing on the special affection that Americans have for small towns and pastoral landscapes.

Marx (1964) argued that the generic appeal of the rural realm is rooted not only in its intrinsic qualities, but also in our negative reactions to city life. Most Americans live and work in urban places, not necessarily because they want to live in the city, but rather because that is where the jobs are. Cities are associated with work, drudgery, and 'city troubles', such as pollution, crime, noise, a frenetic pace of life, and pervasive artificiality. Seen in this context, rural recreation is a form of escape. Harried urbanites temporarily retreat from the city and explore the rural realm to get in touch with a lifestyle that is simpler, quieter, slower, friendlier, and closer to nature and the true wellsprings of human happiness.

To be attractive to urbanites, a town, village, or hamlet need only look and behave like a functional part of the metaphorical 'middle landscape' that lies between the dangerous wilderness and the disliked city (Marx, 1964; Janiskee, 1976). The middle landscape, which is where most Americans lived a few generations ago, is a quiet realm of fields, pastures, streams, woodlots, and small towns; it is wilderness gently tamed. Its basic social unit, the family farm or ranch, is regarded as the perfect environment in which to rear capable citizens with the right kind of values. Its largest social unit, the town, has a tidy scale, a sensible pace, an aura of circumambient friendliness, and other qualities that identify it as the perfect American society in microcosm. Rural festivals of all kinds tend to stimulate thoughts and feelings associated with this pastoral ideal, and festival producers know that this mental behaviour is at least as important as physical experiences.

A rural festival's programmed attractions tend to celebrate the host community's rural lifestyle in a very self-conscious manner. A street parade's cavalcade of marching bands, colourful floats, beauty queens, and elected officials is not just a noisy spectacle; it is a choreographed depiction of the rural community's value system, cultural icons, and social stratification. The stage entertainment can be quite eclectic, but it leans heavily to traditional rural entertainment such as country music and square dancing. Farmers' markets, barnyard animals, hayrides, picnics, bake sales, ice cream socials, and community church services are routine fare. Country style foods like pit cooked beef, whole hog barbecue, corn on the cob, and apple butter are cooked on the premises. Adding to the rustic flavour is a kaleidoscope of exhibits, games, and competitions such as horse shows, roping events, tractor pulls, volunteer firemen's musters, horseshoe pitching, cow milking, hog calling, log sawing, rifle shooting, turtle racing, and frog jumping.

While the underlying message of rural festivals may be fairly simple, the temporal, geographic, and thematic patterns of festival production are quite complex. Most festivals are held in the warmer months, but climate, plant phenology, ethnic composition, and other factors combine to create substantial regional differences in festival timing (Janiskee, 1996c). In the southern States, for example, oppressive heat inhibits the establishment of summer festivals and shifts most outdoor events to the spring and fall. Title themes and programmed activities or attractions also vary from place to place and region to region in accordance with the distribution of economic activities, cultural traits, historically important events, climate, topographic features, and other variables. Broad scale patterns most clearly reflect the distribution of dominant economic activities, especially extractive industries such as farming, grazing, logging, mining, and fishing. Thus, for example, forested regions have more logging festivals, fishing villages tend to have seafood festivals, farming areas celebrate crop harvests, animal products and foods, and rodeos flourish in the grazing lands of the West. Hundreds of festivals represent community celebrations of a local distinction or attraction, such as an ethnic concentration, a folk tradition, the birthplace of a celebrity, the site of a Civil War battle, or a popular recreational beach. There are so many niches available that no two rural festivals need necessarily choose the same title theme or have the same activities schedule.

Preserving the present in Mount Airy, North Carolina

The example of Mount Airy, North Carolina shows that a small town can use festival production very effectively to reinforce an appealing image and attract large numbers of visitors. Located at the foot of the Blue Ridge Mountains in northwestern North Carolina, Mount Airy (pop. 7,200) is the site of the world's largest open-face granite quarry and home of the original Siamese twins (Chang and Eng Bunker), country and western performer Donna Fargo, and southern folk musician Tommy Jarrell. More importantly, it is where popular movie and television actor Andy Griffith was born and reared. Griffith drew upon his boyhood experiences in Mount Airy in creating the fictional town of Mayberry and populating it with Sheriff Andy Taylor, Deputy Barney Fife, Opie, Aunt Bee, Gomer Pyle, Otis, Ernest T. Bass, and the other characters in the enormously popular television series, *The Andy Griffith Show*. A total of 249 episodes were aired during the show's 1960 to 1968 run (Robinson and Fernandes, 1996), and today it is still going strong in world-wide syndication. *The Andy Griffith Show* and its highly successful spin-off, *Mayberry RFD*, have made Mount Airy-cum-Mayberry one of America's most beloved small towns.

Mount Airy's downtown still looks the way that 'Main Street America' did before it was ruined by parking lots, strip malls, and superstores (Figure 10.1). The town is not a fossil or a working model of the past, but rather a living community whose built environment has evolved at a leisurely pace and retains many features typical of bygone eras. This quality, plus traditional small town virtues such as a slow pace of life, friendly neighbours, and strong educational and religious values, made Mount Airy the perfect inspiration for Mayberry.

Mount Airy was settled in the mid-1700s, but did not begin to flourish until the railroad arrived in the late 1880s. The town's core industries then, as now, were

Figure 10.1. Mount Airy is not a moment of history frozen in time, but rather an environment in which people live, work and play. Having evolved at a leisurely pace, and without surrendering its friendly scale or charm, Mount Airy's downtown retains many features of traditional small town business areas. Reproduced with permission.

furniture manufacturing and granite quarrying. Few tourists made this community their destination before the late 1960s and the establishment of the town's Autumn Leaves Festival. Since the 1940s, many tourists had been driving to the mountains to view the fall colours along the Blue Ridge Parkway. The Parkway passed just fifteen miles north of Mount Airy, so Mount Airy Chamber of Commerce leaders discussed various means of attracting some of the tourists. They eventually settled upon a family-style fall festival that would be non-commercial in nature and reflect the community's small town character. The inaugural Autumn Leaves Festival was produced by a Chamber of Commerce committee in 1967, a time when very few street festivals were being staged in the Carolinas. The one-day event, a low budget, logistically simple affair, featured such rustic attractions as ten-cent ham biscuits and bluegrass music.

In the early years, the Autumn Leaves Festival was viewed as little more than a big party. By the early 1980s, however, attendance exceeded 30,000 and festival-related cash flows reached sizeable levels. The festival was given more attention, expanded in size, and extended in duration. Today, the event draws upwards of 200,000 people during its three-day run in early October.

Despite impressive growth, the Autumn Leaves Festival has retained its family-oriented, unmistakably small town flavour. To minimise the threat of commercialisation, prevent outsiders from dictating policy, and keep festival-related income in the community, the producers do not permit commercial vendors and have not solicited sponsorships from major corporations and local businesses. To ensure a wholesome atmosphere, alcoholic beverages are banned and rowdy or immodest behaviour is discouraged. Instead of radio stations blasting rock music from remote broadcast vans, bluegrass bands play the traditional music of Appalachia. Visitors are offered guided tours of the town. Civic and non-profit groups run the food booths, and the cuisine is strictly down-home fare like pork barbecue, hamburgers, and hot dogs. About 100 arts and crafts booths exhibit handmade items, and most of the artisans and crafters are locals.

Producing the Autumn Leaves Festival has yielded many tangible benefits for the Mount Airy community. For three decades, the event has helped to put the community on the map and bring in hundreds of thousands of visitors who otherwise would not have come. The financial benefits of the festival, which have never been systematically studied, are doubtlessly substantial, permeate the community, and yield many improvements. The influx of visitors at festival time fills all the area's motels and markedly increases sales of gasoline, food, sundries, handcrafted items, and other goods. It is highly germane that a large share of the cash flow goes to civic agencies and non-profit organisations who plough the money back into the community. For example, Mount Airy's high school used US$14,000 in festival funds to help start a soccer program.

No gain is won without costs. Merchants complain that downtown streets are closed off and booths back up against their stores. Everyone dislikes the traffic congestion and the vast amounts of litter that must be cleaned up. Nevertheless, the Mount Airy community does not have to give up very much in order to have the festival and its benefits. Monetary outlays are held to a minimum through the liberal use of volunteers, public venues, donated goods and services, and subsidies such as extra law enforcement supplied by Surry County and calendars of events distributed by the State. Since the producer's financial goal is simply to reach the break-even point, fees and charges are held to the level required to cover police overtime, clean-up, and related expenses.

In September 1990, the Surry County Arts Council began producing a new festival called Mayberry Days. The timing was right for this new event, since 1990 was the thirtieth anniversary of *The Andy Griffith Show* and there was a great deal of media interest in the television series and its cast. Publicity in *The Bullet*, the 30,000 circulation newsletter of the Andy Griffith Show Rerun Watchers Club, proved influential. Many ardent fans of the show wanted to visit 'the real Mayberry'. Although Mayberry Days started out small and simple, it quickly grew in size and complexity. In 1991, it expanded to two days, and by 1995, crowds had swelled to over 10,000. As the producers intended, the downtown is awash in tourists during the event and all motels within a 30-mile radius are filled.

Mayberry Days mixes the typical activities of a family-style street festival with a variety of attractions oriented to *Andy Griffith Show* fans. Thus, there is not only a street parade, music and dancing, a golf tournament, a talent show, a 'pig pickin' (pork barbecue), a Volkswalk, a 5km road race, bingo, and a checkers tournament, but also a Mayberry Days Fan Club meeting and dinner, Aunt Bee's Bake Sale, a Mayberry trivia contest, an Andy Griffith filmfest, Mayberry character 'look-alikes', and fan-oriented walking tours. For the latter activity there are temporary displays such as a stage front designed to look like Wally's Service Station and permanent attractions such as Snappy Lunch, Floyd's City Barber Shop, and a prop-filled old jail with a vintage squad car parked outside. Many Mayberry Days visitors return each year. The walking tours have proven so popular with fans, including bus tour groups, that they are now conducted year round.

The Surry County Arts Council takes in enough money to cover current expenses for Mayberry Days, but the near-absence of sponsorship revenues inhibits plans for expanding the event and promoting it more heavily. The Council does not want to ask local businesses to put up sponsorship money because this would reduce contributions to the Council's annual fund raising campaign. Major corporate sponsors have shown little interest because Mayberry Days is a comparatively small event. This latter fact has a positive side. Many merchants and townspeople applaud the event because it brings manageable numbers of well-mannered visitors to town and spreads them around in a way that minimises congestion, does not require street closings, and allows all of the merchants to remain open for business. The fans who march in the parade, participate in Talent Time, and compete in the golf tournament love Mayberry Days because of its small, friendly scale and non-commercial character. In Mount Airy, as in other rural communities, there is growing appreciation that every community celebration has an optimum size, and that bigger is not always better.

Reimaging to the halcyon past

While most rural festivals are used to reinforce the existing image of the host community and the rural realm, festival production can also be used as a tool for reimaging rural communities in the minds of urbanites (the intended consumers of the tourism product). The entire process of creating and maintaining an image of the rural community as a tourist destination is critical to the effective positioning of the tourism product in the urban market and the development of appropriate marketing strategies (Telisman-Kosuta, 1989; Echtner and Ritchie, 1991, 1993). Since a festival's title, theme, and specific activities together constitute a powerful vehicle for shaping thoughts and feelings about the host community, a festival can play a vital role in the process of creating a specific new image for the community.

Reimaging to an old, expired landscape or townscape is a widely available option. Mainstream economic progress has bypassed thousands of small towns, villages and hamlets throughout the rural realm. These off-the-beaten-path places have an obsolete appearance, and many are brimming with vernacular features and forms reminiscent of the historic past. Most rural dwellers are unimpressed by the vernacular relics in their communities, but they understand that urbanites like rural relic landscapes and will invest time and money to enjoy the more interesting examples (Janiskee, 1976; Jakle, 1985).

The desire to promote heritage-based tourism has helped to justify many history-themed projects throughout rural America. Most such efforts have been modestly scaled, involving no more than a building or two, but some have entailed the preservation, renovation, or reconstruction of entire business districts, residential neighbourhoods, or living history museums. Given superior quality and skilful marketing, these undertakings can convert even a moribund backwater into a heritage tourism success story.

Festival production has become a commonplace method of attracting visitors to historic sites and buildings (Janiskee, 1996b). Most events offered in this context are dominated by historical exhibits and living history activities, especially historic house tours, crafts and skills demonstrations, military encampments, battle reenactments, black powder/buckskinner rendezvous, Victorian era life-styles, farming lifestyles and machinery, and holiday celebrations (Janiskee, 1990). Sturbridge, the famed nineteenth-century living history village in Massachusetts, hosts about a dozen festivals each year, focusing on themes such as sheep shearing, militia training, Thanksgiving, and harvest time activities. At Hardin, Montana, Little Big Horn Days attracts 10,000 visitors to large scale reenactments of General George Armstrong Custer's crushing defeat by Indians at the 1876 Battle of the Little Bighorn. At the Hale Farm and Village in Ohio, at Historic Brattonsville in South Carolina, and at hundreds of other historic sites through-out America, managers have learned that special events can dramatically increase attendance.

Producing festivals and other special events is an especially useful strategy for boosting heritage tourism in places that have no nationally significant heritage resources. Famous historic sites or structures are certainly not a prerequisite for heritage tourism. Rural communities in every region of the country attract thousands of tourists with historical features that are simply interesting, entertaining, and educational. Heritage resources that have been exploited successfully to build visitor industry in rural places include such diverse features as farms, plantations, log cabins, barns, covered bridges, grist mills, country stores, courthouse squares, business districts, village greens, churches, mansions, residential neighbourhoods, logging camps, stockyards, mines, railroad depots, Indian mounds, forts, and battlefields. It is the rare community indeed that has no interesting heritage resources to celebrate.

Any rural community that takes stock of its heritage assets and decides that it can build a reputation as a heritage tourism destination is undertaking the task of recreationally packaging history. Many objectives may be deemed important, such as preserving historic sites and folkways or educating people about the authentic past, but the only indispensable component of the managerial equation is getting tourists to come to the community, have a good time, and spend some of their money. Attracting and entertaining people is exactly what festivals do, and that is precisely why heritage resource managers have so eagerly embraced the festival production strategy.

One very important function that a recurring festival serves is to help establish and advertise the specific theme(s) that a community selects for the recreational packaging of its heritage resources. A heritage festival's title and scheduled activities usually reflect a particular historical era and the lifestyles or significant events and people associated with it. The festival therefore provides an effective way to highlight a specific historical concept or event, creates an aura of personal contact with the historic past, and draws attention to community heritage assets whose existence and worth might otherwise escape notice.

A noteworthy feature of heritage festivals is that producers can use living history activities and related tactics to create extraordinary recreational experiences in ordinary settings. For example, a small town can stage a very entertaining Dickens Christmas Festival in its downtown every year even though it has only a modest collection of Victorian era buildings. The historic aura of the special event, promoted with guided tours and the use of artifices such as Victorian Christmas decorations, costumed carollers and crafters, Dickens characters, roasted chestnuts, and horse drawn carriage rides, can be extremely appealing to visitors even if the historic setting is of pedestrian calibre. In addition, different living history festivals can be staged at various intervals in the same setting, drawing both new and repeat visitation. In the case of the Victorian theme, which is riding a crest of popularity in America, this might include a Victorian Independence Day celebration, a Victorian ice cream social, and so forth.

Back to yesteryear in Parke County, Indiana

Parke County, Indiana is one rural community that has relied heavily on history-themed festivals and related special events in a successful campaign to become a major heritage tourism destination (Janiskee, 1974). Parke County is located near the Illinois border about 50 miles west of Indianapolis. Forty years ago, it was a declining farming community with generally dismal economic prospects. Today it is still a small farming community with many welfare families, but it has acquired a year round, multi-million dollar heritage tourism industry that creates jobs, provides supplementary income for many families, generates tax revenues, and lifts the quality of life. The trickle of tourists that came to the area a generation ago has been replaced by a torrent, and Parke County is now one of the premier heritage tourism destinations in the Midwest.

It was a covered bridge festival that got the community started down the road to its lofty status as a heritage tourism destination (Janiskee, 1974, 1976). Parke County has 32 covered bridges, more than any area of its size in America (Figure 10.2). The same economic stagnation that left so many old bridges intact also left a landscape replete with old farmhouses, barns, log cabins, windmills, and other relics. In October 1957, after locals had noticed more and more visitors inquiring about the area's covered bridges, the county's Long Range Planning Committee produced the first Covered Bridge Festival. The community was surprised and delighted when 2,500 people showed up. The festival became an annual event that soon drew visitors by the tens of thousands and then by the hundreds of thousands. In 1995, its 39th consecutive year, the Parke County Covered Bridge Festival was attended by about two million people during a 10-day run that included the second and third weekends of October. Few community festivals in America attract more visitors. This fact has impressed the title sponsor, Buick, which is happy to lend a fleet of 50 new cars for several weeks and pay hefty printing and media reception costs just to get its corporate logo on the maps and brochures distributed free to visitors.

The Covered Bridge Festival is actually a 'confederation' or festival package

Figure 10.2. The numerous covered bridges of Parke County, which visitors find so delightful, stand out boldly in the landscape as powerful symbols of a rural past that is gone but fondly remembered. As this snowy scene suggests, the builders covered the bridges to protect them from the ravages of Midwestern weather. Reproduced with permission.

consisting of eight independent towns and other entities throughout the county that plan and market their own activities in consultation with each other. An umbrella organisation, Parke County, Inc., promotes the Covered Bridge Festival and other special events for the entire county, adding a layer of professional business and marketing expertise that the smaller entities lack (Getz and Frisby, 1988; Stafford, 1993). This mirrors nationwide trends precipitated by heated competition among festivals, rapidly rising production costs, growing legal and financial complexities, and government mandates for the areawide coordination of event tourism.

Like Mount Airy's two major festivals, the Covered Bridge Festival was established by local non-profit organizations, receives only limited advertising help, and routine tax breaks from the state or federal governments, forbids slick advertising by sponsors and others, and has a non-commercialised, distinctively bucolic flavour. The key difference is that Parke County adopted, from the very outset, a turn-of-the-century theme for its special events and tourist-related developments. Covered bridge tours set the tone. Five covered bridge routes for autos and buses loop outward from the county seat of Rockville. These routes let people drive through the scenic countryside and the covered bridges to a variety of festival venues offering heritage-themed live entertainment and related activities. At Rockville, the festival epicentre, two principal venues draw large crowds. One is the downtown area, which has a magnificent French Second Empire courthouse, a thriving courthouse square business area, a courthouse lawn that bustles with heritage activities, and a converted opera house that stages period plays. The other major venue is Billie Creek Village, a museum for the display of historical architecture and living history activities.

Billie Creek Village, organised as a 501-(C)-3 non-profit educational and historical association, was established in 1965 as a direct outgrowth of the Covered Bridge Festival's success (Billie Creek Village, Inc., 1995). The project was intended to enhance the county's appeal as a year round tourist attraction. For the first few years of its existence, the Village was open only during the festival and otherwise served as a repository for a 'rescued' covered bridge and several other transplanted historic structures. It went into year round operation in 1969, received its state charter in 1972, and continued to add historic structures until 1981. Today, Billie Creek Village's annual gross income is in the one million dollar range and includes event sponsorships by local businesses such as banks and Ely Lily. In addition to an inn and education centre complex, a farmstead, and three authentic covered bridges spanning a tree-lined creek, the site has a pseudo-village consisting of a general store (offering one of the largest hand-made consignment craft shops in the Midwest), a one-room schoolhouse, a log cabin, the little frame house of Indiana's first governor, and more than two dozen other historic structures, some of which house costumed artisans and crafters. Horse drawn wagon rides around the Village are popular with visitors, including the 300 tour groups who arrive by motor-coach each year. Horses are such a natural complement to this setting that Anheuser-Busch paid to film its famed Clydesdales in action on the covered bridges.

The 40,000 to 50,000 people who visit Billie Creek Village during the 10-day Covered Bridge Festival account for about half of the Village's gated attendance. The five full-time staff members and other workers are kept busy eleven months of the year, however, with nearly two dozen other heritage-themed special events venued at the Village. The Village's event season begins in late February when it sets up a primitive maple sugaring camp for the Maple Fair, a countywide event. Civil War Days, which was inaugurated in 1976 as part of the country's Bicentennial celebration, occurs in June when 2,000 reenactors entertain a crowd of 5,000 with Indiana's largest Civil War encampment and battle reenactment. Steam Harvest Days, a 'pioneer power' event, takes place on Labor Day weekend (early September), draws a crowd of about 3,000, and features old time tractors, engines, and farm machinery in action or on display. Among the many other events are the July 4th Ice Cream Social, an Arts and Crafts Days, a Quilt Show, School Days, Halloween Fright Nights, an Early Wheels Car Show, and an Old Fashioned Christmas.

The success of the Covered Bridge Festival, Billie Creek Village, and some smaller scale heritage tourism attractions has promoted numerous historic preservation or restoration projects throughout Parke County. Among the rescued, cleaned up, and rejuvenated relics are many covered bridges, a railroad depot, an 1880s roller mill (now a state historic site), an old grist mill, Rockville's Ritz Theatre, and a number of older homes that have been converted into bed and breakfast operations or antique stores.

A university-sponsored financial study of the 1992 Covered Bridge Festival yielded a conservative estimate of US$13 million a year in direct economic benefits to Parke County (Brough and Snedeker, 1992). Measuring the economic impact of festivals and events is a very difficult task, and estimates are frequently wide of the mark (Della Bitta and Loudon, 1975; Mitchell and Wall, 1986; Long et al., 1987; Wall and Mitchell, 1989; Long and Perdue, 1990; Scottish Tourist Board, 1993; Crompton and McKay, 1994). Whatever the total in Parke County, however, it would be dramatically higher were it not for outside vendors and the county's limited supply of lodging facilities. Non-resident vendors pay the US$30 booth rental fees and ten percent sales commissions the producer charges to help defray expenses, but they still siphon money from the county by spending profits elsewhere. Nearly three-fourths of the visitors are aged 46 to 75 and travel 100 or more miles to the festival, and, in addition, although demand for lodging is very high, most visitor expenditures for lodging are diverted to surrounding counties and Terre Haute because Parke County still has very few motels, bed and breakfasts, or other lodging facilities (Brough and Snedeker 1992).

Festival-related income, especially that associated with the sale of handicrafts, artworks, antiques, food, beverages, gasoline, and parking privileges, is earned in Rockville, Bridgeton, Mansfield, Mecca, Rosedale, Tangier, Montezuma, Bellmore, and other towns or locales throughout Parke County. It is highly significant that nearly all the festival money goes to non-profit organisations, small businesses, and individual entrepreneurs. In a county with so many people living on marginal incomes, it really makes a difference when one person can pay for their college education with car parking fees and another can earn US$14,000 in ten days selling fudge.

Parke County's success has attracted a great deal of interest throughout the Midwest and many other areas of the United States. Comparatively few rural communities are so nearly ideally suited for reimaging to their pioneer past, but dozens of towns near and far have been able to copy some of Parke County's tactics in inaugurating new heritage-themed events and history-based tourism projects of their own. Four more covered bridge festivals have been brought on line in Indiana alone.

Reimaging to new futures

A rural community in quest of a larger and better visitor industry may choose to reimage to a new future. This means it either copies a traditionally successful tourism concept (old idea in a new setting), rides a new tourism trend (another setting for a new idea), or explores a new tourism concept (bold new idea). Regardless of whether the reimaging project involved is conventional, trendy, or innovative, it is likely to incorporate festival production as a means of attracting publicity and boosting attendance.

Proven winners

When reimaging themselves, most rural communities copy tourism development and promotion themes that have a long track record of success. By copying proven winners they minimize their risk and their investment of time and energy. One concept that many small towns have been able to use is the birthplace-of-a-celebrity theme, which has yielded dozens of events such as the Glenn Miller Festival in Clarinda, Iowa, and the Judy Garland Festival in Grand Rapids, Minnesota. A popular seasonal theme in the northern states is the winter playground concept, which gives rise to winterfest celebrations with activities such as cross-country skiing, snowmobiling, and ice fishing. Many rural communities have evolved into 'flowertowns' where visitors can see, typically in festival context, unusually attractive displays of azaleas, dogwoods, cherry trees, roses, daffodils, or other flowering vegetation. There are hundreds of traditional concepts like these, including both seasonal and year round attractions.

One of the most successful of the traditional reimaging themes is ethnic tourism. Over the past half-century, dozens of rural communities whose visitor appeal once rested on scenic beauty, historical buildings, water sports, spas, inns, sport hunting, or other attractions have reimaged as ethnic tourism destinations. A community that accomplishes this normally builds from a base of well-defined ethnic traditions and perhaps some visually distinctive ethnic features and forms. The reimaging process involves a concerted effort to develop an infrastructure catering to tourists on a year round or seasonal basis with foods, music, crafts, and other commodities or entertainment that are decidedly ethnic in character. As logic would suggest, the hallmark community celebrations in ethnic tourism destinations tend to be ethnic festivals (Hall, 1992).

Many rural communities in various parts of America were settled by distinctive ethnic groups, including many newly-arrived immigrants. German, Scandinavian, Irish, Polish, Czech, Dutch, Swiss, Greek, Russian, Cajun, and many other ethnic groups are represented. This is reflected in a potpourri of ethnic tourism themes and hundreds of related ethnic festivals such as the Dutch-themed Pella (Iowa) Tulip Festival, the Oklahoma Czech Festival (in Yukon), the Swedish Heritage Festival in Cambridge, Minnesota, and the Wilhelm Tell Festival in the Swiss community of New Glarus, Wisconsin (Hoelscher, 1993). In the typical instance, the ethnic tourism destination is a community whose ethnic character has always been its principal visitor appeal.

America attracted almost as many German immigrants as English, and more German-themed ethnic tourism destinations have been developed than any other type. Success stories abound. In Michigan's Thumb region, an area that attracted many Germans and Slavs, the farming community of Frankenmuth (pop. 4,400) originally developed a visitor industry based on dining at Zhender's, a Bavarian restaurant that served family-style chicken dinners and Frankenmuth beer. In 1959 the town's status as a *bona fide* tourist destination was solidified by the addition of a second large restaurant, the Bavarian Inn. Gradually adopting a Bavarian village motif, Frankenmuth became 'Michigan's Little Bavaria' and now has a year round festival calendar that includes a huge Bavarian Festival (attendance over 150,000) as well as a Maifest and an Oktoberfest (Janiskee, 1997). The Bavarian village strategy has worked so well that Frankenmuth now attracts about two million visitors a year and both Zhender's and the Bavarian Inn perennially rank among the nation's top 15 non-chain restaurants in terms of food volume served. The example of the northeastern Georgia mountain town of Helen shows that a community does not need an ethnic tradition to become an ethnic German tourism hit. Helen was a has-been mining community in the late 1960s when it began, with almost no outside help, a complete makeover of its downtown area into a pseudo Bavarian village, complete with an 1,100-seat Festhalle (Figure 10.3). The Chamber of Commerce inaugurated an Oktoberfest in 1971 to help promote 'Georgia's Alpine Village'. Now one of America's longest Oktoberfests, the event is sponsored by Lowenbrau and Coca-Cola, attracts 30,000 tourists a year, generates over US$350,000 in annual revenues, and accounts for about half of the town's business income.

Emerging trends

Some rural communities reorient their tourism development goals to take advantage of new trends in travel and tourism. In a sense, they jump on a development bandwagon that is new on the scene, but moving fast and quickly gaining speed. In recent years, many communities have implemented tourism development projects and associated festival productions focused on hot-air ballooning, mountain bike riding, microbrew beer tasting, mega-scale Christmas light displays, and other activities or attractions that have surged in popularity.

Ecotourism, one of the most popular tourism trends in the world today, has captured the imagination of many community leaders looking for new directions in tourism development. The popularity of low-impact nature tourism has led hundreds of rural communities to capitalise on the tourist appeal of wildlife watching and other nature appreciation opportunities in their locales. In many rural places, especially remote ones, ecosystem resources constitute the prime visitor attraction and the logical focus of reimaging campaigns. Special events featuring guided nature tours have proven very effective in promoting ecotourism, and many of these events employ the festival format. To name just a few examples, there are community tourism development projects and related festivals focused on wildflowers, whales, salmon, rattlesnakes, eagles, geese, whooping cranes, buzzards, warblers, prairie chickens, pelicans, loons, and moose.

Maine's MooseMainea festival clearly illustrates the reimaging potential of ecotourism themed events. Moose have made a big comeback in Maine, and

Figure 10.3. The Alpine village theme permeates the built environment of Helen's business area. Few of the many thousands of tourists who visit Helen know how unappealing the townscape looked before the Alpine make-over began about thirty years ago. Reproduced with permission.

although these huge animals can be a nuisance in suburbia and a potentially deadly traffic hazard, they are fun to watch. Greenville and Rockwood, two small towns in the hunting-fishing-camping oriented Moosehead Lake region, decided to convince the world that their locale is *the* place to see and photograph moose. The MooseMainea festival they began staging in 1992 has attracted considerable media attention and about 3,000 tourists a year. The May/June event offers, among other festival amenities, moose watching safaris, a children's moose art contest, and promotional gimmicks such the world's largest mousse dessert (5,000 servings) and jewellery made of lacquered moose droppings (now available by mail order).

Endless possiblities

A resourceful rural community has many possible futures as a tourist attraction, since it can successfully promote just about anything it believes in and wants to make happen. The stimulus can be a bright idea, a chance occurrence, or even an unexplained phenomenon. An apt case of the latter is tourism focused on mysterious lights often seen in the desert near Marfa, Texas (pop. 2,551). Inaugurated in 1987, the Marfa Lights Festival has an attendance of about 5,000.

One of the more imaginative reimaging projects was recently undertaken by the little southeastern Kansas town of Sedan (pop. 1,400). In 1988, the economically struggling community decided to build 'The World's Longest Yellow Brick Road' as a way of capitalising on the rural Kansas setting of the film classic 'The Wizard of Oz'. By 1995, at least 40,000 tourists a year were coming to Sedan to view the more than one mile-long road, which is actually a steadily lengthening sidewalk constructed of more than 9,500 yellow concrete paving blocks imprinted with the names of purchasers, including celebrities, from 24 countries. Each Memorial Day weekend since 1989, Sedan has hosted a Yellow Brick Road Festival (one of several in the state) to celebrate and promote the town's principal tourist attraction. The festival, which draws about 4,000 visitors, offers not only routine fare such as a parade, a beauty pageant, a mock gunfight, and hot-air balloon rides, but also special features such as a Wizard of Oz character look-alike contest, a brick stacking contest, and a guest stint by an original Munchkin from the 1938 film production. As a publicity bonus, the event producer draws attention to the town's lesser visitor attractions, such as the 'world's largest sunflower' (a 20-foot wide painting on the tourism office floor) and America's largest flower bedding facility. The community is delighted with the results of its tourism initiatives, and some boosters claim that the Yellow Brick Road, the festival, and the town's tourist appeal 'could keep on growing forever'.

Conclusions and implications

It is easy to understand why community festivals have blossomed all over rural America in recent decades. Festival production is a versatile, highly effective means of publicizing a community's appealing features and attracting tourists who might otherwise never visit. As a delightful bonus, the beneficial effects of festivals extend well beyond generating tourism dollars and include strengthening rural communities and enriching the quality of small town life.

From the tourism planning and promotion perspective, it is vital to remember that rural festivals are produced in places that appeal to urbanites primarily because they are simpler, quieter, slower, friendlier, and closer to nature than the city. A rural festival is not about thrill-a-minute excitement. On the contrary, it works by creating a relaxing, homey atmosphere of simple, wholesome pleasures served up at a gentle pace.

It is very clear that the typical rural festival is meant to reinforce the existing image of the host community, but it is also clear that festivals have a role to play in helping some communities reimage to the past or to a new future. The experiences of Parke County, Sedan, Helen, Greeneville/Rockwood, and other reimaged communities show that festival production can be an effective tool for reorienting the way that people think about specific rural locales and evaluate them as tourist destinations.

It is highly germane that the typical rural festival functions primarily to generate event-based tourism, not to promote a community's tourism assets. Thus, even though helping to publicise new or previously neglected community attributes is a praiseworthy contribution of festivals, their main value rests on the fact that they provide, if only temporarily, entertainment that dramatically increases a community's visitor appeal. This works to the advantage of many communities, of course, since they can generate significant event-based tourism by simply hosting differently-themed festivals at appropriate intervals throughout the year.

It is a very strong advantage that the vast majority of rural festivals are produced with little appreciable assistance from the state or federal governments. In this era of risky and expensive tourism development projects, festival production seems to be one of the true bargains. This goes a long way toward explaining why festival production has increased so greatly in recent years.

A cautionary note is in order. Some areas have become glutted with rural festivals and others are quickly approaching saturation point. In addition, the novelty aspect of rural festivals is wearing thin with many urbanites. There is growing concern that slackening visitor interest and fierce competition may combine to trigger a downturn and weed out many festivals. Festival producers throughout rural America will need to remain keenly attentive to emerging trends, improve the quality of existing products, and create better strategies for new product development and marketing. This not only portends an expanding niche for professionally trained festival producers, but also the greatly increased use of tactics such as planning and coordinating festivals on an areawide basis.

References

Amusement Business, 1996, *Directory of North American fairs, festivals & expositions*, Amusement Business, Nashville

Billie Creek Village, Inc., 1995, *Annual membership report*, Billie Creek Village, Inc., Rockville

Brough, K. and Snedeker, C., 1992, *Preliminary 1992 Covered Bridge Festival economic impact study*, Unpublished report, Terre Haute Area Small Business Development Center, Indiana State University

Chacko, H.E. and Schaffer, J.D., 1993, The evolution of a festival: Creole Christmas in New Orleans, *Tourism Management*, **14** (6): 475–82

Crompton, J.L. and McKay, S., 1994, Measuring the economic impact of festivals and events: some myths, misapplications and ethical dilemmas, *Festival Management & Event Tourism: An International Journal*, **2** (1): 33–43

Della Bitta, A.J. and Loudon, D., 1975, Assessing the economic impact of short duration tourist events, *New England Journal of Business and Economics*, **1** (Spring): 37–45

Echtner, C.M. and Ritchie, J.R.B., 1991, The meaning and measurement of destination image, *Journal of Tourism Studies*, **2** (2): 2–12

Getz, D., 1991, *Festivals, special events, and tourism*, Van Nostrand Reinhold, New York

Getz, D. and Frisby, W., 1988, Evaluating management effectiveness in community-run festivals, *Journal of Travel Research*, **27** (1): 22–27

Hall, C.M., 1992, *Hallmark tourist events: impacts, management and planning*, Halsted Press, New York

Hoelscher, S.D., 1993, Old European homelands in the American Middle West, *Journal of Cultural Geography*, **13** (2): 87–106

Jakle, J.A.,1985, *The tourist: travel in Twentieth-century America*, University of Nebraska Press, Lincoln

Janiskee, R.L., 1974, Rural relic landscape as a recreational resource: the case of Parke County, Indiana. Unpublished doctoral dissertation, University of Illinois at Urbana-Champaign

Janiskee, R.L., 1976, City trouble, the pastoral retreat, and pioneer America: a rationale for rescuing the middle landscape, *Pioneer America*, **8** (1): 1–7

Janiskee, R.L., 1980, South Carolina's harvest festivals: rural delights for day tripping urbanites, *Journal of Cultural Geography*, **1** (1): 96–104

Janiskee, R.L., 1990, History-themed festivals: a special events approach to rural recreation and tourism. In *Proceedings of the applied geography conferences*, vol. 13., J.W. Frazier, F.A. Schoolmaster III, and J.D. Lord, eds., pp. 111–117, Department of Geography, SUNY-Binghamton, Binghamton

Janiskee, R.L., 1991, Rural festivals in South Carolina, *Journal of Cultural Geography*, **11** (2): 31–43

Janiskee, R.L., 1994, Some macroscale growth trends in America's community festival industry, *Festival Management & Event Tourism: An International Journal*, **2** (1): 10–14.

Janiskee, R.L., 1996a, Community festivals in the Carolinas. In *Snapshots of the Carolinas: landscapes and cultures*, G. Bennett, ed., pp. 57–61, Association of American Geographers, Washington, DC

Janiskee, R.L., 1996b, Historic houses and special events, *Annals of Tourism Research*, **23** (2): 398–414

Janiskee, R.L., 1996c, The temporal distribution of America's community festivals, *Festival Management & Event Tourism: An International Journal*, **3**: 129–137

Janiskee, R.L., 1997, Oktoberfest—American style. *Festival Management & Event Tourism: An International Journal*, **3**(4): pp. 197–199.

Long, P.T. Perdue, R.R. and Behm, J., 1987, *1986 Carbondale Mountain fair visitor survey: an evaluation of nonresident expenditures*, Center for Rural Recreation Development, University of Colorado, Boulder

Long, P.T. and Perdue, R.R., 1990, The economic impact of rural festivals and special events: assessing the spatial distribution of expenditures, *Journal of Travel Research*, **28** (4): 10–14

Marx, L., 1964, *The machine in the garden: technology and the pastoral ideal in America*, Oxford University Press, New York

Mayfield, T.L. and Crompton, J.L., 1995, Development of an instrument for identifying community reasons for staging a festival, *Festival Management & Event Tourism: An International Journal*, **3** (3): 37–44

Mitchell, C. and Wall, G., 1986, Impacts of cultural festivals on Ontario communities, *Recreation Research Review*, **13** (1): 28–37

Mohr, K., Backman, K.F., Gahan, L.W. and Backman, S.J., 1993, An investigation of festival motivations and event satisfaction by visitor type, *Festival Management & Event Tourism: An International Journal*, **1** (3): 89–97

Mules, T. and McDonald, S., 1994, The economic impact of special events: the use of forecasts, *Festival Management & Event Tourism: An International Journal*, **2** (1): 45–53

Robinson, D. and Fernandes, D., 1996, *The definitive Andy Griffith Show reference*, McFarland & Company, Inc., Publishers.

Saleh, F. and Ryan, C., 1993, Jazz and knitwear: factors that attract tourists to festivals, *Tourism Management*, **14** (4): 289–297

Schmader, S.W. and Jackson, R., 1990, *Special events: inside and out*, Sagamore, Champaign

Scottish Tourist Board, 1993, Edinburgh festivals study: visitor survey and economic impact assessment summary report; February 1992, *Festival Management & Event Tourism: An International Journal*, **1** (2): 71–78.

S.E.N., Inc., 1996, *Special events directory*, SEN, Inc., Palmyra

Stafford, J., 1993, Standards & [sic] certification for event professionals, *Festival Management & Event Tourism: An International Journal*, **1** (2): 68–70

Telisman-Kosuta, N. 1989, Tourist destination image. In *Tourism marketing and management handbook*, S.F. Witt and L. Moutinho, eds., pp. 557–561, Prentice Hall, Hemel Hempstead

Ukman, L., ed., 1993, *IEG Directory of Sponsorship Marketing*, 6th ed., International Events Group, Inc., Chicago

Uysal, M., Gahan, L. and Martin, B., 1993, An examination of event motivations: a case study, *Festival Management & Event Tourism: An International Journal*, **1** (1): 5–10

Wall, G. and Mitchell, C., 1989, Cultural festivals as economic stimuli and catalysts of functional change. In *The planning and evaluation of hallmark events*, G.J. Syme, B.J. Shaw, D.M. Fenton, and W.S. Mueller, eds., pp. 132–141, Avebury, Aldershot

Part Four:
Social and Economic Dynamics

11 Rural landholder attitudes: the case of public recreational access to 'private' rural lands

JOHN M. JENKINS AND EVI PRIN

Introduction

Rural areas have become increasingly important locations and backdrops for tourism and recreational activities. Whereas much of the focus of recreational and tourism activity and related research and public policy making in rural areas has been on public lands, attention to the potential and roles of private lands in the provision of recreational opportunities is relatively lacking, particularly in such countries as Australia and Canada.

The amount of private land available in any area for recreation is largely dependent on the goals and attitudes of landholders (Coppock and Duffield, 1975; Cullington, 1981; Pigram, 1981; 1983; Sanderson, 1982; Butler, 1984). Research concerning public access to private lands for recreation has been conducted in Canada, North America and the United Kingdom (e.g., see Conservation Council of Ontario, 1975; Troughton, 1975; Bull and Wibberley, 1976; Cullington, 1981; Middleton, 1982; Swinnerton, 1982; Butler, 1984; Butler and Troughton, 1985; Centre for Leisure Research, 1986; Perdue, *et al.*, 1987; Wall, 1989). Such research indicates that landholder attitudes are determined by: landholder values and personal beliefs; legal, economic, social and ecological concerns; national, local and family traditions; government incentives; the type and volume of recreational activities; and past encounters with recreationists (Cullington, 1981). However, research findings in particular localities may be site or regional specific and therefore have little application outside their context because of different institutional arrangements, legal situations, historical development processes, land use intensities and, in all likelihood, the different attitudes to land by landholders.

In Australia, despite the increasing use of the countryside for recreation and tourism, and the attention given to the potential for these activities to contribute to rural regional development and more specifically farm incomes, information concerning landholder attitudes to recreational access to private rural lands is scant. Therefore, the aims of this chapter are:

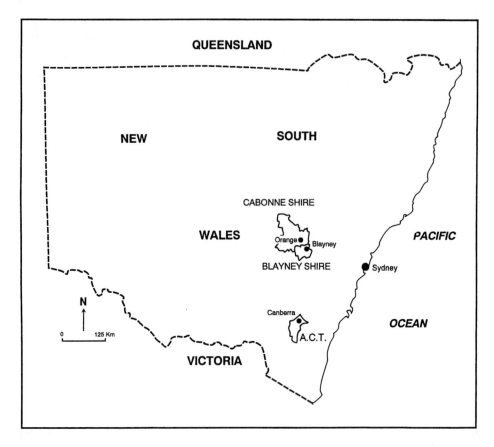

Figure 11.1. New South Wales: study area

- to outline recent research and developments concerning recreational access to private rural lands in the UK, Canada and Australia (also see Chapter Five for a brief discussion of access related issues in New Zealand); and
- to examine landholder attitudes to recreational access to private lands in central western New South Wales (NSW), Australia (Figure 11.1).

Attitudes and approaches to providing recreational access to public and private lands vary around the globe. These variations relate to different historical developments (landscape images; public policy; private development), land ownership rights and attitudes (the latter perhaps reflecting historical trends and issues), government initiatives or lack thereof, and past and present legislative provisions (which may reflect past public policy experience and practice). In Australia, there is no parallel system to the rights of way network which gives people access to much of the countryside in England and Wales. Conflict in the use of private rural lands for public recreation is common, but has yet to attract much attention from planners and policy makers.

Table 11.1. Positive and negative impacts of recreational activities

Impacts	Negatives	Positive
Environmental	– erosion of trails, campsites, picnic sites, and water-side areas – loss of vegetation and disturbance of livestock – pollution of streams from farm land effluent – dumping of garbage	– increased environmental awareness and education – greater support for financial support for the environment
Economic	– damage to property (crop damage, livestock loss, vandalism and theft) – littering, gates left open, fire risk, illegal shooting – cost of providing and maintaining recreational facilities e.g. picnic sites, road, trails – legal (liability) and account-ancy fees, fire insurance, policing and other costs stemming from recreational provisions – changes to farming practices or other such requirements	– sale of goods and services to recreationists – leasing land to groups or government agencies – sale or lease of land for recreational development – income for recreational ventures
Legal	– occupier liability – limiting access and trespass – compensation for property damage and related civil costs	– legislation of access is cheaper than land acquisitioned, avoids problems associated with land severance – secures desirable public rights – compensation to farmers for maintenance, including conservation activities
Social	– differing attitudes between recreationists and residents – increased stress, crowding, traffic congestion – lack of/or reduction of privacy – change in lifestyle and quality of life on a seasonal or permanent basis – non-permitted activities (e.g., indiscriminate use of firearms, trail bikes, fire lighting)	– political change resulting from increased representation of seasonal or temporary urban residents – urban rural interaction – escape for city dwellers – altruism
Other	– change in status quo – gradual urbanisation of rural areas – increasing loss of control over rural areas by rural residents (this could relate to all the above concerns)	– wider (e.g. political) recognition of importance of recreation and the need for strategic recreational planning and development strategies – educational programmes

Source: Adapted from Cullington, 1981; Pigram, 1981; Sanderson, 1982; Butler, 1984.

Context and settings

Rural recreation is just one competitor for the use of non-urban/metropolitan land and water (Green, 1977). Other uses include primary production (e.g., agricultural, aquatic, horticultural, pastoral and timber production), conservation or preservation of the natural and built environment (e.g., national parks, wilderness areas), and transport and communication networks.

Rural tourism and recreation activities are often extensive in that they require large tracts of land (e.g., bushwalking) and water (e.g., boating), but are largely non-consumptive and can be incorporated into a multiple land use situation. Therefore, rural recreation and tourism are often compatible with other forms of land use such as agriculture, forestry, horticulture and water supply (see Green, 1977). However, the relationships between rural tourism and recreation and other land and water uses are largely influenced by landholder attitudes. Landholders include individuals (e.g., farmers), businesses (e.g., agribusiness; tourist resort) and groups (e.g., recreation clubs) with private ownership rights, leaseholders (whose land use may be regulated by public agencies), and resource management agencies (e.g., national parks, forestry, nature/wildlife reserves, public owned recreational facilities, water reservoirs). In short, there is a wide variety of individuals and agencies with different value sets and interests with respect to the rural environment, and with different rights as landholders according to land tenure and other institutional, legislative or contractual arrangements.

The complexity of institutional and ownership arrangements and the multi-functional character of rural areas has led to conflict between competing uses, and between land managers. Land ownership and the exercise of landownership rights are thus critical elements in the supply of tourism and recreation opportunities because access to land and water in this context is generally contingent upon legislation, public policy interpretations, and landholder/management attitudes (Pigram, 1981; Corfield, 1987). Perhaps unsurprisingly, debates between what are often seen as competing, or even complementary, values and interests can be vociferous and thereby attract much public attention, e.g., between forestry agencies and conservationists, between national parks agencies/managers and tourists, and even within resource management agencies themselves as different branches within an agency grapple with balancing conservation versus recreational objectives.

Agreements and compromise between recreationists, responsible agencies and landholders are often difficult to achieve. On the one hand, as farmers seek to improve productivity (e.g., through more intensive land use practices, including the development of cattle feed lots), 'aesthetic and functional' changes to the landscape occur and impact on recreational supply and visitor experiences and satisfaction (see Chapter Seven). On the other hand, rural recreation activities can become more contentious as their environmental impacts increase (e.g., large numbers of people visit sensitive sites; the use of such recent and potentially destructive recreational technologies as four wheel drive vehicles and snowmobiles). Recreational activities such as hiking, camping, fishing and nature observation may be passive and therefore, although depending on the sensitivity/fragility of the environment, have less inherent and actual potential to cause conflict between participants and land managers. However, landholder attitudes, perceptions and experiences may be influenced by small numbers of people who fail to consider the relationship between the type and intensity of their activities and the resulting impacts on the environment, including other people. Indeed, there are those whose intentions and activities are deliberately environmentally destructive and criminal (e.g., indiscriminate shooting of stock, and stealing). Clearly, an understanding of land use involves both an understanding of the values of the physical, biological, productive, spatial, and visual/aesthetic attributes of land, and 'an awareness of the different standpoints from which land use may be considered' (Mather, 1991, p. 6). Increased understanding and awareness of landholder attitudes to public access to private lands for recreation should contribute to our knowledge of land use values generally, and to our knowledge of the different standpoints from which land may be considered for recreational use specifically. As noted in Chapter One, the future of recreation and tourism in rural areas depends heavily upon the successful integration of the traditional and the new forms of leisure with the traditional and the new forms of other economic activities and social/cultural mores.

The United Kingdom

In the UK, private land has a long history of use for recreation, and 'A central theme to the development of countryside recreation policies has been that of access' (Groome, 1993, p. 5). However, recreational use of the countryside is not 'a public prerogative. It constitutes use of a domain owned mainly (87 per cent) by private individuals, and with public access dependent on certain legal rights or lenient attitudes on the part of landowners. Even the national parks, areas designated specifically for landscape protection and public amenity, are largely in private ownership' (Shoard, 1987, in Glyptis, 1992, p. 156). British landowners have a long developed tradition of exclusive control of the countryside (Shoard, 1996, p. 13). To make the matter more complex still, there are signs that land ownership is gradually becoming concentrated in the hands of fewer people rather than spreading more widely while counterurbanisation is bringing new, affluent and mobile residents who are accustomed to urban standards of service provision (Glyptis, 1992).

Nevertheless, with respect to Australia and Canada, the UK has enjoyed comparative ease of access to rural lands for recreation where the broad aim has been to promote and market leisure to as wide a public as possible (Pigram and Jenkins, 1994). For instance, recent policy development in rural recreation and tourism has 'resulted in a change from the perceived need to control the public, to their wholesale encouragement. This has happened quite swiftly and has taken place in tandem with a fundamental reappraisal of the primary role of agriculture in rural areas' (Robinson, 1990, p. 132). Yet, as discussed later in this section, despite initiatives to enhance public recreational access to the countryside in the UK, there are still concerns about landholder attitudes, the ineffectiveness of such initiatives in many cases, and, ultimately, the lack of access.

In 1986, the Countryside Commission undertook a review of the selected accessibility mechanisms that are most commonly used or that provide the most scope for recreation provision. These were:

(i) Common law rights of access
  • public rights of way
  • access rights to commons
(ii) Public intervention to secure access
  • local authority purchase for recreational purposes
  • access agreements and orders; management agreements
  • financial incentives
(iii) Private agreements to enable access
  • purchasing and leasing by recreational and sporting organisations
  • licences and permission.

Public rights of way and securing of access

The National Parks and Access to the Countryside Act, 1949, provides for National Parks and Areas of Outstanding Natural Beauty (AONB) which, between them, cover more than 18 per cent of England and Wales. Also in the Act was provision to improve actual access to the countryside. The 1949 Act gave powers to local authorities to negotiate access agreements and required them to prepare definitive maps of public rights of way on bridle paths and footpaths (Patmore, 1983). Another feature of the Act was legislation for the creation of Long Distance Footpaths, making up a national system of rights of way through some of the most striking upland and coastal scenery (Patmore, 1983; Countryside Commission, 1986). A recent estimate indicates that the network of footpaths, bridleways and byways amounts to 193,000 km (Glyptis, 1992).

The Countryside Act, 1968, requires that County Councils (highway authorities) signpost public paths where they leave metalled roads. However, such a requirement is often ignored. For instance, in Gloucestershire, up to 90 per cent of paths lacked signposts where they left the roads, and 11 that were provided pointed in the wrong direction (Shoard, 1987, in Glyptis, 1992). Moreover, the Countryside Commission (1989, in Glyptis, 1992) found that people on a two-mile walk, planned with a map, stand a two in three chance of not being able to complete their walk because of obstacles.

The recreational potential of public rights of way may be enhanced by the more recent Rights of Way Act, 1990. Under that Act:

> farmers have wider rights to plough or disturb cross-field paths, if this cannot be avoided, at any stage of cultivation. But they are under a much stricter duty to restore paths quickly – within two weeks when preparing a seed bed, or within 24 hours of any other operation – and to make sure that the line of paths can be clearly seen. All paths must be kept free of crops that would interfere with people's use of them (Countryside Commission, 1990, p. 2).

If a farmer fails to restore or clear paths, highway authorities can do so at the farmer's expense.

Access agreements

In many open-country areas in Britain (namely areas which are wholly or predominantly mountain, moor, heath, down, cliff or foreshore landscapes – all agricultural land except rough grazing was excluded) local authorities can and do make access agreements with landholders to ensure that the public can wander freely over that land. This is a more flexible arrangement than with a footpath right of way that does not grant the public any right to linger on the path. Where agreement is not reached, the authorities can make an order and, as a last resort, may secure access through compulsory purchase (Cloke and Park, 1985). Access agreements represent a promising policy initiative to be sure, however, such agreements are scarce. Less than one half of one per cent of the land surface of England and Wales is covered by access agreements (Shoard, 1996).

Water catchment lands were the main focus of early agreements and water authorities were one of the main objectors (Pigram and Jenkins, 1994). However, the increased effectiveness of water treatment processes has, to some extent, reduced real and apparent pollution risks, and has enabled water authorities to adopt more positive access policies. Some concern has been expressed about recreation opportunities following privatisation of water supplies in Britain (Saddler, 1989). Although new legislation provides for public access to water authority land, the provisions are vague and open to interpretation and thus disputes over access continue. In the 1990s, aroused by concerns that the privatisation of the water industry and Forestry Commission would reduce public access rights on private land, the Rambler's Association (under the banner of 'Forbidden Britain') organised mass trespasses over such lands. 'With the sale of over 250,000 acres of Forestry Commission woodland since 1981, there are real fears that private owners will seek to restrict public access, and that commercial pressures will further diminish the stock of available countryside' (Spink, 1994, p. 66). Access is therefore a high profile political issue in rural areas.

Despite policy and legislative developments concerning recreational access to the countryside in the UK, several important problems have been identified, including problematic trespassing laws, and the levels of landholder compensation (Duffield and Owen, 1970; Butler and Clark, 1992; Shoard, 1996). Butler and Clark have categorised these problems in economic, environmental and social terms. In economic terms, arguments for rural recreation and tourism tend to be based on the assumption that tourism, in particular, can boost declining rural economies and provide employment for the local population. Although the diversification of rural economies can benefit a region, the type of employment that tourism generates is often poorly paid and subject to seasonality (Pearce, 1989). As the countryside still has more seasonal tourism than the cities it thus less likely to provide attractive year round employment for local people. In environmental and social terms, rural recreation and tourism are often perceived as being destructive (e.g., by way of water and noise pollution, erosion and traffic congestion) to the very qualities that attracted people in the first place.

A recent policy initiative for access to the countryside is the Countryside Commission's 'Countryside Stewardship Scheme' (CSS), which was launched in 1991. CSS encouraged farmers and landowners to conserve and re-create the beauty of five traditional English landscapes (chalk and limestone grassland, lowland heath, waterside landscapes, coastal land, uplands), and their wildlife habitats, and to give opportunities for informal public access. 'The long term objective is to develop a basis for a comprehensive scheme to achieve environmental and recreational benefits as an integral part of agricultural support' (Countryside Commission, 1991, p. 1). Farmers and landholders were granted annual payments of up to £300 a hectare, a commitment costing the government £13 million for the first three years. 'Typical annual payments ranged from £50 a hectare for managing limestone grassland to £275 a hectare for creating riverside meadows and opening them for people to enjoy' (Countryside Commission, 1991, p. 1). Additional annual payments of £50 per hectare were available in return for agreements that allow access to the landscapes, including suitable enclosed land in upland areas, for quiet enjoyment (Countryside Commission, 1991). According to Knightbridge and Swanwick (in Ravenscroft, 1996, p. 43), 'Not surprisingly, the CSS has proved particularly popular with many farmers and rural landowners, with over 25,000 heactares being brought into the scheme in its first year of operation, of which about one-quarter had provision for new access'. However, concerns have been raised as to whether the access payments have secured access, with many open access areas difficult to locate.

Many other examples of recent initiatives to secure access to the UK countryside, and in particular private rural land, abound (see Watkins, 1996). However, there is much debate with respect to such initiatives. Shoard (1996, p. 21) argues:

> Farmers now get £247 per mile per year merely for allowing people to walk along access strips ten metres wide along the sides of or across fields in ESAs [Environmentally Sensitive Areas] and £145 under the NRSA [Non-Rotational Set-Aside] (MaFF, 1994, p. 6–7). The landowners of the past who established the idea of a right of exclusion would be amazed to learn the size of the potential bounty they have created for their descendants.
>
> The right of exclusion is being increasingly used to turn access into a tradeable asset. The government's endorsement of the right of the landowner to charge others to set foot on his or her land puts the official seal of approval on the notion that access to the countryside is a commodity to be bought from landowners rather than a free public good. This is like bestowing on one group a whole new form of wealth.

Yet, in the same volume of works (Watkins, 1996), Curry (1996, p. 34) argues that one means of 'improving opportunities for access to closed land ... should be pursued through direct payments from the consumer to the farmer and landowner since, in the absence of non-excludability, this is both more efficient and more equitable'.

There are no right or wrong answers or simple solutions to the access issue because of the disparate views on landowner's rights and the nature and outcomes of government intervention, and such a situation is unlikely to change markedly in the near future. The restructuring of rural economies and the difficulties that have been faced by some rural producers and communities in tandem with an increased demand for recreational and tourist use of the countryside, mean that public sector incentives or disincentives and user pays fees are likely to become even more attractive to landholders. However, if according to Shoard (1996, p. 21), 'The only honest and effective way of opening the countryside to the people is to require landowners to relinquish some of the rights in their asset which they are otherwise bound to defend and exploit', then, in the absence of blanket public policy establishing such access (and this is not only opposed by some public officials as it is politically dangerous) a significant reordering of landholders' values will be needed*. So, as Shoard notes, while general rights to roam and wander which exist in countries such as Switzerland and Denmark might be an ideal situation, it is unlikely to eventuate in the UK in the short to medium term. Before such a turnaround in values can be contemplated, an acute understanding of landowner attitudes is needed. To some extent, such understanding is becoming increasingly evident and detailed in the expansive literature on recreational access in the UK (see Watkins, 1996), but it is sadly lacking across Canada and Australia.

Canada

During the settlement of much of Canada, rural life provided few opportunities for recreation participation. According to Butler (1984), recreational use of rural areas began with the establishment of cottages and hunting/fishing forays which were frequented by British army officers and members of the 'Canadian aristocracy' in the second half of the nineteenth century. Prior to this period, many forms of recreation in rural areas were acts of survival (e.g., hunting and fishing) or part of social and agricultural life (barn-building bees, agricultural fairs and community picnics).

As the urban population expanded, demand for recreational space intensified. With improved transport, the development of the steamship, railway and later the automobile, weekend escapes to the countryside became possible. This increase in personal mobility was mirrored by an increase in the establishment of formal recreation areas, including national and provincial parks, private campgrounds, and resorts (Butler 1984). In Ontario, for instance, variables such as population growth, urbanisation, higher standards of living, increased levels of leisure time, more personal mobility, American tourism and a younger more educated population all helped bring about the crisis in outdoor recreation that occurred in that Province in the late 1940s. Generally, however, the notion of the private cottage epitomised the Canadian vacation from the turn of the century until well after the Second World War. 'Going to the cottage' was the Canadian equivalent of the British 'going to the seaside' (Butler and Clark, 1992, p. 169).

In the 1980s when rural areas began to receive vastly increased numbers of visitors, two main concerns arose. First, the alienation of land. For example, in Ontario the sale of Crown Land to non-residents was halted, and only leases were allowed for cottage developments because of similar pressures on shorelines. Second, the abuse of rural property through trespass and problems of owner liability (Ironside, 1971; Butler and Troughton, 1985; Conservation Council of Ontario 1975, in Butler and Clark 1992, p. 170). As a result, legislation in Ontario was amended in order to reduce owner liability and to limit access to private land (see Butler and Clark 1992, p. 170). Despite these developments, the major problems in southern Ontario continue to include trail route securement, non-permitted activities, and the need to provide compensatory payments to landholders. More than 20 years ago,

* Editor's note: The newly-elected UK governement has indicated that such a blanket policy may be introduced in 1998.

Troughton (1975) argued that there is much scope for Ontario to increase the supply of private land available for recreation by way of management agreements, but significant developments in this area have not been forthcoming. The situation is little different today.

Butler (1984) divided the positive and negative impacts which result from recreational activities into five categories: environmental economic, social, legal, and other (also see Cullington, 1981; Sanderson, 1982; Butler and Clark, 1992). These are included in Table 11.1, but with specific reference to recreational access to private lands. As in the UK (and Australia – see the following section), conflict in Canada tends to occur primarily as a result of differences in attitudes, demands and expectations concerning the purpose and use of rural lands by permanent residents and recreational users. For example, a study conducted in Cavan Township by Anslow (1994), reported that: (1) general public access to private land is virtually an unattainable goal largely because of landholder attitudes and concerns, and (2) there appears to be no correlation between increased access and improved land stewardship, an issue which requires further research.

People have limited time to pursue their recreational activities, and as they are in a sense 'on holidays', obligations and responsibilities which they may have ordinarily practised in the context of their home environment may be neglected. Problems such as littering, neglecting to close gates and disturbance of livestock do occur (Butler, 1984). To a recreationist who may or may not return to the area again, these problems may not seem of great significance. However, to the landowners who have a commitment to the land and are often dependent on it for their livelihood, such problems can be antithetic to their primary interests of maximising the property's economic productivity (Butler, 1984). According to Sanderson (1982), landholders in Alberta do not consider recreational use of the land to be a major problem. Rather, they attribute many of the problems to ignorance and thoughtless disregard for private property (e.g., by way of vandalism) (Sanderson, 1982).

Australia: a case study of Central Western New South Wales

Participation in rural recreation in Australia has grown rapidly since World War Two, and particularly since the 1960s (Pigram, 1983). The rates of recreational participation have been affected by such factors as greater available leisure time; higher disposable incomes; increased mobility of people (by way of the development of private motor vehicles and other forms of transportation); the influence of commercial interests; the promotion of high-risk recreational activities; emphasis on health and fitness programmes; increasing environmental awareness; and a growing focus on human services (Pigram, 1983; Parker and Paddick, 1991).

Several writers have drawn attention to the lack of research and substantive results in rural recreation and tourism studies, and especially the absence of sound theoretical frameworks in Australia (Pigram and Jenkins, 1994) and overseas (see Butler and Clark, 1992). In Australia, research in rural recreation and tourism has attracted only spasmodic interest (Pigram and Jenkins, 1994). Landholders' attitudes to public recreational access is one aspect of rural recreation which requires much more research attention. According to Pigram (1981, p. 111), in Australia,

Table 11.2 Trespass damage in New South Wales

Damage category	Number reporting (n = 38)
Gate problems	30
Fire hazard	34
Litter	34
Shooting	35
Stock disturbance	28
Violence/vandalism	23
Theft	19
Other	28

Source: Graziers' Association of New South Wales, 1975 in Pigram (1981: Vol. 21.1, 118). Reproduced with permission.

> the concept of inviolate rights of property is widespread and generally acceptedè ... Landowners generally regard access to private land for sport and recreation as a privilege, not a birthright, which may be earned by good behaviour and responsibility. The landholders' attitude is typified by this statement made by the Graziers' Association of New South Wales: 'This Association will not consent to accept the entry upon private land, without the permission of owners or occupiers, of any persons who are not performing a statutory function, as other than trespass'.

As part of its submission to the NSW State Government Committee of Enquiry into the fishing industry, the Graziers' Association of New South Wales (1975) conducted a survey of its members in order to obtain factual evidence to substantiate objections to easing entry on private lands. Permission to enter private lands was granted by less than 50 per cent of rural landholders, and these cases were dependent on specific conditions being met. According to the study, graziers were concerned about guns, dogs, litter, gates, unattended fires, and disturbance to stock. Further enquiries indicated that the farmers' reservations concerning public access were justified as 'evidence gathered covered a wide range of damaging incidents and potentially dangerous situations' (Graziers' Association of New South Wales, 1975, in Pigram, 1981, p. 117–118) which are summarised in Table 11.2.

Following this report the Committee of Enquiry supported the view that 'it would be a major and serious departure to in any way interfere with the rights of property owners... by allowing free public access for whatever purpose' (Pigram, 1981: 118).

A 1987 study of landholder attitudes toward public recreation access to private rural land in North-Western NSW reported on the substantial reluctance of landowners to permit such access. Only 20 per cent of respondents were willing to allow access to the wider public (ie. excluding friends and relatives), while only 21.6 per cent showed any willingness to even consider possible government measures to improve the access situation (Corfield, 1987).

In late 1995, the authors undertook surveys of rural landholders in the Shires of Blayney and Cabonne, central western NSW (see Figure 11.1). The following section outlines the study aims, research method and some of the findings of that study.

Study aims

The aim of the study was to examine rural landholder attitudes to recreational access to private lands in NSW. It was designed to assist in the identification of barriers to recreational access to private lands, the reconciliation of conflicts in the recreational use of private lands, and to enhance the spectrum of recreational opportunities in the countryside.

Given these broad aims, the specific objectives of the study were:

• to identify rural landholder attitudes to recreational access;
• to identify the underlying dimensions which explain those attitudes, and therefore to determine whether attitudes differ because of ownership, land tenure, government incentives, income and other arrangements;
• to review the systems of incentives and disincentives under which landholders are operating; and
• to identify means of ameliorating rural land use conflict by way of incentives and removal of disincentives identified by landholders.

The study is significant because it is one of few studies (and statistically the largest), to address the subject of rural landholder attitudes to public access to private lands for recreation in Australia (also see Pigram, 1981; Corfield, 1987).

Study method   A systematic random sample of 200 landholders in Blayney Shire (response rate 51 per cent) and 500 landholders in Cabonne Shire (response rate 54 per cent) were selected from lists of landholders whose properties were designated 'farmland'. Lists of landholders were provided by the Blayney and Cabonne Shire Councils. Only landholders whose properties were designated 'farmland' were included in the sample. A mail out pilot study of 20 respondents in Blayney and 50 in Cabonne (response rate with one mail out – 38 per cent) was undertaken in October, 1995. Subsequent, minor alterations were made to survey content and presentation.

Section 493 of the Local Government Act, 1993, requires that NSW local councils categorise land into one of four categories – 'farmland', 'residential', 'business' or 'mining'. The definition for each category is contained in that Act. Section 515(1) of the LGA sets out the prerequisites for occupied land to be categorised as 'farmland'. Section 519 facilitates the categorisation of vacant land and it should be noted that scope exists for vacant land to be categorised as 'farmland' in certain circumstances via those provisions.

For land to be categorised as 'farmland' in terms of section 515 it must be a parcel of rateable land, valued as one assessment, the dominant use of which is for farming (that is, the business or industry of grazing, animal feedlots, dairying, pig-farming, poultry farming, viticulture, orcharding, beekeeping, horticulture, vegetable growing, the growing of crops of any kind, forestry, or aquaculture within the meaning of the Fisheries Management Act, 1994, or any combination of those businesses or industries) which has a significant and substantial commercial purpose or character, and which is engaged in for the purpose of profit on a continuous or repetitive basis (whether or not a profit is actually made).

Study findings and discussion

Respondents were predominantly males (Blayney – 70.5 per cent; Cabonne – 78.9 per cent), which in itself raises questions of gender distributions in land ownership and attitudes with respect to access; and 40 years of age or more (Blayney – 89.6 per cent, over a third of whom were 60 years of age or more; Cabonne – 82.4 per cent, of whom nearly 30 per cent were 60 years of age or more). Respondents' levels of education attained, occupation, and membership of leisure or sporting organisations are shown in Tables 11.3, 11.4 and 11.5.

In response to the question 'Do you or would you allow any members of the public to use your land for recreational purposes?', 73 per cent of respondents from Blayney and 63 per cent of respondents from Cabonne replied 'No'. The most popular reasons cited for denying access were:

- damage to crops;
- disturbance of stock;
- failure to shut gates;
- littering and associated problems;
- vandalism to property; and
- indiscriminate shooting.

Table 11.3   Membership of leisure and sporting organisations

Element	Cabonne Results (%)	Blayney Results (%)
Yes	37.143	38.043
No	62.857	61.957
Total	100.00%	100.00%

Table 11.4   Main occupation

Occupation	Cabonne Results (%)	Blayney Results (%)
Farmer	67.355	61.957
Retired	3.719	3.261
Professional	14.050	17.391
Trade	2.479	2.174
Clerical	2.066	3.261
Home duties	3.306	7.609
Unemployed	0.000	0.000
Social Services	0.000	0.000
Student	0.413	0.000
Other	6.612	4.348
Total	100.00%	100.00%

Table 11.5 Highest level of education attained

Level	Cabonne Results (%)	Blayney Results (%)
Primary School	2.834	11.828
High School	37.247	46.237
TAFE/College certificate	21.457	17.204
TAFE/College diploma	8.502	2.151
University diploma	8.907	2.151
University degree	12.955	11.828
University post-graduate degree	4.858	6.452
Other	3.239	2.151
Total	100.00%	100.00%

The problem of access is also manifested in people using property without landholder permission. In response to the question 'Have you ever had any members of the public use your land for recreational purposes without your permission?', 61 per cent of respondents from Blayney and 60 per cent of respondents from Cabonne replied 'Yes'.

Perhaps unsurprisingly, and reflecting, in part, the findings of earlier studies, landholders in Blayney and Cabonne expressed little or no interest in entering into incentives or agreements for recreational access to their property with the following:

- the then Labor Federal government (86.8 per cent in Blayney and 81.4 per cent in Cabonne respectively) (in March, 1996, the conservative Liberal/National Party coalition ascended to power);
- the then NSW Department of Land and Water Conservation (86.8 per cent and 78.9 per cent);
- the NSW National Parks and Wildlife Service (80.4 per cent and 80.2 per cent);
- Local government (81.1 per cent and 76.3 per cent); and
- private recreation organisations (81.3 per cent and 76.5 per cent).

Contrastingly, a number of conditions hold some promise as means of encouraging recreational access to private land. Positive ('Yes') responses to the question 'Would any of the following conditions encourage you to allow or increase public access to your land for recreational purposes' were as follows:

- only certain types of recreational activities be allowed (25.8 per cent in Blayney and 33.3 per cent in Cabonne respectively);
- that activities be confined to a particular area of your property (26.1 per and 30.6 per cent);
- that activities be limited to set times of the day (19.8 per cent and 21.6 per cent);
- that activities be limited to certain seasons (24.1 per cent and 24.3 per cent);
- that people arrange times with you (30.3 per cent and 35.8 per cent);
- that you can prevent people from undertaking recreational activities if the conditions you agreed to are not being kept (42.7 per cent and 46.1 per cent);
- that legal liability not rest with the landholder (40.7 per cent and 45.8 per cent); and

Table 11.6 Landholders' comments

- The bible says to forgive your trespasses. We don't. We shoot the bastards.
- Government should provide the land for public recreational activities, for example, State forests...the farmers and landholders have a big enough responsibility just surviving.
- A lot of people have no idea about farming. If they come onto your place they are just as likely to drive over new crops etc and do damage or get bogged and then you have to pull them out. Irresponsibility with fire is our major fear, dog control also worries us.
- Most people that visit the property are honest and attempt to do the right thing. We are concerned about the small number of less civic minded souls who do on occasion turn up. They ruin the property, owner's confidence and trust and make one wary of strangers in general.
- If we were to adopt a socialist agenda it must apply to all urban and rural lands, i.e., open house to all. This must be a decision by all people to affect all people not just a minority ie rural landholders.
- We feel that private property should be just that. Access on invitation only.
- Once access is given it's very hard to stop people – they think that they have an inalienable right to your place.
- Would you like people camping in your garden without permission?
- Surely there is enough land controlled by crown lands to satisfy the bush walkers, etc. without the farmers of Australia having to put up with yet another intrusion into their privacy.
- Have you asked these questions of town or suburban land owners?
- Having been burgled... to the extent of $15,000, I am now very reluctant to draw any attention to our remoteness, as we are not in residence permanently.
- I am entitled to have quiet enjoyment of my own land. This is given by the Law of the Land and must be retained unless I choose to give up those rights.
- Would you like the general public camping and walking around your front yard?... we like our privacy as much as city dwellers.

- that people pay for using your property for recreational purposes (20.7 per cent and 25.2 per cent).

Clearly, the ability of landholders to regulate recreational activities and the absence of legal liability of farmers for people who use lands for recreational activities appear to be aspects which (1) warrant further research, and (2) present potential public policy avenues for increasing recreational access to private lands.

This study indicates that there is much resistance, if not direct opposition, to the use of private rural lands for public recreation in the Blayney and Cabonne shires (Table 11.6 provides examples of comments that were far from supportive). Earlier studies (Graziers' Association of New South Wales 1975; Pigram, 1981; Corfield, 1987) indicate similar findings in other areas of NSW. Nevertheless, there are avenues for increasing recreational access to private rural lands. In short, the results of the surveys in the Blayney and Cabonne Shires largely support the findings of Corfield (1987) and reflect some of the concerns raised in Canadian studies. The views of respondents largely reflect those views expressed almost twenty years earlier in the Submission of the Grazier's Association of NSW.

Conclusion

> Leisure has become a vital part of the lives of all Australians; in an increasingly
> complex society, the task of creating and enhancing leisure environments will call
> for many fresh initiatives. At the same time, participation in outdoor recreation is
> very much a function of available opportunities. The challenge of rural
> accessibility planning is to expand the supply of opportunities by enlarging the
> space-time prisms available for outdoor recreation. Perhaps access to countryside
> is a good place to begin (Pigram, 1981, pp. 122–123).

Whatever one's stance on the issue of public access to private lands, and there are
diverse opinions with respect to landholders' rights, more empirical research on this
issue is needed in Australia, and indeed in the UK and Canada, particularly with
respect to how and why landholder attitudes vary spatially and even with respect to
land tenure. Unfortunately, however, with the increasing emphasis on economic
returns on public sector investment, and with well established rural land ownership
rights and ethics, particularly in Australia, much rural recreation research and
planning is likely to remain conservative and unimaginative, lacking in sound
theoretical frameworks, and tied mainly to tangible initiatives.

Unfortunately, we are likely to see policy-making and planning with respect to
recreational access to private rural lands remain somewhat neglected but complex
issues. Yet, such access goes to the core of landholder rights, perceptions and
attitudes, characterised by entrenched values and interests, which relate, in part, to
inviolate rights, and therefore the right to exclude. Yet we should raise several
critical questions. Is the concept of inviolable rights attaching to land ownership
appropriate to lands in private ownership? Should policy-makers take care 'that land
is used to satisfy the needs of the majority and not of the few with some special
interest [because] it is no more legitimate to advocate closing the countryside to the
population to avoid pollution or the loss of native flora and fauna than it is to close
the roads to motorists as a means of preventing car accidents' (Davidson, 1972,
p. 212)? Are landholders merely stewards or custodians of 'their' property, holding
and using it on trust for later generations?

Who does 'own' the land? Who does have a right to access? These questions are
being raised not just in limited circles with respect to recreational and tourist access
to private lands, but very much more widely with respect to indigenous land rights,
mining and other issues, such as heritage. Interestingly, in Australia, there is strong
opposition from landholders to Aboriginal land rights which have been upheld by
the High Court of Australia and supported, to different degrees in legislative,
institutional and policy developments, among the Australian States. In attempting to
reach solutions to these and other similar complex problems, Lowenthal's ideas are
worth recounting

> To be effective...planning and design should be grounded on intimate
> knowledge of the ways people think and feel about the environment; this calls
> for a substantial familiarity with social and intellectual history, with psychology
> and philosophy, with art and anthropology. All these fields contribute to our
> knowledge of how we see the world we live in, how vision and value affect
> action, and how action alters institutions (Lowenthal, 1968, in Mitchell, 1989,
> p. 144).

Interestingly, studying tourism, an often disputed or underrated discipline (Hall and Jenkins, 1995), and recreation issues offers a very useful position to contribute to our understanding of the ways people think and feel about their environment because the study of tourism and recreation is fluid and transcends disciplinary boundaries. Surely indigenous peoples want rights or access to 'their' land for recreational activities as much as the other aspects of their lives which seem to receive greater attention. The study of rural tourism issues, including research on landholder attitudes to public recreational access can, then, make a much wider contribution to our understanding of society than perhaps first appears.

References

Anslow M.C., 1994, Public access to private land in Cavan Township, Peterborough County: incentives, agreements, and attitudes, Unpublished Master's thesis, Trent University, Ontario.

Bull, C. and Wibberley, G., 1976, *Farm-based recreation in South-East England.* Studies in Rural Land Use No. 12, Countryside Planning Unit, School of Rural Economics and Related Studies, Wye College

Butler, R.W., 1984, The impact of informal recreation on rural Canada. In *The pressure of change in rural Canada.* Geographical Monograph 14, M.F. Bunce and M. J. Troughton, eds., Downsview, York University, Ontario.

Butler, R.W. and Clarke, G., 1992, Tourism in rural areas: Canada and the United Kingdom. In *Contemporary rural systems in transition: economy and society.* I.R. Bowler, C.R. Bryant and M.D. Nellis, eds., CAB International, Wallingford

Butler, R.W. and Troughton, M.J., 1985, *Public use of private land.* University of Western Ontario, London

Centre for Leisure Research, 1986, *Access to the countryside for recreation and sport: Report to the Countryside Commission and the Sports Council by the Centre for Leisure Research.* Countryside Commission, Cheltenham

Cloke, P. and Park, C., 1985, *Rural resource management.* Croom Helm, London

Conservation Council of Ontario, 1975, *Private land, public recreation and the law.* Conservation Council of Ontario, Toronto

Coppock, J.T. and Duffield, B.S., 1975, *Recreation in the countryside: A spatial analysis.* Macmillan Press, London

Corfield, R., 1987, *Recreational access to private rural land.* Unpublished Bachelor of Arts with Honours thesis, University of New England, Armidale

Countryside Commission, 1986, *Access to the countryside for recreation and sport: Report to the Countryside Commission and the Sports Council by the Centre for Leisure Research.* Countryside Commission, Cheltenham

Countryside Commission, 1990, *Countryside Commission News.* Sept/Oct. Countryside Commission, Cheltenham

Countryside Commission, 1991, *Countryside Commission News.* July/August. Countryside Commission, Cheltenham

Cullington, J.M., 1981, *The public use of private land for recreation.* Unpublished Master of Arts thesis, Department of Geography, University of Waterloo, Waterloo, Ontario

Curry, N., 1996, Access: policy directions for the late 1990s. In *Rights of way: policy, culture and management,* C. Watkins, ed., Pinter, London

Davidson, B.R., 1972, Agriculture and rural land use. In *Australia as human setting: approaches to the designed environment.* A. Rapoport, ed., Angus and Robertson, Sydney

Duffield, B. and Owen, M., 1970, *Leisure and countryside: a geographical appraisal of countryside recreation in Lanarkshire.* University of Edinburgh, Edinburgh

Glyptis, S., 1991, *Countryside recreation.* Longman, Harlow

Glyptis, S., 1992, The changing demand for countryside recreation, In *Contemporary rural systems in transition: economy and society*, I.R. Bowler, C.R. Bryant and M.D. Nellis, eds., CAB International, Wallingford

Graziers' Association of New South Wales, 1975, *Submission to select committee of the Legislative Assembly upon the fishing industry*, Graziers' Centre, Sydney

Green, B. 1977, Countryside planning: compromise or conflict? *The Planner*, **63**: 67–69

Groome, D., 1993, *Planning and rural recreation in Britain*, Avebury, Aldershot

Hall, C.M. and Jenkins, J. 1995, *Tourism and public policy*, Routledge, London

Ironside, R.G., 1971, Agriculture and recreation land use in Canada – potential for conflict or benefit? *Canadian Journal of Agricultural Economics*, **19** (2): 1–12

Mather, A., 1991, *Land use*. Longman Scientific and Technical, Harlow

Middleton, V.Y.C., 1982, Tourism in rural areas, *Tourism Management*, **3**: 52–8

Mitchell, B., 1989, *Geography and resource analysis*, 2nd. ed., Longman Scientific and Technical, Harlow

Parker, S. and Paddick, R., 1991, *Leisure in Australia: themes and issues*. Longman, Melbourne

Patmore, J.A., 1983, *Recreation and resources: leisure patterns and leisure places*, Basil Blackwell, Oxford

Pearce, D.G., 1989, *Tourist development*, Longman Scientific and Technical, Harlow

Perdue, R.R., Long, P.T. and Allen, L., 1987, Rural resident tourism perceptions and attitudes, *Annals of Tourism Research*, **14**: 420–9

Pigram, J.J., 1981, Outdoor recreation and access to the countryside: Focus on the Australian experience. *Natural Resources Journal*, 107–123

Pigram, J.J., 1983, *Outdoor recreation and resource management*, Croom Helm, London

Pigram, J. P. and Jenkins J.M., 1994, The role of the public sector in the supply of rural recreation opportunities. In *New viewpoints in outdoor recreation research in Australia*, D. Mercer, ed., Hepper Marriott and Associates, Williamstown

Ravenscroft, N., 1996, New access initiatives: the extension of recreation opportunities or the diminution of citizen rights? In *Rights of way: policy culture and management*, C. Watkins, ed., Pinter, London

Robinson, G., 1990, *Conflict and change in the countryside*, Belhaven Press, London

Saddler, R., 1989, *National Parks Today*, **24**: 1–3

Sanderson, K., 1982, *Recreation on agricultural land in Alberta: summary*, Environment Council of Alberta, Edmonton

Shoard, M., 1996, Robbers v. revolutionaries: what the battle for access is really all about. In *Rights of way: policy, culture and management*, C. Watkins, ed., Pinter, London

Spink, J., 1994, *Leisure and the environment*, Butterworth-Heinemann, Oxford

Swinnerton, G.S., 1982, *Recreation on agricultural lands in Alberta*, Environment Council of Alberta, Edmonton

Troughton, M.J., 1975, Agriculture and the countryside. In *The countryside in Ontario*. M.J. Troughton, J.G. Nelson and S. Brown, eds., University of Western Ontario, London

Wall, G., 1989, *Outdoor recreation in Canada*, John Wiley, New York

Watkins, C., ed., 1996, *Rights of way: policy, culture and management*, Pinter, London

12 Wine tourism in Australia and New Zealand

C. MICHAEL HALL AND NIKI MACIONIS

Introduction

Wine and food have long been regarded as an important component of the tourist experience. However, despite the extent to which they are featured not only in tourism advertising and promotion at the destination or business level, and the extent to which they contribute to tourist attractions such as festivals, little has been written about the role that wine and food play in rural tourism development.

This chapter is divided into three main parts. First, it provides an overview of the way in which wine tourism has developed around the world and the manner in which it is integrated, or otherwise, into rural tourism product. Second, it will provide an analysis of wine tourism in Australia and New Zealand, two New World wine regions that have begun to place substantial emphasis on the possible interrelationships between the wine and tourism industries. Finally, the chapter will discuss the impediments towards viticultural and tourism linkages and the manner in which such impediments may hold lessons for attempts to better integrate tourism with other rural sectors, including agriculture.

Wine tourism

Wine tourism can be defined as visitation to vineyards, wineries, wine festivals and wine shows for which grape wine tasting and/or experiencing the attributes of a grape wine region are the prime motivating factors for visitors (Hall, 1996; Macionis, 1996). Although tourism is important for many wineries in terms of the ability to sell wine either directly to visitors through cellar sales or to place such customers on a direct mail order list but if mentioned at all, it is often seen in very disparaging terms with the implication being of course that those who are seriously interested in wine are not tourists (e.g., Bradley, 1982).

Visiting wineries, sightseeing, attendance at festivals, visiting other attractions, socialising, recreation and visiting friends and relatives are recognised as the main reasons for visiting wine regions (Reid, 1990; Tourism South Australia, 1991; Macionis and Cambourne, 1994; Maddern and Golledge, 1996). Maddern and Golledge also note that 72 per cent of winery visitors incorporate food related activities as part of their trip to the region. This motivation and focus is also recognised in the South Australian Tourism Plan 1996–2001 (South Australian Tourism Commission (SATC), 1996, p. 22), which aims to position South Australia as the Australian state for 'gourmet living' by 'encouraging working links between the tourism, wine and food industries'.

Specific motivations for visiting wineries include:

- sampling and purchasing;
- festivals and events;
- socialising with family and friends;
- country setting/vineyard destination;
- other attractions and activities;
- learning about wine and winemaking;
- eating at winery (restaurant, cafe or picnic);
- tour of a winery;
- meeting the winemaker; and
- entertainment (Macionis and Cambourne, 1994; Maddern and Golledge, 1996; SATC, 1996).

Within the context of the motivations of winery visitors and visitors to wine regions, wine tourism can be conceptualised in terms of an activity/destination hub model (Figure 12.1) (Macionis, 1996). In some cases, the motivations for engaging in wine tourism will revolve around the destination hub, where the wine region is the primary motivational factor. In other cases, the motivations will revolve around the activity hub, where the opportunity to engage in wine tasting is the primary motivational factor for participating in wine tourism, and where food, wine and gourmet experiences, educational opportunities, regional prestige, festivals and events, the rural setting and other attractions enhance or contribute to this activity experience. The destination and the activity are explicitly interconnected. As the *South Australian Tourism Plan 1996–2001* (1996, p. 10) stated: 'it's not only great wine – it comes from a special place'.

The notion of place plays an important part in both wine and tourism. As Dickenson and Salt observed: 'The geography of wine is an experience of place . . . Its production is intensely geographical, with wines being identified more by location than anything else' (1982, pp. 149, 159). For example, the concept of *terroir* is extremely significant in terms of French viticulture. No precise English equivalent exists for the term. However, major elements are climate (from macro through to meso), sunlight, topography, pedo-geomorphology, and hydrology (Dickenson, 1990). The concept of *terroir* is important because it underlies the notion of appellation control which is a form of geographical delimitation which seeks to establish a distinctive identity for the wine that is produced within a specified region or place (de Blij, 1983). Elements of appellation controls include: production area, vine varieties, viticulture (including vine density, pruning regime, vine-training system, and irrigation), yields, grape ripeness, alcoholic strength, and wine making and distillation. The concept is extremely significant in world winemaking terms not just because of the influence of French wine and wine making but because of the development of European Union agricultural and wine policies and consequent development of international accords on labeling requirements which may serve to reinforce regionality in wine.

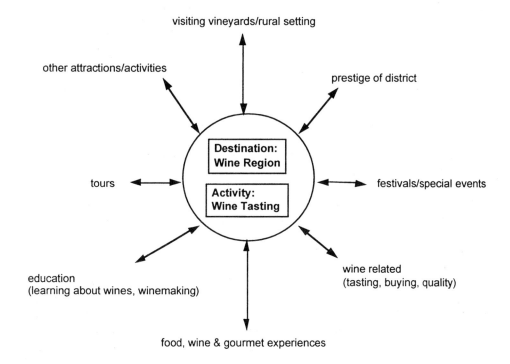

Figure 12.1. Activity/destination hub model for wine tourism

Ideas of place or *terroir* associated with wine are also related to notions of cultural and regional identity. As de Blij (1983, p. 1) notes

> viticulture is the most expressive of all agricultural industries. Not only does it involve considerations of climate and soil, the availability of water and threat of disease, local and regional methods of cultivating the vine and widely varying harvesting practices; the geography of viticulture also extends to the development of distinct cultural landscapes and the perpetuation of regional traditions.

It is this cultural landscape, de Blij argues, that gives identity to a region. Wine and food can therefore be expressive of regional culture as well as a regional environment. Such a relationship is extremely significant for tourism because of the possibilities of utilising wine and the associated vineyard landscape as a means of establishing a strong regional identity in the tourism marketplace. However, while the destinational appeal of wine regions and wineries is generally acknowledged, very little research has been conducted on wine tourism development, marketing and impacts (Hall, 1996; Macionis 1996).

In her standard work on wine, Robinson (1994) records that

> Wine-related tourism has become increasingly important. For many centuries not even wine merchants traveled, but today many members of the general public deliberately make forays to explore a wine region or regions. This is partly a reflection of the increased interest in both wine and foreign travel generally, but

also because most wine regions and many producers' premises are attractive places. Vineyards tend to be aesthetically pleasing in any case, and the sort of climate in which wine is generally produced is agreeable during most of the year. Getting to grips with this specialist form of agriculture combines urban dwellers' need to commune with nature with acquiring privileged, and generally admired, specialist knowledge. And then there is the possibility of tasting, and buying wines direct from the source, which may involve keen prices and/or acquiring rarities (1994, p. 980).

Visits to vineyards have been a part of organised travel at least since the time of the Grand Tour, and likely even since the times of ancient Greece and Rome (Vandyke Price, 1985). However, it was not until the mid-nineteenth century that wine began to appear as a specific travel interest. Several factors came together at this time. First, the transport revolution created by the development of the railways. Second, a social revolution in terms of the growth of a wealthy middle-class that sought to emulate some of the 'refinements' of the aristocracy. Finally, the publication of the 1855 *Classification of the Wines of the Gironde*. This classification, which had government sanction, of the wines of Bordeaux, was the result of recommendations made by the Syndicate of Bordeaux Wine brokers for use during the Paris Exhibition of 1855 (de Blij, 1983). The classification served as the basis for the system of appellation control which exists to this day in France, but not only did it reinforce the quality and regional characteristics of Bordeaux wine, it also served to provide a marketing tool for the region and identified specific chateaux as possessing classified growths which in themselves became visitor attractions.

The development of wine roads

Of more explicit relation to tourism is the system of wine trails or roads which have been established in Europe. Wine trails have been a part of the German tourism industry since the 1920s. According to Johnson (1986, p. 158) the *weinlehrpfad* (instructional wine path) 'help to explain and therefore sell German wine, and by the end of the 1970s practically all the eleven wine regions had their own *Weinstraßen* [wine roads]'. More recently, Eastern European countries, such as Hungary, have begun to establish wine trails in an effort to attract Western European tourists. For example, Hungary's first wine road, the Villány Siklós Wine Road, was established in Baranya county in 1995 (Tourinform Baranya, nd). Similarly, Portugal has begun to develop wine routes in regions, such as the Alentejo, in order to develop wine related cultural and rural tourism (ATEVA, nd), while wine routes are being established in Languedoc-Roussillon in France in order to increase the value of viticulture to the economy through tourism (Comté Régional du Tourisme de Languedoc-Roussillon Prodexport, 1994).

Many of the wine trails and routes in Europe are being developed with the assistance of the Europäische Weinstrassen (European Council of Wine Routes) based in Bordeaux. The Council is an organisation which is incorporated within the European Council of Wine Regions (Assembleia das Regioes Europeias Viticolas (AREV)) which was created within the framework of the Dyonisos multimedia network of European wine producing regions which was established in 1992 with European Community support and now encompasses more than 60 European wine regions. The goal of Europäische Weinstrassen is 'to improve the quality of the service of all wineries on the trails, while at the same time promoting the individual characteristics of the wineries' (translated from Europäische Weinstrassen, nd). According to the Europäische Weinstrassen:

> For the region which establishes a winetrail, it is the best framework for cooperative work between government, private enterprises and associations, the tourism industry, wine and the local council. It is a productive factor, which harnesses the energies of all involved with regional development, for the benefit of creating jobs and economic and cultural development. It is one of the best means to stimulate the activities of the local environment which would otherwise suffer from the decline in the rural market and migration from the country (for economic reasons).
>
> An opportunity exists for the winegrower to establish advantageous connections and a strategically important means of obtaining trade in high quality produce which encourages the development of direct sales and levels of awareness, and consolidates the image of products as well as creating a loyal consumer market (translated from Europische Weinstrassen, nd, p. 1).

Various regions have also established wine tourism and wine trail organisations. In Italy, the Movimento del Turismo del Vino (Wine Tourism Association), founded in 1993, has the mission to increase the flow of visitors to the sites where wine is produced, 'on the strong belief that wine cellars can attract visitors like a museum or a resort' (Movimento del Turismo del Vino, 1995). With over 450 members in nearly all of the country's wine producing regions, the Association argues that wine tourism has many positive effects:

- it increases chances of economic development, product diversification and new occupational levels in the wine areas;
- it helps teach people how to discover the right wine. It deepens the knowledge of wine, and allows the understanding of the different flavours and perfumes;
- it increases the image and the reputation of Italian wines, especially of the high quality ones;
- it increases the commercial capabilities of wine cellars both in direct sales and through ordinary distribution channels;
- it promotes rural areas as a unique mixture of environmental, cultural and productive components, and contributes to the discovery and protection of the ancient traditions of rural villages; and
- it suggests new tourist destinations adding value to landscapes, foods, art of the Italian wine counties, creating a good opportunity to meet people of these areas (Movimento del Turismo del Vino, 1995).

The development of wine routes and trails has also been substantial in new world wine regions, such as South Africa and North America. In the United States and Canada the interdependence between wine and tourism is explicitly recognised in several areas. The Indiana Wine Grape Council reported US$1.8 million in wine sales to tourists in 1993, while estimates of regional wine tourism expenditure range from US$30 million per annum for the Long Island, New York, wine region to US$75 million per annum for Oregon (Moynahan, 1995; Oregon Wine Advisory

Board, 1995), which promotes its Pinot Noir wines through the hosting of an annual Pinot Noir festival. The Napa Valley in California is probably the foremost wine region of the United States in terms of wine tourism promotion. It holds a series of festivals in the region, possesses a well-established system of wine trails and wine tours, and actively utilises wine promotion in imaging the region as a tourist destination (for further information see http://www.freerun.com/napavalley/mwinerie.html).

The North American and European experiences indicate (1) the potential economic contributions that wine tourism can make to rural communities, and (2) the varied recognition by government of the potential linkages between wine and tourism. Indeed, despite its long history as a wine region, it was not until 1993 that Languedoc-Roussillon (France), launched a tourism strategy to develop new products in its historic towns and countryside, which included a focus on the rich cultural heritage, gastronomic tradition and celebrated wines of the region (Klemm, 1996). The somewhat belated recognition of wine tourism as a significant element in rural tourism is not isolated to Europe. Tourism and wine have long been perceived as separate and unrelated industries in Australia and New Zealand.

Wine tourism in Australia and New Zealand

The Australian wine industry

From the beginning of European settlement, the pursuit of viticulture and wine making was an important aspect of Australia's culture. After 200 years, the Australian wine industry has become a major rural industry. In 1993, Australia was ranked tenth amongst the major wine producing countries of the world, producing 1.8 per cent of the volume of the total world production of 25,927 mega-litres. In 1994/95, the total wine grape crush totaled 629,883 tonnes, and is projected to increase to in excess of 800,000 tonnes in 1996/97 (Deves, 1995). In 1994/95, the industry recorded wholesale sales of around $114 billion, with exports valued at around $370 million. The Winemakers' Federation of Australia (1996) reports that 1995/96 export earnings increased to Aus.$450 million.

In 1996, there were 892 wine producers in Australia, an increase of approximately 11 per cent since 1994, located in every State and Territory. Of these 892 wine producers, 739 have cellar door outlets (Deves, 1995). An analysis of winery size by categorising them according to tonnage crushed, shows that the industry is dominated by two categories: very large and very small. Of the 892 wineries in Australia, 450, or just over 50 per cent, crush less than 50 tonnes (many with a crush of typically less than 20 tonnes), with only 32 wineries crushing more than 10,000 tonnes (Committee of Inquiry into the Winegrape & Grape Industry in Australia, 1995; Deves, 1995). Table 12.1 provides a breakdown by State of total number of wine producers, cellar door distribution, and each State's percentage of national wine production.

While the wine production figures may be impressive, they hide the fact that four major companies control the vast bulk of wine production in Australia. Nevertheless, it is the small, 'boutique' wineries, with their emphasis on cellar door sales, which continue to provide the greatest impetus to wine tourism.

Table 12.1 Distribution and total number of wine producers in Australia 1996

State/territory	Major regions	Total number of wine producers	Number of cellar door outlets	Percentage of national production
NSW	• Hunter Valley • Riverina • Mudgee • Cowra/Young	162	142	19.4
ACT	• Murrumbateman /Hall/Bungendore	16	13	0.05
Victoria	• Central Victoria • Western Victoria • North East Region • Yarra Valley • Mornington Peninsula • Geelong • Murray River Valley • Gippsland	274	227	30.2
QLD	• Primarily Stanthorpe Area	29	29	0.1
South Australia	• Adelaide Hills & Plains • Barossa & Eden Valleys • Clare Valley • Coonawara • McLaren Vale • Murray Valley • Eyre Peninsula	211	170	48.5
Northern Territory	• Alice Springs	1	1	–
Western Australia	• Margaret River • Great Southern • Swan Valley • North-east Perth, South-west Coastal, Pemberton, Perth Hills	149	117	1.4
Tasmania	• Pipers River • Tamar Valley • 5 smaller regions	50	40	0.17
Total		892	739	100

Source: Deves 1995

The emergence of wine tourism is the result of several catalysts, which significantly increased the accessibility and appeal of wine to the Australian public. A continued physical expansion of the Australian wine industry resulted in the development of new wine growing regions and the appearance of new varieties and styles of wine. The influence of cultural factors such as post-war immigration and greater exposure to European lifestyle broadened the appeal of wine as a lifestyle product. Coupled with marketing and technological innovations such as the 'bag in the box' or wine cask, and a generally increasing level of affluence in Australian society, these factors led to the 'wine boom' of the 1950s and 1960s which strengthened markets both quantitatively and qualitatively (Renwick, 1977).

The boutique winery boom

In 1963, Max Lake established his *Lake's Folly* winery in the Hunter Valley in New South Wales, the first new winery in the region since the Second World War. With this he became the first of many hundreds of what James Halliday refers to as 'weekend winemakers', who established their own vineyards and wineries for lifestyle reasons above economics. These adventurous new winegrowers, growing grapes and making and selling wines, on a small scale, and with a personal touch and flair heralded and, ultimately, constituted the 'boutique boom' (Rankine, 1989).

The significance of Max Lake's vision cannot be overstated. With the production of his first foot-trodden wine in 1966, and then his first commercial vintage in 1967, he showed that even a rank amateur could establish a winery in Australia and produce a reasonable wine. In the words of James Halliday, Max Lake 'had not so much rubbed Aladdin's Lamp, he had opened Pandora's box' (Halliday, 1995, p. 26).

By the 1970s, the destinational and recreational appeal of the wine industry in the Hunter Valley was beginning to receive some recognition. Wilson (1972, p. 10) reported that 48 per cent of visitors to the Cessnock, Maitland and Kurri areas listed visiting vineyards as the primary purpose of their trip. He further noted that these areas 'could benefit from a greater number of visitors' and that 'this affords an inducement for local authorities to provide greater amenities where needed and to generally promote the attractions of these areas'. Renwick (1977, p. 4) was even more positive about the effects of the boutique boom:

> the vineyards of the Hunter Valley are to be treasured and promoted for their aesthetic and recreational values, as well as for economic and financial reasons...
> In addition to passive recreation, the vineyards of the Hunter region also offer active leisure and tourism attractions, bringing people to the region as well as entertaining the resident population. The spin off to other businesses is self evident, and it would not be ambitious to claim that vineyard visiting has become the largest new recreational and tourist activity of the region during the last decade.

Renwick (1977, p. 1) did note however that for the wine industry to be sustainable there needs to be a 'reduction of acreage, control of production, reduction of winery facilities [and a] reduction of winery facilities (probably down to about 8 wineries for the region)'.

The growth in small-scale wineries was not restricted to the Hunter region; all over the country there was a proliferation of small 'boutique' wineries. 'It was almost as if every prosperous person who had ever sipped a glass of wine wanted their own vineyard' (Beeston, 1994, p. 238). For instance, in the 1960s, in Victoria, Reg Egan established Wantrina, in what is now the Yarra Valley wine region. Balgownie winery emerged around Bendigo, and the Seftons established their Idyll Vineyard near Geelong.

A new wave of boutique winemakers also emerged in South Australia with the first Redman's of Coonawarra vintage in 1966, St Halletts in the Barossa Valley in 1967, and the establishment of wineries such as Wirra Wirra in McLaren Vale in 1968. At the same time, new wineries such as Vasse Felix, Moss Wood and Plantagenet were emerging in Western Australia (Halliday, 1995).

The 1970s witnessed the continued growth of the boutique winery phenomenon. Victoria continued its winery resurgence with the establishment of the Goulburn Valley, the Pyrenees and the Mornington Peninsula regions as wine producing districts, and rejuvenation of the North Eastern region around Rutherglen. New South Wales saw the rebirth of the Mudgee region with the establishment of wineries such as Botobolar and Montrose, as well as the first plantings in the Hilltops region around Young (Barwang and Nioka Ridge wineries). Canberra, the nation's capital, was also caught up in this boutique boom with the establishment of Lake George Vineyard and Clonakilla Winery in 1971. In 1972, the emergence of the boutique wine industry spread to Tasmania with the establishment of Piper's Brook near Launceston in the north of that State.

The Lake's Folly phenomenon extolled confidence in small wineries. These boutique wineries appealed to the Australian public because they presented the small winemaker as an underdog, competing against the anonymous face of large winemaking organisations. To the weekend visitor and tourist, the local wineries of large, national winemakers were often closed. The small boutique winery was 'winemaking with a human face' (Beeston, 1994, p. 220).

Despite the opinions of industry leaders of the time who dismissed the boutique boom as 'distracting the wine buying public from the major producers' (Beeston, 1994, p. 236), it is these small wineries involved in growing grapes and making and selling wines with a personal touch and flair, that are the driving force behind the burgeoning wine tourism industry. Although these small boutique wineries account for only a tiny percentage of the national crush (3 per cent in 1989), their approach and existence finds considerable sympathy with consumers who can relate to an individual winemaker in a small winery, and perhaps fulfill popular images of the 'romance' of winemaking as opposed to the reality of the large-scale, 'industrial' winemaking of the major companies. As a result, the small, boutique wineries have achieved an importance in the wine tourism industry far out of proportion to the volume of wine which they produce (Rankine, 1989; Halliday, 1995).

Recognition of the tourism potential of wine

By the 1980s the tourism potential of the wine industry was beginning to receive attention throughout Australia. In 1984, the Victorian Government's Economic and

Budget Review Committee commissioned a Report on the Wine Industry in Victoria, which, among other things, had in its terms of reference an evaluation of the wine industry's involvement in marketing and tourism, and an examination of Victoria's relative position to other States in terms of the wine industry's tourism potential (Victorian Parliament Economic Budget Review Committee, 1985). This report was the first comprehensive study of the Victorian wine industry and significantly (and prophetically), noted that: 'the committee believes that there is scope to develop a tourism policy for the Victorian wine industry and integrate this policy with State and regional tourism strategies' (1985, p. 181). It also provides an indication as to the nature of the fledgling wine tourism industry at this time. The Committee reported that while around 86 per cent of wineries participating in the inquiry 'allow and encourage the general public to visit', there was no consistent policy regarding opening times which could frustrate intended tourist visits, and went on to record that 'tourist facilities are relatively restricted at both small and intermediate wineries. Sales facilities, picnic areas and separate tasting rooms being the most frequently reported' (1985, p. 183).

The Committee of Inquiry expressed a concern that 'many small and intermediate wineries had not realised the potential of winery based tourist facilities' and that

> if wineries are to attract visitors, one way is to increase the range of facilities available – both sales facilities and special features. This would encourage not only increased private and family patronage, but also coach tours to those wineries with suitable facilities. Such developments would benefit the winery directly, and contribute to the growth of tourist related services in the region itself (1985, p. 186).

Nevertheless, the enquiry also indicated that assessment of visitation to Victorian wineries was difficult because 'in some cases it was clear that the winery had little, if any, idea of the breakdown of cellar door sales by wine type or of the number of visitors to the winery' (1985, p. 113). Furthermore, almost 50 per cent of Victorian wineries had either no record of visits, or had records which they admitted to being somewhat vague (1985).

The situation in the 1990s

Wine tourism is now being explicitly recognised as part of the Australian tourism product. In Australia, with only 25 per cent of domestic tourists and 30 per cent of international visitors venturing outside capital cities or major gateways (Langton, 1995), many regional areas are aiming to build upon the production of regional foods and wines to market new travel and destinational experiences. Wine tourism has therefore emerged as a strong and growing area of special interest tourism in Australia, and has become an increasingly significant component of the Australian regional tourism product. Australia's federal and State governments, and regional tourism associations are recognising the benefits of promoting their wine districts as tourism attractions in their own right.

Previous federal governments have supported regional wine tourism development through the Rural Tourism Development Program and the Regional Tourism Development Program (1993–1995). Projects funded included:

- the development of food and wine trails (Albury-Wodonga, New South Wales (NSW), and Geelong, Victoria);
- the building of wine interpretive and visitor centres (Barossa Valley and McLaren Vale, South Australia);
- the provision of signage systems for vineyard areas (Cessnock, NSW); and
- the development of food, wine and cultural tourism strategies (Barossa Valley, South Australia; Hunter Valley, NSW; Augusta-Margaret River, Western Australia).

In addition, the Australian Tourist Commission designated 1997 to be the 'Year of Good Living' concentrating on marketing Australia as a culinary tourism destination to overseas tourists.

In 1992, the Victorian State Government established the Victorian Wineries Tourism Council, to take advantage of Victoria's growing reputation as a wine tourism destination. With wine becoming one of the main foci of the tourism drive in South Australia (SA), the SA Government has followed suit with the formation of the South Australian Wine Tourism Council in 1996. According to the South Australian Premier, Dean Brown, 'wine tourism is there to be developed' and 'is going to be a big money earner for South Australia' (*Weekly Times*, 1995, p. 22). The South Australian Premier's support for wine tourism is reflected in that State's tourism marketing and promotion. The Chief Executive of the South Australian Tourism Commission, Michael Gleeson, for instance, stated that: 'we're so good at wine tourism we have made it the single most important focus for tourism in our marketing for the next two years' (Innes, 1996, p. 5).

The marketing opportunities of wine promotion are also being seen as having great potential in increasing the benefits of regional tourism in NSW. According to the NSW Tourism Minister, Brian Langton, 'NSW will embrace food and wine as an integral part of the visitor experience and the focus on food and wine will broaden the destinational appeal of NSW, and encourage more first time visitors to come back for seconds' (Langton, 1995, p. 3). Indeed, the 1996 NSW Tourism Week was designed to profile the food and wine hospitality sectors of the tourism industry, while Tourism New South Wales launched a strategy document on food and wine tourism in November 1996.

The economic significance of wine tourism in Australia

The Bureau of Tourism Research (BTR) (1996) estimated that 282,400 visitors, or almost 1 in every 11 international visitors, visited wineries during their stay in Australia in 1995. This represents an increase of 20 per cent from 1993 figures. Recent data from the BTR also indicates that 45 per cent of all international visitors to South Australia in 1995 visit the state's wineries (Ruberto, 1996). Other states' estimates of the size of the wine tourism market are also substantial. For example, Tourism New South Wales estimate that approximately 1.5 million domestic and international tourists will visit a winery in that state, while the Victorian Wine Tourism Council reported almost two million visits to Victorian wineries in 1994–95, generating almost Aus$120 million for regional Victoria (Macionis, 1996).

The Winemakers' Federation of Australia estimates total Australian wine tourism figures to be in the order of 5.3 million visits, worth $428 million in 1995 (Winemakers' Federation of Australia, pers comm., 1996). The value of wine tourism is expected to grow substantially to $1100 million by 2025 (Australian Wine Foundation, 1996). Although little systematic research is available, the regional impact of wine tourism may also be substantial. For example, in South Australia, the McLaren Vale Winemakers have estimated that the annual value of the region's wine tourism industry is in excess of Aus$50 million, of which Aus$8.7 million is attributable to wine sales alone. In New South Wales, the Hunter Valley Vineyards Association estimates annual visitation to the region's vineyards to be in excess of 500,000 visitors. Based on an average expenditure of Aus$246 per visitor, the total tourist expenditure generated by the wine industry is estimated at Aus$123 million per annum, with additional indirect expenditure of approximately Aus$158 million per annum (Committee of Inquiry into the Winegrape and Wine Industry, 1995).

In the Margaret River region of Western Australia, the presence of a wine industry is seen as being the major reason for tourists visiting the area. According to the Margaret River Wine Industry Association:

> Margaret River is the most visited tourism destination in Western Australia, recording over 158,000 visitors in 1993. This is the highest visitation rate of any bureau in the state. Of the visitors coming through the doors, it is estimated by bureau staff, close to 80 per cent of customers seek information about the vineyards (in Committee of Inquiry into the Winegrape and Wine Industry, 1995).

The nature and extent of tourist facilities at Australian wineries has also increased markedly during the last decade, with substantially more wineries now possessing cellar door and sales facilities, restaurant, catering, barbeque facilities and picnic areas. An analysis of tourist facilities at Australian wineries in 1996, segmented by State (see Table 12.2) indicates that the provision of basic visitor infrastructure at wineries, such as cellar door facilities, is similar for all States. This suggests similar levels of tourism involvement and development. However, it is interesting to compare the percentage of those which offer such facilities on weekends or by arrangement only. These figures are perhaps more indicative of the level of wine tourism development and involvement in each State, reflecting a longer or more sustained wine industry history (NSW, South Australia) or a greater tourism history or dependence, such as Western Australia, where in regions such as the Margaret River tourism has flourished because of the growth of the wine industry.

The development of organisational structures

In Australia the economic potential of wine tourism has been recognised at State government level (1) in terms of explicit promotion of wine tourism packages by State tourism commissions, especially New South Wales, South Australia, and Victoria, and (2) through the establishment of wine tourism organisations in South Australia and Victoria, to provide better coordination between the wine and tourism industries.

In 1993, the Victorian State Government formed the Victorian Wineries Tourism

Table 12.2 Tourist and visitor facilities at Australian wineries in 1995

Tourist visitor facilities	NSW		VIC		SA		ACT		QLD		WA		TAS	
	No.	%	No.	%	No.	%	No.	%	No.	%	No.	%	No.	%
Total number of wineries	162	100	274	100	211	100	16	100	29	100	149	100	50	100
Total cellar door	142	87.65	227	82.85	170	80.57	13	81.25	29	100	117	78.52	40	80.00
Cellar door open weekends or by arrangement only	32	22.53	98	43.77	20	11.76	8	61.54	5	17.24	33	28.21	18	45
BBQ	30	18.52	39	14.23	13	6.16	2	12.50	3	10.34	11	7.38	1	2.00
Tours	9	5.56	12	4.38	5	2.37	0	0	3	10.34	6	4.03	0	0
Function facilities	4	2.47	9	3.28	9	4.27	2	12.50	1	3.45	7	4.70	1	2.00
Festivals	2	1.23	1	0.36	0	0	0	0	0	0	3	2.01	0	0
Children's facilities (playground, etc)	4	4.27	8	2.92	6	2.84	0	0	1	3.45	4	2.68	0	0
Total restaurant/catering available weekends or by arrangement only	8	32.0	17	43.58	4	15.38	1	50.0	2	50.0	4	13.33	1	16.66
Accommodation	8	4.94	9	3.28	10	4.74	1	6.25	1	3.45	3	2.01	8	16.00
Picnic	12	7.41	31	11.31	19	9.00	3	18.75	3	10.34	9	6.04	2	4.00
Historic building/museum	14	8.64	25	9.12	35	16.59	1	6.25	0	0	5	3.36	4	8.00
Resort	1	0.62	1	0.36	0	0	0	0	0	0	0	0	0	0
Conference facilities	2	1.23	4	1.16	6	2.84	1	6.25	0	0	0	0	1	2.00
Craft/produce/gallery	11	6.79	2	0.73	18	8.53	1	6.25	0	0	13	8.72	0	0
Souvenirs	3	1.85	0	0	1	0.47	0	0	1	3.45	0	0	0	0
Other activities (golf, cricket, camel rides, fishing etc)	2	1.23	11	4.01	2	0.95	0	0	0	0	0	0	0	0
Visitor centre	0	0	2	0.73	0	0	0	0	0	0	0	0	0	0
Other wines (mead/fruit wine)	4	2.47	6	2.19	5	2.37	1	6.25	3	10.34	4	2.68	1	2.00
Disabled facilities	0	0	1	0.36	1	0.47	0	0	0	0	1	0.67	0	0

Council (VWTC), with the terms of reference of developing strategies to promote the wineries of Victoria as important State tourism assets and productions in their own right (Golledge and Maddern, 1994; Maddern and Golledge, 1996). South Australia followed suit in 1996, with the formation of the South Australian Wine Tourism Council, a joint wine and tourism body given the task of 'championing' wine tourism in SA and based on the successful VWTC model. While New South Wales has yet to institute a specific wine tourism body, it has constituted a Culinary Tourism Advisory Committee, which released a food and wine tourism development strategy in November 1996. The functions, aims and activities of these organisations are detailed in Table 12.3.

In a regional context the Australian wine industry is also organised around a number of regional winemakers' and grapegrowers' associations which are responsible for activities such as the organisation of wine shows and field days, industry representation and regional promotion (Deves, 1995). *Winetitles* lists the organisation of regional events and festivals as the responsibility of a number of these regional associations (Deves, 1995). However, it is interesting to recall the comments from a member of the MIA Winemaker's Association, who stated: 'yes, we organise and conduct a number of festivals throughout the year, but we don't really have anything to do with tourism'.

Nevertheless, several regional wine industry associations are quite proactive with regard to wine tourism development. For example, the activities of the Vineyards Association of Tasmania include the development and promotion of regional 'Wine Trails', participation in a Statewide calendar of events, and an appellation scheme which defines the authenticity and regionality of Tasmanian wines.

The Barossa Wine and Tourism Association Inc. details a number of wine tourism specific objectives in its business plan, including the development and encouragement of festivals and special events, branding the region as 'a taste for the good life' and developing and maintaining quality promotional material regarding wineries, events and attractions. The Augusta Margaret River Tourism Association and Margaret River Wine Industry Association list devising an inventory of winery tourism facilities, understanding winery visitor needs, improving the standard of cellar door services and facilitating and improving wine industry and tourism industry linkages and involvement as their main foci.

The Australian situation stands in contrast with that of New Zealand. Both countries have similar histories with respect to the development of wine regions, the importance of the export market for wine sales, and the use of tourism as a component of national economic restructuring, but formal recognition of the significance of wine tourism in New Zealand lags behind that of Australia.

The New Zealand wine industry

In New Zealand, the wine industry has been established for almost as long as in Australia but has only received substantial international recognition over the past decade. Similarly, the role that wine plays as a component of the country's tourism product is only just getting recognition.

The first grapes were probably planted in New Zealand by Samuel Marsden at

Table 12.3. Functions, aims and activities of State wine tourism bodies in Australia

Organisation/strategy	Victorian Wineries Tourism Council	South Australian Wineries Tourism Council	Tourism New South Wales 'food and tourism' plan
Year formed	1993	1996	1996
Mission	To increase the economic contribution to Victoria by increasing the number of visitors to Victoria's wineries and wine regions	Raising the profile and championing wine tourism in South Australia	To weave food and wine into every part of the tourist experience and its promotion
Priority aims and issues	1. Product development and regional tourism promotion through: • the production of promotional material such as Great Victorian Winery Tours Booklet • the development and marketing of a comprehensive calendar of events • the development of a conventions and events marketing strategy • supporting the development of regional festivals 2. Promotion of Victorian Wines • encourage participation and promotion of the wineries category of the Victorian Tourism Awards • Promote and support wine shows and festivals	1. Product development and infrastructure • ensure provision of appropriate development in wine regions, such as specialised accommodation and convention facilities • provide wine tourism education forums • develop tourism infrastructure and interpretive material in wine regions 2. Promotional activities • production of motivational brochures • extend visiting journalists' program • maximise the benefits of ATC is theme year of 'Good Living' (1997) • develop wine region positioning and branding activities such as SATC logo	1. To package and market food as an integral part of the tourism experience • feature the food and wine experience as a major component in packaging and promotional activities • promote industry and community awareness of culinary tourism • expand and enhance food and wine tourism experiences • explore food and wine visitation-based promotions and trade shows 2. Encourage the delivery of food and wine experiences • develop wine growing regions of centres for quality food, wine and experience

Table 12.3. cont.

Organisation/strategy	Victorian Wineries Tourism Council	South Australian Wineries Tourism Council	Tourism New South Wales 'food and tourism' plan
	3. Industry communication • develop a database of key wine and tourism bodies • develop and cultivate relationships with key industry publications and editors • support journalist familiarisation programs 4. Identify impediments to and opportunities for Victorian wine tourism • undertake research on tourism numbers	3. Research • identify wine tourism motivations and experience gaps • undertake competitive analysis 4. Develop attractions within wine regions • further develop wine-based festivals • develop facilities including restaurants, guided tours, and food and wine trails • establish a national wine centre	• develop achievement awards which recognise the development of quality food and wine tourism packages 3. Foster greater coordination and operation between the food, wine, agricultural and tourism industries • access appropriate sectoral experience • encourage cooperative marketing and wine tourism packages

Source: Macionis 1996. Reproduced with permission.

Kerikeri in the Bay of Islands on 25 September 1819 with vines that were brought from Port Jackson in New South Wales (Thorpy, 1971). The first recorded consumption of New Zealand wine was by the French explorer Dumont d'Urville who visited the vineyard of James Busby at Waitangi in 1840, proclaiming the light white wine to be 'delicious to taste' (Thorpy, 1971, p. 24; Cooper, 1993, p. 8). Coincidentally, Busby may also be regarded as the father of viticulture in Australia, planting a model vineyard of forty acres in the Hunter Valley in 1831 and publishing the first textbook on viticulture in the Southern Hemisphere in 1825 (Thorpy, 1971).

New Zealand wines have gone through many ups and downs since the time of Marsden and Busby (see Moran, 1958; Thorpy, 1971; Cooper, 1993; George, 1996). While the nineteenth century was full of hope for winemaking because of both the influx of experienced European winemakers and classic grape varieties, the dreams of the early settlers were shattered by diseases, pests and most significantly 'prohibitionist zealots' (Cooper, 1993, p. 8) for most of this century. It is only since the 1960s that there has been a substantial push from within the wine industry itself to aim to produce quality table wine.

Auckland was for long the focal point for grapegrowing in New Zealand. Then, as urban expansion intruded into the vineyards and as other areas expanded, Auckland became more of a centre of winemaking. Since the 1970s, the area of vines for producing table wine has been growing rapidly with considerable expansion in areas such as Canterbury, Hawkes Bay, Martinborough, Marlborough, Nelson and Central Otago. Indeed, it is worthwhile noting that Marlborough, the country's leading wine region, was only first planted in 1973. The Central Otago area, near the resort town of Queenstown, is currently the fastest growing wine region in the country, although admittedly it is starting from a small base. As in Australia, boutique wineries have been a major factor in the development of new wine regions. The state of the New Zealand wine industry is illustrated in Tables 12.4 and 12.5.

The first New Zealand wine to be exported was made in Wanganui in 1874. Nevertheless, the modern period of wine exporting did not commence until 1963 when the first exports of a Corbans' medium-sweet sherry were made to the British Columbia Liquor Control Board. Growth in export sales of table wine did not start to occur in substantial amounts until the early 1980s, although then, as now, the emphasis was on white wine. The primary overseas markets are Australia, North America, Sweden, Finland, Germany, Japan and the United Kingdom (UK). The UK is an especially important market for New Zealand with wine sales of NZ$40.6 million (7.4 million litres) for the year to June 1996, up from $26.6 million (5.3 million litres) for the previous 12 months (Dominion, 1996). In the UK, New Zealand wines have a strong quality and value image, led by Sauvignon Blanc, which can be regarded as the flagship wine which has paved the way for attention to be given to New Zealand chardonnays, sparkling wines and pinot noirs.

Wine tourism in New Zealand

One method of assessing the degree to which winery operations may be integrated with the tourism industry is to analyse the extent to which they have cellar door sales and possess visitor infrastructure such as cafes, restaurants, bars or accommodation.

Table 12.4 New Zealand wine industry statistics, 1985–1995

	1985	1986	1987	1988	1989	1990	1991	1992	1993	1994	1995
Total Vine Area (ha.)	6 000	4 500	n/a	4 880	5 437	5 800	5 980	6 099	6 680	8 039	8 293
Producing Area (ha.)	5 900	4 300	4 300	4 300	4 370	4 880	5 440	5 800	5 980	6 107	6 108
Average Yield (tonnes per hectare)	13.2	12.7	11.6	12.0	13.8	14.4	12.1	9.3	7.1	8.8	12.2
Tonnes Crushed	78 000	54 694	49 727	51 509	60 335	70 265	65 708	55 500	42 621	54 000	74 500

Source: After Wine Institute of New Zealand, various; Cooper, 1993; George, 1996

Table 12.5 New Zealand wine regions: area, production and tonnage 1994–1995

Region	Producing area (ha.) 1994	1995	% Change	Total vine area (ha.) 1992	1994	1995	% Change (94/95)	Production (tonnes)* 1994	1995	% Change
Marlborough	2 095	2 123	1	2 071	3 000	3 233	7	18 851	24 509	30
Hawke's Bay	1 642	1 776	8	1 614	2 268	2 276	0	15 116	20 632	36
Gisborne	1 427	1 356	-5	1 503	1 464	1 514	3	17 555	22 289	27
Canterbury	208	216	4	198	260	325	20	197	756	384
Wairarapa	188	189	0	189	275	271	-1	501	933	86
Auckland	248	215	-15	241	272	248	-9	1 185	1 874	58
Otago	48	47	-3	35	237	152	-56	125	168	34
Nelson	92	70	-32	81	102	137	25	366	683	87
Waikato/Bay of Plenty	159	118	-35	161	161	137	-18	505	617	22
Total	6 107	6 108	0	6 099	8 039	8 293	3	51 491	72 846	41

* Refers to the results of the New Zealand Wine Institute Annual Vintage Survey

Source: After Wine Institute of New Zealand, various; Cooper, 1993; Talmont, 1995; George, 1996

Table 12.6   New Zealand wine tourism 1995

Region	Wineries	Cellar door sales	%	Restaurants/ cafes/bars	%
Auckland	52	27	52	5	10
BOP/Waikato	10	6	60	3	30
Canterbury	20	11	55	7	35
Central Otago	7	5	71	1	14
Gisborne	9	6	67	1	11
Hawkes Bay	27	19	70	4	15
Marlborough	36	18	50	4	11
Nelson	9	7	78	3	33
Wairarapa	19	14	74	1	5
Total	193	116	60	29	15

Source: derived from Deves 1995

Table 12.6 provides an analysis of New Zealand wineries. Table 12.6 was derived from a content analysis of the *Australian and New Zealand Wine Industry Directory* (Deves, 1995) which provides a full breakdown of winery characteristics.

Approximately 60 per cent of New Zealand wineries offered cellar door sales in 1995 with a high of 78 per cent of wineries in the Nelson region and a low of 50 per cent in the Marlborough region. These figures are substantially below that of Australian wine regions in which, on average, approximately 80 per cent of wineries offer cellar door sales (Deves, 1995; Macionis, 1996), and also appear below that of the Washington wineries in the United States (Folwell and Grassel, 1995). However, the small number of wineries which have cafes or restaurants is similar to that of Australia. Other tourist attractions, such as art galleries, museums, and on-site accommodation exist in some regions, but the number of wineries which run such tourist operations is extremely small. However, in the case of some vineyards, e.g., Ponder Estate and Hunter's Wines in Marlborough, such complementary activities are an integral component of the visitor experience (Hall, 1996). Other wineries also utilise traditional features of European wineries to attract visitors by reinforcing the romantic image of winemaking. For example, Johanneshof Cellars winery in Marlborough and Gibbston Valley winery in Central Otago both have underground cellars for wine storage. Johanneshof Cellars were the first to develop their underground cellars and it has allowed them to continue to attract an increasing number of visitors particularly as it has been featured on two New Zealand television travel programmes. The tourism significance of the winery is such that it has also received a local tourism award. Nevertheless, it should be noted that the cellars at Johanneshof were constructed for practical wine storage reasons and not just for tourism, visitation being an incidental or secondary component of the development of the cellars.

There is also a substantial difference between various wineries as to the extent to which they attach importance to cellar door sales (Hall, 1996). Larger wineries, such as Montana, tend to perceive cellar door sales as a public relations exercise which does not contribute much either directly to sales or indirectly in terms of later purchasing behaviour. In contrast, smaller boutique wineries see cellar door sales as vital to their survival, particularly when they are geared primarily to the domestic market. For example, Johanneshof Cellars winery, noted above, relied on cellar door and mail sales for approximately 80 per cent of its sales in 1996. Indeed, they have made the personal contact available through cellar door sales an essential ingredient of their business philosophy:

> Although our decision not to enter any wine shows remains in place, Johanneshof Wines are now to be found in fine wine shops and restaurants from Auckland to Invercargill. Our preferred emphasis is still to maintain direct contact to you, our most favoured clients, through cellar door and mail order custom (Johanneshof Cellars, 1996).

For many boutique wineries, the cellar door sale is an opportunity to place customers on to a direct mail-order list and to create brand-loyalty amongst some of their customers because of the positive experience with winery personnel that may be provided. Even in the case of wineries which have built up substantial export markets cellar sales are regarded as important. For example, the Cloudy Bay winery in Marlborough regards wine tasting as an opportunity to further reinforce the quality image of its wine with both domestic and overseas customers and to generally play a role in customer education which may be regarded as being of benefit to the entire wine industry (Hall, 1996). Indeed, some regions have now developed substantial wine trails and an Automobile Association guidebook to the wineries and vineyards of New Zealand has now been produced (Talmont, 1995). However, while wine may feature in the branding and advertising of several destination regions (e.g., Central Otago, Hawkes Bay, Marlborough, Nelson, Waiheke Island), no regional wine tourism associations have been established as in Australia and there is relatively little integration between the wine and tourism industries.

The wine tourism market

Substantial confusion exists over who the wine tourists actually are. For instance, McKinna (1979, in Macionis, 1996) identified wine tourists as 'the passing tourist trade who thinks a "winery crawl" is just a good holiday', whereas McKenzie (1986, p. 7) describes wine tourists as wine buffs who seek out 'trendy, exclusive or almost unattainable wines direct from the producer'. Indeed, many wineries have very little knowledge of who their customers actually are, with research typically being focussed more on what goes in the wine bottle than the person(s) who consume it (Hall, 1996; Macionis, 1996).

From a series of interviews with winemakers, vineyard management and service staff, Hall (1996) identified three wine tourism market segments – 'wine lovers', 'wine interested', and the 'curious tourist'. Table 12.7 sets out some of the characteristics of these markets. The size of each market will depend on:

- the individual characteristics of each winery and wine region in terms of its accessibility;
- the profile of its wine;
- the types of wine produced;
- marketing and promotion;
- attractiveness; and
- facilities.

Table 12.7 Wine tourism market segments

Market segment	Characteristics
Wine Lovers	• Extremely interested in wines and wine making • Wineries may be sole purpose of visit to destination • May be employed in wine and food industry • Likely to be mature with high income and education levels • Likely to be regular purchaser of wine and food magazines, e.g. *Australian Gourmet Traveller, Cuisine, Wine Spectator, Vogue Entertaining* • Will have visited other wine regions • Highly likely to purchase at winery and add name to any mailing list
Wine interested	• High interest in wine but not sole purpose of visit to destination • Likely to have visited other wine regions • Familiar with wine making procedures • Moderate to high income bracket, tend to be university educated • 'Word of mouth' and wine columns in newspapers may be important for arousing interest in region • Occasional purchaser of wine and food magazines, regular purchaser of 'lifestyle' magazines • Likely to purchase at winery and add name to any mailing list • Potential for repeat purchase of wine through having visited winery
Curious Tourists	• Moderately interested in wine but not familiar with wine-making procedures • Winery tour a byproduct of visit to region as visiting was for unrelated purposes • Wineries seen as 'just another attraction' • May have visited other wine regions • Curiosity aroused by drinking or seeing winery product or general tourism promotion or pamphlets • Moderate income and education • Opportunity for social occasion with friends and/or family • May purchase at winery but will not join mailing list

Sources: interviews with wineries, tour operators, regional tourism organisations, and Macionis and Cambourne, 1994.

Interestingly, it may also depend on the interaction between the various markets. For example, during a series of interviews with wineries in the Marlborough and Martinborough wine regions in New Zealand (Hall, 1996), one of the most common factors to emerge was the extent to which large bus tours could serve not only to swamp a winery for little return but may also deter potential 'serious' wine consumers from sampling wine because of perceptions that the buses might be full of tourists who were there to 'drink' rather than 'taste' (Figure 12.2). Nevertheless, such problems can be alleviated, if not completely avoided, by sensitive tourism development. For instance, National Capital Wine Tours, the leading wine tour operator in the Australian Capital Territory, ensures a return to each winery visited

Figure 12.2.   Wine tourism at Te Kairanga Vineyard, Martinborough, New Zealand (C.M. Hall)

by paying a service fee, providing regional wines with the tour lunch and carefully scheduling tours so as to avoid conflict with other visitors and peak periods of the day.

Difficulties in managing the interaction between the wine markets segments may also extend to wine and food festivals and events. In the case of the Marlborough Wine and Food Festival in New Zealand, for example, the event has grown to such a stage that there is difficulty for the organisers in distinguishing what the event is actually aiming to achieve, i.e. educate and promote fine food and wine, which was the original goal of the event, or provide a party (Hall, 1996). Clearly, there can be a substantial overlap between the two, but given the desire of many stakeholders to promote the quality of Marlborough produce, the image of a large drunken party may not be the most conducive for the overall promotion of the region.

In the case of wine and food festivals, many regions increasingly seek to make the events more exclusive and focused on specific activities, e.g., 'Toast Martinborough' in New Zealand which seeks to integrate the wineries and music with Wellington restaurants which provide food out at the vineyard; and the 'Tour de Muscat' event at Rutherglen in Victoria, Australia, which is a cycling and tasting tour of the wineries. However, the proliferation of wine and food festivals and the difficulties this creates in promoting a clear image for each event in the marketplace is only one issue amongst several that face the development of wine tourism in rural Australia and New Zealand.

Conclusions

Just as the rapid growth of the Australian and New Zealand wine industries from the 1960s through to the present day has presented serious problems with regard to development and sustainability, so too has the growth of wine tourism. While the interdependence of the wine industry and the tourism sector is gaining increased recognition, tourism is essentially a secondary product for wine makers, and the wine industry in general. As a consequence, the Australian and New Zealand wine industries exhibit an almost exclusive product orientation with regard to product development and marketing. Additionally, wine tourism practitioners often suffer from a lack of know how, experience and entrepreneurial ability. As Gray (1981, cited in Macionis, 1996, p. 165) stated, wine makers must 'recognise that buying wine is a tourist experience, that is also a learning or entertainment experience, not just wine'.

In general, the concept of strategic marketing does not appear to be well understood within the wine industry (Spawton, 1986; Edwards, 1989). Spawton (1991 in Macionis, 1996) observed that 'marketing is perceived often, even by successful small wine companies and quite large family wineries, as something not for them' and noted that participants in panel discussions at the Wine 2000 Conference at Cambridge in 1990 'admitted to having a production oriented philosophy (with some implying that marketing was a dirty word)'. Such a conclusion is also supported by Welsh (1994), who reported that:

- the wine makers involved in his study described marketing in clear product terms;
- less than half of his study group could provide a reasonable definition of marketing (less than 10 per cent of his subjects engaged in market or consumer research);
- most wine makers had difficulty identifying any unique characteristics that might distinguish them from competitors and consequently had little understanding of the need for identification, development or promotion of true uniqueness; and
- few could accurately discern their core market segments.

In relation to this last point, Welsh recorded comments such as: 'I don't think that there is in our case [a core customer profile]', and 'your target audience?... that's got to be the biggest bloody question of the lot!' (1994, pp. 151–152). Nevertheless, market considerations should be of primary significance to wineries and wine tourism businesses at the local level and to those concerned with rural development at the macro level. As Gannon (1993, p. 58) asserted, 'development starts with marketing because the motor for marketing is customer needs. Therefore, product providers must understand the customer and the tourist features and benefits they seek'. Producers, whether they be in wine, tourism, or both, cannot sell a product unless there is market.

Of considerable concern to the development of wine tourism is the substantial lack of cohesion, understanding and integration between the wine and tourism industries. For example, the Augusta-Margaret River Tourism Association in Western Australia noted a general lack of co-operation between the wine and tourism industries: 'because of the wineries' primary focus on producing premium wines rather than facilities and secondly, because of the poor understanding of tourism operators about boutique wineries' (1994, p. 2).

The South Australian Tourism Plan (South Australian Tourism Commission 1996: 139) more explicitly notes the common wine industry perception of 'co-operative arrangements between the wine industry and the tourism industry benefit only the tourism industry', going on to state that 'if the way in which the wine and tourism industries currently operate in relative isolation to one another can be changed and a stronger working partnership forged, there will be simultaneous benefits to both industries'. While such issues are acknowledged by wine and culinary tourism bodies, such as the VWTC, SAWTC and the NSW Culinary Tourism Advisory Committee, the continued growth of wine tourism in Australia and New Zealand and its potential contribution to rural development appears very much dependent upon the encouragement of greater linkages between the wine and tourism industries. While government bodies at the regional and local levels are particularly important in creating and encouraging the development of networks between the wine and tourism industries under the wine tourism umbrella, the regional nature of both wine and tourism may also serve as a contributing factor to greater cooperation and integration.

Elements of the idea of appellation control, at least in terms of ensuring that wines labeled as coming from a particular region were at least picked and made in that region, may offer considerable potential with regard to regional branding and consequent destination identity in Australia and New Zealand.

In the case of a number of areas, such as Marlborough, Central Otago and Martinborough in New Zealand, for instance, or Coonawarra, Clare Valley, Yarra Valley, or Tamar Valley in Australia (Figure 12.3), it can be argued that not only do certain wine varieties convey distinctive regional characteristics but that the region also becomes a key element in the potential attractiveness of the wine in the marketplace, particularly in Europe, where regional branding may be regarded as a benchmark of quality. However, the identification of appellations is fraught with difficulties and controversies, not only because of the debate over where does one draw the line for the boundaries of any region but also because the effectiveness of such schemes may be questionable. Although in well-established wine producing countries, such as France and Portugal, it has created order and a systematic classification of wines, it has been suggested that they are not necessarily a reliable guarantee of origin or quality, and that they have stymied progress and produced a distorted picture of where the best wines are grown (Victorian Parliament Economic and Budget Review Committee, 1985). In Australia and New Zealand appellation or regional authentication schemes are largely voluntary or self-regulatory, with legislated European style authentication schemes often perceived to be inhibitory to industry development. A number of Australian wine regions, such as Western Australia, Victoria, Mudgee and the Hunter Valley have investigated and implemented authentication schemes (Victoria Parliament Economic and Budget Review Committee, 1985), but they have met with only limited success, primarily due to the high costs of administration and voluntary involvement. Furthermore, existing Food and Drug Standards regulations regarding wine labelling would need to be altered in order to develop strict appellation controls along the French model.

Nevertheless, there is a direct impact on tourism in the identification of wine regions because of the inter-relationships that may exist in the overlap of wine and destination region promotion and the accompanying set of economic and social

Figure 12.3 Visitors to a winery in the Tamar Valley, Tasmania (C.M. Hall)

linkages. Clearly, the potential for regional branding between the wine and tourism industries is an area which deserves substantially more research in the context of rural development, yet it may also be useful to note that such regional identification may also be carried over into other rural produce. Indeed, one possible area for examination is the role that regional authentication and identification schemes may play in ensuring quality tourism as well as wine and food product, as many people probably do not realise that, in France, appellations as regards to regional origin and quality exist for food as well (Crewe, 1993).

The inter-relationship between wine and tourism in terms of rural regions environment and culture is something which strikes to the core of contemporary economic and cultural debate about processes of globalisation and localisation (Hall, 1997). At a time of substantial restructuring in many of the world's rural regions, policy responses require the encouragement of greater linkages between industries and a greater ability to promote places in order to attract investment and visitors and encourage employment. Wine and tourism are two rural industries which have enormous potential to contribute to each other and serve as a strong base for the development of a healthy rural economy. Wine tourism provides just that opportunity. Unfortunately, however, the greatest barrier to such developments often remains the failure of the wine and tourism industries to understand and work with each other.

Acknowledgements

The authors would like to acknowledge the assistance of Brock Cambourne, Gabriela Kraft-Somogyi, and Kirsten Short in the preparation of this chapter.

References

ATEVA, nd, *Alentejo's wines route*, ATEVA, Évora

Augusta-Margaret River Tourism Association, 1994, *The cellar: opening the door to tourism*, unpublished funding proposal to Commonwealth Department of Tourism, Regional Development Program 1995/1996

Australian Wine Foundation, 1996, *Strategy 2025: the Australian wine industry*, Winemakers' Federation of Australia, Adelaide

Beeston, J., 1994, *A concise history of Australian wine*, Allen & Unwin, Sydney

Bradley, R., 1982, *The small wineries of Australia: a guide to the best winemakers*, McMillan, South Melbourne

Bureau of Tourism Research, 1996, *International visitor survey*, Bureau of Tourism Research, Canberra

Committee of Inquiry into the Winegrape and Wine Industry, 1995, *Winegrape and wine industry in Australia*, final report, AGPS, Canberra

Comté Régional du Tourisme de Languedoc-Roussillon Prodexport, 1994, *Route des vins en Languedoc-Roussillon: projet de valorisation du patrimone viticole par le tourisme*, Comté Régional du Tourisme de Languedoc-Roussillon Prodexport, Blaye

Cooper, M., 1993, *The wines and vineyards of New Zealand*, 4th ed., Hodder & Stoughton, Auckland

Crewe, Q., 1993, *Foods from France*, Ebury Press, London

de Blij, H.J., 1983, *Wine: a geographic appreciation*, Rowman & Allanheld, Totowa

Deves, M., ed., 1995, *The Australian and New Zealand wine industry directory*, 13th annual ed., Winetitles, Marleston

Dickenson, J., 1990, Viticultural geography: an introduction to the literature in English, *Journal of Wine Research*, **1**: 5–24

Dickenson, J.P and Salt, J., 1982, An introduction to the geography of wine, *Progress in Human Geography*, **6** (2): 159–189

Dominion, 1996, New Zealand wine sales skyrocket in Britain, *The Dominion*, 12 October: 12

Edwards, F., 1989, The marketing of wine from small wineries: managing the intangibles, *International Journal of Wine Marketing*, **1** (1): 14–17

Europäische Weinstrassen (European Council of Wine Routes) nd, *La route des vins*, Europäische Weinstrassen, Blaye

Folwell, R.J. and Grassel, M.A., 1995, How tasting rooms can help sell wine. In *Direct farm marketing and tourism handbook*, pp. 11–15, Cooperative Extension, College of Agriculture, University of Arizona

Gannon, A., 1993, Rural tourism as a factor in rural community economic development for economies in transition. In *Rural tourism and sustainable rural development*, B. Bramwell and B. Lane, eds., pp. 50–60, Channel View Publications, Bristol

George, R., 1996, *The wines of New Zealand*, Faber and Faber, London

Golledge, S. and Maddern, C., 1994, *A survey of tourism activity at Victorian wineries*, Victorian Wineries Tourism Council, Melbourne

Hall, C.M. 1996, Wine tourism in New Zealand. In *Tourism down under II, towards a more sustainable tourism, conference proceedings*, G. Kearsley, ed., pp. 109–119, Centre for Tourism, University of Otago, Dunedin

Hall, C.M., 1997, Geography, marketing and the selling of places, *Journal of Travel and Tourism Marketing*, **6** (3/4) in press

Halliday, J., 1985, *The Australian wine compendium*, Angus & Robertson, Sydney

Halliday, J., 1995, *A history of the Australian wine industry (1949–1994)*, The Australian Wine & Brandy Corporation, Winetitles, Marleston

Innes, S., 1996, Pacesetting SA wineries, the toast of tourism, *SA Advertiser*, 6 March: 5

Johanneshof Cellars, 1996, *Johanneshof Cellars Newsletter*, December

Johnson, H., 1986, *The atlas of German wines and traveller's guide to the vineyards*, Mitchell Beazley, London

Klemm, M., 1996, Languedoc Rousillon: adapting the strategy, *Tourism Management*, **17** (2): 133–147

Langton, B., 1995, News, *Tourism NSW Newsletter*, Spring

Macionis, N. and Cambourne, B, 1994, *Marketing the Canberra district wineries*, unpublished research report, National Capital Wine Tours, Canberra.

Macionis, N., 1996, Wine tourism in Australia. In *Tourism down under II: towards a more sustainable tourism, conference proceedings*, G. Kearsley, ed., pp. 264–286, Centre for Tourism, University of Otago, Dunedin

Maddern, C. and Golledge, S., 1996, *Victorian Wineries Tourism Council cellar door survey*, Victorian Wineries Tourism Council, Melbourne

McKenzie, M., 1986, The premier wine state set to fight back, *Grapevine, South Australian Tourism News*, December: 6–7

Moran, W., 1958, *Viticulture and winemaking in New Zealand*, unpublished MA thesis, University of Auckland, Auckland

Movimento del Turismo del Vino 1995 http://ulysses.ulysses.it/mtv/

Moynahan, M., 1995, East End wineries boost Long Island tourism, *Long Island Business News*, 7 August: 17

Oregon Wine Advisory Board, 1995, *History and character of the Oregon Wine Industry*, Oregon Wine Advisory Board, Portland

Rankine, B., 1989, *Making good wine – a manual of practice for Australia and New Zealand*, Pan Macmillan Publishers, Sydney

Reid, A., 1990, *Grape expectations? An exploratory study of the tourist potential of the New Zealand wine industry*, unpublished diploma dissertation, Centre for Tourism, University of Otago, Dunedin

Renwick, C., 1977, *A study of wine in the Hunter region of NSW*, Hunter Valley Research Foundation, Newcastle

Robinson, J., 1994, Tourism. In *The Oxford companion to wine*, J. Robinson, ed., pp. 980–981, Oxford University Press, Oxford

Ruberto, A., 1996, Visitors to wine regions, *BTR Tourism Update*, Summer: 4

Reid, A., 1992, *New Zealand cuisine as a tourist attraction*, unpublished diploma dissertation, Centre for Tourism, University of Otago, Dunedin

South Australian Tourism Commission, 1996, *South Australian tourism plan 1996–2001*, South Australian Tourism Commission, Adelaide

Spawton, T., 1986, Marketing planning for small winemakers, *Australian and New Zealand Wine Industry Journal*, **1** (3): 89–91

Talmont, R., 1995, *New Zealand wineries & vineyards 1996: a wine trail guide*, AA Leisure Guides, Hodder Moa Beckett, Auckland

Thorpy, F., 1971, *Wine in New Zealand*, Collins, Auckland

Tourinform Baranya, (no date), *The Villány Siklós wine road (brochure)*, Tourinform Baranya, Pécs

Tourism New South Wales, 1996, *Food & wine in tourism: a plan*, Tourism New South Wales, Sydney

Tourism South Australia, 1991, *Marketing strategy*, Tourism South Australia, Adelaide

Vandyke Price, P., 1985, *Wine: lore, legends and traditions*, Hamlyn, Twickenham

Victorian Parliament Economic Budget Review Committee, 1985, *Report on the wine industry in Victoria*, Parliament of Victoria, Melbourne

Weekend Australian, 1986, Slab hut to vintage success. *Weekend Australian*, 26 May: 28.

Weekly Times, 1995, Wine tour push, *Weekly Times*, 1 November: 22

Welsh, A., 1994, An analysis of marketing factors contributing to success amongst geographically clustered small businesses in the Australian wine industry, unpublished thesis, University of South Australia, Roseworthy

Wilson, W., 1972, *Tourism and the visitor industry in the Newcastle/Hunter region NSW*, Hunter Valley Research Foundation, Newcastle

Winemakers' Federation of Australia, 1996, *Annual report 1994/5*, Winemakers' Federation of Australia, Adelaide

13 Farm tourism in New Zealand

MARTIN OPPERMANN

Introduction

Pigram (1993, p. 156) may have best summarised the research endeavours into farm and rural tourism when he described it as a 'spasmodic interest'. More recently, Oppermann (1995, p. 63) appraised that 'the field of rural and farm tourism still lacks a comprehensive body of knowledge and a theoretical framework'. He also suggested that this is caused by (a) definitional problems concerning what constitutes rural tourism (also see Bramwell and Lane, 1994); (b) a lack of data sources on small, rural tourism enterprises and data coherency; and (c) the small size of farm/rural enterprises which makes rural tourism much less obvious and signifies much more tedious work for researchers in their quest for data in the form of operator or guest questionnaires. Yet there seems to be a slowly growing body of knowledge in this field with studies conducted by a number of researchers in different countries (e.g., Oppermann 1995, 1996). Nonetheless, very few of these studies have gone beyond a simple data collection and presentation stage and attempted more theoretical or philosophical approaches.

Farm tourism is often considered an economic alternative for farmers who are facing decreasing profits and require a second or third economic footing (e.g., Embacher, 1994) (also see Chapters Two and Three). This concept is based on the notion that disadvantages of rural areas with regard to industrial development serve as advantages for tourism development. Hence, encouragement of tourism on farms, or in rural areas for that matter, is commonly considered as a means to overcome low incomes and provide employment opportunities (e.g., Maude and van Rest, 1985; Crotts and Holland, 1993; Gannon, 1994). Some early research into farm tourism and euphoric results (e.g., Ager, 1958) may have contributed to the persistence of this opinion despite several studies indicating otherwise (e.g., Frater, 1983; Staudacher, 1984).

In the New Zealand context, very little has been conducted into the arena of farm tourism. Pearce's (1990) study is the only one that was returned from an extensive bibliographical search through international journals in the fields of tourism, geography, agriculture and sociology as well as through several generic and tourism bibliographies. Hence, there is a dearth of published material on this topic in New Zealand, despite the agricultural landscape constituting one of New Zealand's primary tourist attractions and arguable tourist icons in form of sheep.

This chapter examines a range of issues within the domain of farm tourism in New

Zealand. After a more in-depth literature discussion it will discuss the results of a survey of 264 farm tourism operators undertaken in 1996. Specifically, the objectives of this chapter are:

• to analyse the supply and demand for farm tourism;
• to provide insights into the structure and marketing distribution channels used; and
• to uncover any problems that might arise between hosts and guests.

Tourism in New Zealand

Geographically, New Zealand can be considered as one of the most isolated destination countries in the world. Located in the southwest Pacific, New Zealand is a long-haul destination for the major tourist generating markets of North Asia, North America, and Europe. As much as this isolation acts as an attraction by itself, it also constitutes an obstacle to the tourism industry. Relatively long distances from the major tourist source markets have kept travel costs to New Zealand at a comparatively high level. In addition, the limited number of air carriers actually serving New Zealand has further reduced the potential for airfare discounts due to a lack of competition.

Not surprisingly, New Zealand is a relatively small player on the international tourism scene with more than 1.4 international million tourist arrivals in 1996 (Table 13.1). However, New Zealand has been able to show relatively consistently high growth rates in tourist arrivals over the last few years and decades. For example, tourist arrivals in 1996 were up more than 50 per cent over 1990 and 140 per cent over 1985 estimations.

Table 13.1   Tourist arrivals to New Zealand, 1950–1996 (years ending March)

Year	Visitors	Year	Visitors
1950	14,716	1991	967,062
1960	36,557	1992	999,714
1970	154,991	1993	1,086,557
1980	445,195	1994	1,213,318
1985	596,995	1995	1,343,003
1990	933,431	1996	1,441,838

Source: NZTB 1994, 1996a

Table 13.2 provides an overview of the major accommodation forms used by international visitors in the year 1995/96. It clearly indicates the impact of length of stay in the various accommodation forms on the share distribution. While some three per cent of the international visitors experienced at least one night on a farm or homestay, this accommodation type accounted for seven per cent of all nights spent in New Zealand. However, as the NZTB (1996b) pointed out, a large share of the total nights, especially in homestays and rental houses, can be attributed to a very small number of people. Nonetheless, farmstays do play their role in accommodation provision in New Zealand for international visitors.

Table 13.2. Accommodation used by international visitors, 1995/96

Accommodation type	Used (%)	Share in nights
Motel	27	13
Private Home/Friends	26	36
Mid Range Hotel	15	6
Top Hotels	13	4
Budget Hotel	9	3
Backpacker/Hostel	9	11
Campervan/Camping Ground	7	7
Luxury Lodge	4	1
Farmstay/Homestay	3	7
Bed and Breakfast	3	1
Rented Home/Time share	2	6
Conservation Department Hut	1	1
Other	4	4

Source: NZTB 1996b

Unfortunately, much less is known about domestic tourism in New Zealand, both with respect to total size of the domestic market and its travel behaviour. While some attempts are under way to rectify this situation, there is a critical gap in understanding of the domestic market. Considering that domestic tourism remains the major part of total tourism demand in New Zealand, even in most primary tourist hubs but particularly in the lesser visited regions and destinations, this information deficiency impinges on the planning abilities for this vital industry.

Methodology

The *New Zealand Bed & Breakfast Guide* (Thomas and Thomas, 1995) was used as the primary source of addresses of farm tourism operators. This was complemented by information available from regional tourist bureaus although most such obtained addresses were redundant. In total, some 264 addresses were collated. Given this relatively small population size and the lack of other comparative data, it was decided on a full census survey. A questionnaire for self-completion was mailed out along with a cover letter and a freepost return envelope. This first mailing yielded 137 usable responses and nine addresses where the business was either no longer ongoing or the owner/operator was away for an extended period as it was the slow winter period. Two weeks after the initial mailing, a second mail out was sent out to the remaining 118 farm operators in the sample, with a slightly modified cover letter and a freepost envelope. The second mailing rendered a further 35 usable responses for a total of 172 respondents at the cut-off date four weeks after the initial mailing. Another eight questionnaires were returned after the cut-off date but not included in the study. The 172 usable responses constitute a 65 per cent response rate based on the original 264 operators in the list and an adjusted response rate of 67 per cent after those operators who were no longer in business were taken out. It was decided that this was sufficient, both with respect to response rate as well as in regard to the total number of responses. The almost complete lack of previous inquiries into farm

Table 13.3. Starting year of operation

Year	Number of operators in %
1995/96	14
1994	10
1993	11
1992	11
1991	4
1990	8
1985–1989	24
1980–1984	7
1970–1979	6
before 1970	none

tourism in New Zealand might very well have been a contributing factor to this good response rate as operators did not feel too overwhelmed by continuous surveys.

Results

The operators and operations

Almost 50 per cent of all respondents had started their farm tourism operation in the 1990s and over 80 per cent during the last 10 years (Table 13.3), a time of tremendous change in New Zealand agriculture. Traditional subsidies were abolished during the Labour Government of David Lange, starting in 1984. This has meant a much closer relationship between global economic developments and local farm incomes and, therefore, dependence on fluctuations in overseas market prices for agricultural products which have been quite dramatic. For example, the recent export boom of lamb meat to the United Kingdom in the aftermath of the meat scare ('mad cow disease') in that country has resulted in a huge price leap for lamb meat, easily recognised by consumers in New Zealand who have faced an almost 100 per cent price increase between mid-1995 and mid-1996. Market over-supply of the same product in 1985/86 resulted at that time in wholesale sales prices of about NZ$5 for a whole lamb. Hence, if ever, the last 10 years were a time period when farmers required a more stable economic footing that would help them balance their fluctuating income from farming. In addition, the tremendous influx of international tourists to New Zealand in the same time period (see Table 13.1) dramatically boosted the demand for farm tourism. Approximately 75 per cent of the total demand to the surveyed farm operations were international visitors. Hence, the real and perceived need of an additional economic footing coupled with a simultaneous expansion of the tourist demand base appear as logical reasons behind the rapid establishment of farm operations over the last decade.

Most other operations were established in the early 1980s and only 6 per cent pre-dated the year 1980. Obviously this analysis is flawed by the methodology used, namely restriction of the survey to current operators. No information was available on those who might have started in the 1960s or 1970s or any other time and at one stage decided to discontinue that venture. In this survey seven questionnaires were returned as undeliverable or the recipient wrote back that they had discontinued offering accommodation on their farm. Perhaps, too, some of the current operators may actually not have started their farm tourism business, but bought into it along with acquiring the whole farm. This was the case with at least one respondent who mentioned that fact. A glance through the rural real estate market also regularly yields farms with tourism accommodation for sale. The small scale of many of these operations results in very low entry and exit barriers.

Another reason people begin farm tourism enterprises are the social contacts it brings the farmers who often live in relatively remote areas. Some 41 per cent of the respondents stated social contacts ahead of economic gain as their main reason to venture into farm tourism (Table 13.4). Notably, eight per cent of the respondents mentioned some sort of outside suggestion, either in the form of guests asking for accommodation ('demand not met by others'), tourism information bureaus or others in the business ('outside suggestion'). Ten per cent mentioned the availability of rooms, either because children had left home or a new property was bought, as their major reason for venturing into farm tourism. Hence, the opportunity of utilising existing accommodation facilities appears to be a major influencing factor in establishing a farm tourism enterprise. Clearly, this lowers the entrance costs considerably as little investment needs to be made to provide accommodation.

As mentioned above, most operations are very small. On average, the operators offered just 2.4 rooms with 4.9 beds (Table 13.5). Since many of these rooms are often connected, most operators can only accommodate one 'group' at any time.

Table 13.4. Main reason to start farmstay

Reason	%
Meet people/share with others/fun	41
Money/security/investment	32
Spare room available	8
Experienced it elsewhere	4
Demand not met by others	4
Outside suggestion	4
Work at home/retirement programme	2
Personal development/diversification	2
New property allowed to offer	2
Other reasons	2

Table 13.5. Number of rooms

Number of rooms	Operators (%)	Number of Beds	Operators (%)
1	16	2–3	16
2	45	4	39
3	31	5	15
4	5	6	16
5–10	2	7–10	12
> 10	1	> 10	2

Table 13.6. Accommodation charges

Cost (NZ$)	Single (%)	Double (%)
< 35	8	n/a
35–39	26	n/a
40–44	24	1
45–49	12	n/a
50–54	14	1
55–59	4	7
60–64	4	22
65–69	2	12
70–74	2	21
75–79	n/a	5
80–89	2	12
90–99	n/a	12
100+	1	8
Mean (in $)	44	73
Median (in $)	40	70

Some operators even indicated that they never take more than one group, in spite of being able to do so, in order to provide that group a better and more intensive experience.

The average cost of renting the rooms in New Zealand was quite substantial when compared to similar operations in Central Europe, albeit more in line with prices charged in North America and Australia. According to those operators who responded to the survey, single occupancy costed an average of NZ$44 (median $40) and double occupancy was NZ$73 (median $70) (Table 13.6).

The primary marketing channel used by the respondents was the *New Zealand Bed and Breakfast Book*. Other channels were the internet, roadside signs, overseas travel agencies, flyers, combined brochures with other operators, newspaper advertisements and the local tourist bureau. In terms of effectiveness, almost all respondents indicated that they received most of their enquiries and bookings based on the *New Zealand Bed and Breakfast Book*, particularly among overseas guests. Newspaper advertisements tend to be more targeted at domestic visitors and seem to be used more in the off-season.

The demand side

As mentioned previously, the clear majority of the guests were international. When asked to provide a breakdown into domestic and international customers, the respondents indicated that on average 73 per cent of their guests were international and 27 per cent of domestic origin. Not surprisingly, demand is heavily concentrated in the summer months from December through to March with a brief shoulder season in November and April (Table 13.7). From May through September, occupancy dips to about 10 per cent. Due to low demand some operators 'close' altogether because of high heating costs. Nonetheless, even in the peak summer months January and February, occupancy reaches only about 55 per cent and is,

Table 13.7. Average monthly occupancy rates

Month	Average occupancy (%)
January	55
February	58
March	48
April	33
May	12
June	8
July	8
August	8
September	11
October	22
November	33
December	40

Table 13.8. Occupancy per year in nights

Nights	Number of operators (%)
< 40	15
40–69	22
70–99	16
100–149	25
150–199	11
200+	9
Mean	98.9 nights
Median	90 nights

therefore, far below capacity. This results in a fairly low yearly mean room occupancy rate of just below 100 nights and a median of 90 nights (Table 13.8).

According to studies conducted elsewhere (see Oppermann 1995, 1996), 100 nights is often considered as the crucial barrier below which the enterprise is considered unprofitable. However, profitability may well depend on whether, and to what extent, labour costs by the hosts are realistically calculated into the equation. If little or no capital investment is required, for example, in the case where rooms formerly occupied by children is used, the profitability threshold is evidently lower than where such investment is necessary. Similarly, when the labour time could not be used for other income purposes, for example, because there is no other part-time and/or work at home available, time investments into farm tourism yield an income not otherwise available although at a low hourly rate. However, the apparent interest in social interactions (Table 13.4) can make farmstay a very attractive income alternative as one might derive a high degree of personal satisfaction in addition to the economic gain.

Very few operators mentioned difficulties or problems with their guests. Language problems were indicated by two respondents. Other areas of potential conflict were a different sense of humour, and different cultural background and/or eating habits (e.g., vegetarian).

The guests remain very briefly at each farm stay. The respondents indicated that the average length of stay was 1.5 nights. Most guest groups consisted of a couple (80 per couple) and about 10 per cent each of single travellers or couples with children. This could very well be a function of the dominance of international demand with international travellers coming to New Zealand being much less likely to be families with children due to cost reasons (i.e. flight costs). Moreover, the predominant type of intranational travel patterns by international visitors to New Zealand, namely to tour the country and visit as many places as possible (Oppermann, 1993, 1994) could be a major factor behind the short average length of stay of the farm guests.

Conclusion

These results, from what appears to be the first baseline survey of farm tourism in New Zealand, indicate the radical shift in the supply side over the last decade. As farmers needed to restructure their operations in the wake of major agricultural policy changes, more and more farmers decided to venture into farm tourism. A rough calculation of the average gross income earned from the farm tourism operation shows that this amounts to about NZ\$17,000 per annum (2.4 rooms × 100 nights × \$73). The low entry barrier to running a farm tourism operation, due to ready availability of existing accommodation facilities, is certainly a major incentive for many 'to try it out'. Existing accommodation is generally used rather than new rooms being built, for example, when children move out of their parents house. The availability of existing rooms was mentioned by almost 10 per cent of the respondents as their primary reason to offer farm tourism. On the other hand, there is also an equally low exit barrier and the hosts can essentially decide on a daily basis to terminate their involvement in farm tourism while maintaining the agricultural activities on their farm. As there is no comprehensive database that would track farm tourism operations from their start until cessation, very little information is available on: the total number of farm tourism operators; the length of operation of each farm tourism enterprise; and, perhaps most importantly, why some have ceased to offer farm tourism. While a lot can be learned from successful examples of running farm tourism operations (e.g., Oppermann, 1997), equally a lot can be gleaned from operators that have given up (Leiper, 1997), because it is the 'negative' reasons that need to be more thoroughly understood in order to give interested parties more rounded advice. To use an analogy, 'how to recognise and avoid the grevasses when crossing glaciers is more important than to know another person moved across yesterday, because the situation may have changed'.

References

Ager, T., 1958, Der Fremdenverkehr in seiner Bedeutung für die Gebirgsbevölkerung und für die Bergbauernbetriebe, *Agrarpolitische Revue*, **14**: 455–468

Bramwell, B., 1994, Rural and sustainable tourism. In Rural tourism and sustainable development, B. Bramwell and B. Lane, eds., pp. 1–11, Channel View, Clevedon.

Crotts, J.C. and Holland, S. M., 1993, Objective indicators of the impact of rural tourism development in the State of Florida, *Journal of Sustainable Tourism*, **1**:112–119

Embacher, H., 1994, Marketing for agri-tourism in Austria: strategy and realisation in a highly developed tourist destination, *Journal of Sustainable Tourism*, **2**: 61–76

Frater, J., 1983, Farm tourism in England: planning, funding, promotion and some lessons from Europe, *Tourism Management*, **4**: 167–179

Gannon, A., 1994, Rural tourism as a factor in rural community economic development for economies in transition, *Journal of Sustainable Tourism*, **2**: 51–60

Leiper, N., 1997, Big success, big mistake, at Big Banana: marketing strategies in road-side attractions and theme parks, *Journal of Travel & Tourism Marketing* **6** (3/4): in press

Maude, A.J.S. and van Rest, D.J., 1985, The social and economic effects of Farm tourism in the United Kingdom, *Agricultural Administration*, **20**: 85–98

New Zealand Tourism Board (NZTB), 1994, *New Zealand international visitor arrivals, March 1994*, NZTB, Wellington

New Zealand Tourism Board (NZTB), 1996a, *New Zealand international visitor arrivals, March 1996*, NZTB, Wellington

New Zealand Tourism Board (NZTB), 1996b, *New Zealand international visitor survey 1995/ 96*, NZTB, Wellington

Oppermann, M., 1993, German tourists in New Zealand, *The New Zealand Geographer*, **49** (1): 31–34

Oppermann, M., 1994, Regional aspects of tourism in New Zealand, *Regional Studies*, **28**: 155–167

Oppermann, M., 1995, Holidays on the farm: a case study of German hosts and guests. *Journal of Travel Research*, **34** (1): 63–67

Oppermann, M., 1996, Rural tourism in Southern Germany, *Annals of Tourism Research*, **23**: 86–102

Oppermann, M., 1997, Rural tourism operators in Southern Germany. In *The Business of Rural Tourism*, D. Getz and S.J. Page, eds., Routledge, London

Pearce, P.L., 1990, Farm tourism in New Zealand: a social situation analysis, *Annals of Tourism Research*, **17**: 337–352

Pigram, J.J., 1993, Planning for tourism in rural areas: bridging the policy implementation gap. In *Tourism research – critique and challenge*, D.G. Pearce and R.W. Butler, eds., pp. 156–174, Routledge, London

Staudacher, C., 1984, *Invention, Diffusion and Adoption der Betriebsinnovation 'Urlup auf dem Bauerhof' – Beispiel Niederösterreich*. *Zeitschrift für Agrargeographie*, **2**: 14–35

Thomas, J. and Thomas, J., 1995, *The New Zealand bed and breakfast book: homestay, farmstay, private hotel*, Moonshine Press, Wellington

14 The significance of tourism and economic development in rural areas: a Norwegian case study

JENS AARSAND SAETER

Introduction: tourism as a rural development strategy

Most Norwegian counties and municipalities encourage tourism as a strategy for job creation and economic development. Tourism is widely regarded as a growth sector which can generate new employment and partly replace jobs lost through economic restructuring. Despite the general enthusiasm for tourism development by local and regional politicians and planning officials, questions remain as to the indirect effects of the tourist industry on local economies. Disagreement exists as to the overall extent of multiplier effects and the sectors which will most benefit from linkages with tourism. Therefore, there is a clear need by planners and policy makers for a more stringent understanding of the connections between tourism and other parts of the economy, and the direct and indirect economic effects of tourism development.

The aim of this chapter is to provide a practical understanding of the nature of the tourist product. It highlights (1) the significance of tourism in a rural economy, and (2) how tourism affects other economic sectors by way of cross deliveries of commodities and services. The chapter includes a case study of the total economic impact of tourism in a rural economy, Roeros, a former mining town in South Troendelag county in southern Norway, near the Swedish border. An input-output funded regional-economic model is applied for the calculation purpose, with the total tourist demand being estimated on the basis of a field examination of the tourist consumption behaviour. The chapter also emphasises the extent to which economic impacts will be closely related to the extent of tourist demand, and the individual structure of the economy that is being analysed.

Analysing the economic impacts of tourism

Substantial research has been undertaken on the economic impact of tourism (e.g., Bull, 1995). Tourism is often referred to as an economic sector, but it is not in the traditional sense, and is not even a so-called multi-product industry (Briassoulis, 1991). Economic impact studies of tourism require a limitation of tourist related economic activities within an economy. This limitation problem leads to the fundamental and substantial question: 'What is tourism?'.

Smith (1988) introduced 'the supply side view', where the tourism industry was described as consisting of two kinds of suppliers. One group exclusively delivers commodities and services to tourists, and these suppliers were described as 'tier 1' or 'pure tourism'. Another group of suppliers delivers commodities and services to a mixture of tourists and other customers, and these suppliers were described as 'tier 2'. The distinction between two different kinds of tourism suppliers has much in common with the analytical foundation of several Norwegian tourism impact studies (Reiersen, 1980; Akselsen, 1986; Hovland, 1989). These studies operate with a group of suppliers that are referred to as the tourism *core*, and the demand for commodities and services from these suppliers is the direct economic effect. The tourist demand for commodities and services outside the core is described as the *irrigation effect*. The limitation of the core determines what are the direct and irrigation effects. Accommodation, restaurant and food services, attractions and activities are usually defined to be within the core. The irrigation effects usually occur in groceries, transport and different kinds of personal services. However, absolute conventions on how different economic activities should be categorised have not been established.

The tourist industry has an economic impact due to the demand for commodities and services from tourists. The tourist-share of demand in each sector, within and outside the 'core', is an expression for the *direct effects* of tourist demand. The *indirect effects* consist of the generation of cross deliveries between sectors, and consumption and investment generated effects.

How to limit tourism within the framework of a traditional sector classification

As discussed above, tourism products are an amalgam of commodities and services from different economic sectors. Figure 14.1 illustrates how the demand for commodities and services in various sectors distributes tourist (T) and non tourist demand (N). For some sectors, the demand comes from both tourists and others. For other sectors, one can imagine that the tourists are representing the whole demand. However, in practice, it will be difficult to find a sector that is fully based on tourist demand if the sector classification in the national account is applied. This includes the hotel and restaurant sector, which is dependent on non-tourist consumers as well, even if the tourists in most cases consume the greatest share of total sector production. This means that the 'tier 1' suppliers in Smith's terminology, the core, or 'pure' tourism activities, can be hard to identify within the framework of traditional economic sectors. The tourist influenced sectors are based on sales to both tourists and others, and the tourist industry in that case occurs as a *pure cross-sectoral activity*. On the other hand, it is easy to imagine production sectors in which no direct demand from tourists exist.

The tourism sector consists of economic activity that has its origin in tourist demand for commodities and services. In principle, this is analogous with the 'supply side view' of Smith (1988, 1989), certainly with respect to other industrial sector classifications. However, Leiper (1990) described this as 'the demand side view', because it is the demand for commodities and services that delimits the tourism

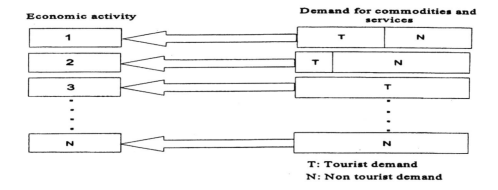

Figure 14.1. An illustration of how the tourists represent a part of total demand in different sectors

industry. The tourism sector is therefore a 'dynamic sector', compounded by contributions from various economic sectors. It will be different from one site to another, and varies temporally because of composition shifts in the tourist population, or changed tourist motivations and preferences. This is a strictly practical and pragmatic attitude to the question 'what is tourism?', and one which escapes analytical, methodological and operational problems in applied economic impact studies.

Economic impacts and the integration of tourism in Roeros

The following discussion outlines the findings of a study of the impacts and integration of tourism in the economy of Roeros, a former mining town in South Troendelag county in southern Norway, near the Swedish border. Roeros is a town of 5,400 inhabitants, with an economic base mainly built on tourism but which also has highly specialised furniture manufacturers and some summer agricultural and grazing activity. Roeros is on UNESCO's World Heritage List, and is a high profile destination in Norwegian government tourism promotion. Cultural and heritage tourism is the basis of the region's attraction as a tourist destination. The main attraction is the historic old town, 'Bergstaden', with its wooden houses, the church, and the mines. The town also has several museums which are the principal interpretation centres for conveying information about the cultural and mining heritage.

The study is based on a field-examination of tourist consumption and official statistics from the Norwegian Central Bureau of Statistics. The calculations were undertaken with use of an input-output funded regional-economic model, which consists of 30 economic sectors. The sector classification follows the standardized system of national accounts.

Table 14.1. Tourist expenses divided into main economic activities

Economic activity	Expenses	
'Hotel and restaurant'	(1)	Accommodation
	(2)	Food service
'Wholesale and retail trade'	(3)	Fast food and groceries
	(4)	Alcoholic drinks
	(5)	Souvenirs
	(6)	Gas/garage
'Domestic transport and communications'	(7)	Taxi
	(8)	Public transport
	(9)	Guided bus tours
	(10)	Car–rentals
'Other personal services'	(11)	Entertainment
	(12)	Museum/exhibitions
	(13)	Playgrounds and family parks
	(14)	Sports and fitness centres
	(15)	Hunting/fishing/nature
	(16)	Parking
	(17)	Other

Sector distribution of the tourists' demands for commodities and services

During the summer of 1991, staff and students from Oppland College, Lillehammer, undertook an extensive survey of tourists' consumption patterns in the case area. Tourists were asked to give an account of their consumption the previous day to being surveyed, according to 17 different spending categories. These categories, along with the corresponding production sectors, are stated in Table 14.1.

The connections between spending categories and production sectors are at times more obvious in some cases than others. In the official hotel and restaurant statistics, the expense of accommodation, food-service, and fast food is reported. Besides groceries, the official wholesale and trade statistics includes alcoholic drinks (bought at special state monopoly shops). A large proportion of the sales of souvenirs and petrol will also be included in these statistics. Taxis, collective transport, guided bus tours and car rental expenses are classified under the sector 'domestic transport and communications', whereas for expenses for entertainment, museums and exhibitions, playgrounds and family parks, parking, sports and fitness activities, hunting, fishing and other nature-based experiences, several classification candidates can be identified. National and local government agencies, together with the private sector, are involved in the arrangement and supply of these services. Theoretically, we should analyse the supply structure of these services in the host community, and then undertake the sector classification. In practice, expenditures are not significant in comparison with other sectors. We have, therefore, simplified the classification of all these spending categories under the sector 'private services'. According to this classification, tourism is integrated with four economic sectors. Although the choice of sectors is somewhat arbitrary, the uncertainty of the data means that a more detailed classification would be unlikely to provide a higher level of precision.

The tourists' share of total sector production

The number of visitor nights per year for hotel and camping guests is available through the official hotel and camping statistics. The estimation of annual tourist volume within the other visitor night categories is not accessible from official data, and is estimated from other sources. Table 14.2 shows the number of guests in each accommodation category.

The total tourist demand in each sector is calculated by multiplying the average consumption with the annual number of visitor nights. Table 14.3 indicates the total sector production, total tourist demand, and its share of total sector production in each of the four direct tourist-influenced sectors. As Table 14.3 illustrates, tourist demand accounts for three-quarters of the total sector production in the hotel and restaurant sector, 11 per cent in the grocery sector, and 6 per cent in the other personal services sector. The tourist share of total production in the domestic transport and communications sector was only 1.5 per cent. Therefore, we have disregarded this activity as a direct tourist-influenced sector.

Table 14.2. Calculated number of visitor nights per year in Roeros by accommodation

Accommodation type	Visitor nights
Hotel	89,644
Other tourist accommodation	10,000
Private accommodation	285,000
Campgrounds	22,041
'Wild' camping	5,000

Table 14.3. Tourist sales per year in Roeros (all figures in Norwegian crowns (NOK), 1991 value)

Economic activity	Value of total sector production ('000)	Calculated value of tourist sales ('000)	Tourist share of total sales (%)
Hotel and restaurant	89,000	68,000	76
Wholesale and retail trade	383,000	41,000	11
Domestic transport and communications	51,000	750,000	1.5
Other personal services	35,000	2,000	6

The input-output based regional economic model

The applied model is a part of the so-called *panda-system*, developed at Sintef/ Norwegian Technical University. The system includes both databases and models, made for use in regional analysis and strategic planning in county municipalities and at lower geographic levels. The regional economic model unit works according to input-output principles, and also includes a consumption and investment function.

Input-output techniques have been widely used in the analysis of tourism's economic impact (e.g., Groenewold *et al.*, 1986; Fletcher, 1989; Archer and Fletcher, 1990; Heng and Low, 1990). However, the majority of studies on the impact of tourism's contribution to the economy tend to be carried out at the national level in terms of contribution to Gross National Product. Regional and local economic impact studies are relatively uncommon.

Input-output analysis is based on assumptions that involve, in part, great simplifications regarding national and regional economies. A very good account of these assumptions and simplifications is provided by Briassoulis (1991). A most significant assumption is that the production is assumed to be homogeneous. This implies that an exogenous change in the final demand in a sector will induce an accurate predictable response in a given amount of sectors that produce cross deliveries to this sector. The connection between employment and gross production in every sector is also assumed to be linear. This means that any economies of scale and any 'sill values' in the production are not taken into consideration. In practice, a sector can reach a level of production that is critical for its existence, and the activity can suddenly fall to zero if the production falls beyond this level. A hotel, for instance, which loses 50 per cent of its demand can very likely be forced to close down. It is also apparent that sill values among several businesses will occur in the other direction as well. Another limitation of input-output models is that the economic fabric in the economy is determined through fixed input-output coefficients. This implies a rigidity that does not allow any sector to substitute cross deliveries as a response to, for instance, changes in relative prices.

Input-output analysis is especially suitable for analysing dependency between economic activities. Connections between the various sectors in an economy are modelled in a matrix of cross and final deliveries. The model calculations are based on assumptions regarding exogenous growth parameters, such as public and private consumption, investments and export. The parameters are specified on the basis of general national estimates. Another key factor behind the calculations is productivity development. In the calculations this factor was assumed to be changing at a rate corresponding to the average for the period 1980–91. The employment in each sector was calculated according to a linear function of the production level. The final deliveries from hotel and restaurant, wholesale and trade, and private services were stated exogenously, according to our assumptions regarding the tourists' share of these sectors.

Because of changes in final deliveries, indirect effects can be divided into three categories:

- Alterations in cross deliveries between sectors, according to the input-output fabric, fixed in the model. The matrix of input-output coefficients is broken down at county level from national figures, and is therefore not an accurate description of the economic fabric in the county. When this structure is projected down to municipality level, it is expected that the production structure on the county level matches the structure on the municipality level. This is obviously an assumption which suggests that production-generated indirect effects should not be interpreted too fundamentally.
- Alterations in final deliveries will generate alterations in investments which affect the construction sector in particular.

- Household income is a linear function of the final production. Increased final production will create a growth in consumption, which at the next turn will create increased gross production.

Calculation alternatives and results

The calculations consist of three alternatives. First, we have made a reference path, called the *zero-alternative*, which describes the development without any exogenous changes in any of the direct tourist influenced sectors. The employment in each sector will then be determined by the general growth parameters, and the productivity growth. The zero-alternative is not a description of the actual development. The purpose of the zero-alternative is to establish a basis of comparison with the results of the other calculation alternatives. The deviations between the zero-alternative and the calculation alternatives are of interest, not the reference path itself.

Alternative I describes a situation in which the gross production value in the sectors hotel and restaurant, wholesale and retail trade, and private services, is reduced in proportion to the tourist share of the total demand. The reduction was made gradually, during the three-year period 1991–1993, with identical annual reductions. The result of this manipulation is a 10 per cent decline in total employment in comparison with the zero-alternative. Calculation results are presented in Table 14.4. For the most part, the reduction comes in the direct tourist-influenced sectors, especially in the hotel and restaurant sector and wholesale and retail trade. Only one tenth of the total effects is caused by indirect effects. The indirect effects occur in such sectors as agriculture and hunting, manufacture of food, and business services.

Alternative II describes a situation in which the gross production value in the hotel and restaurant, groceries, and personal services sectors, is gradually increased, and corresponding to a 50 per cent increase in the tourist share of total demand during the three-year period 1991–1993, and with identical annual increases. This means that the final deliveries from the direct tourist-influenced sectors are increased, and the tourist share of total demand in these sectors increases somewhat. The results from these calculations are also shown in Table 14.4. Total employment increases by 4 per cent under this regime. By far the greatest part of this increase appears in the hotel and restaurant sectors, where the employment is about 30 per cent above the reference alternative. One might expect similar findings in the commodity trade and personal services sectors as well. However, these sectors do not seem to be affected by the increase in tourist demand. The interpretation of this is that the general growth will affect these two sectors just as much as the 50 per cent increase in the tourists' share of demand in these sectors. Ideally, the growth in tourist demand should support the general growth. This is not possible in the model, and must clearly be stated as a limitation. The calculation of results regarding the direct tourist-influenced sectors are therefore somewhat underestimated.

In the analysis the direct tourist-influenced sectors are managed exogenously simultaneously. Technically, this means that production-generated effects between

Table 14.4. Calculations and forecasts on employment in different economic sectors, under absence of tourist demand (alternative I) and 50% increase in tourist demand (alternative II)

Economic activity	Zero–alternative number of employed	Alternative I %deviation from the zero-alt.	Alternative II % deviation from the zero-alt.
Agriculture and hunting	222	−5	3
Forestry and logging	1	−	−
Mining and quarrying	1	−	−
Other manufacture of food	80	−5	4
Manufacture of textiles and wearing apparel	16	−	−
Manufacture of wood and wood products	221	−	−
Printing and publishing	34	−3	−
Manufacture of chemical products	4	−	−
Manufacture of mineral products	52	−	−
Manufacture of metal products, machinery and equipment	137	−1	−
Electricity supply	24	−	4
Construction	166	−	1
Wholesale and retail trade	333	−16	0
Hotel and restaurant	248	−75	31
Ocean transport	3	−	−
Domestic transport and communications	148	−4	3
Post and telecommunications	47	−4	4
Financing and insurance	57	−2	2
Business services	29	−14	7
Other personal services	59	−10	−
Production sectors, local government	724	0	0
Production sectors, central government	65	−	−
Gross Employment	2,635	−10	4

these sectors will vanish. If these effects were to be taken into consideration we would have to run the model with exogenous changes in one sector at a time. However, this is more of a theoretical than practical interest, and has a very little influence on the results.

Discussion and concluding remarks

The results indicate that the tourism sector, directly and indirectly, accounts for approximately 10 per cent of the employment in the study area. Such an amount will be considered significant by many people, but the indirect effects only account for one-tenth of this.

As stated in the introduction, indirect effects are often central to the economic and political debates which surround tourism development projects, but also economic development as a whole. Development projects stimulate other economic activities, such as the need for delivery of goods and services, improved communications, establishment of service companies, increased incomes, sales, consumption. Focusing on such indirect effects can make almost every development project appear profitable to a community. However, the calculations indicate that the focus should be turned more towards the direct economic effects of tourism than on indirect effects. It is also important to distinguish between the effects of tourism development in areas of high and low employment. In areas with low employment, the contributions of economic development projects to employment generation provide a substantial economic argument for undertaking such projects. However, in areas with high employment the effects of the project may deter or drive away other economic activity because of, for example, increased costs and reduced access to human and physical resources. Therefore, in an area with high employment, a 50 per cent growth in tourism can deter or drive away other sectors. In such cases, it will be vital to weigh tourism development strategies against development in other economic fields.

The calculations predict that a 50 per cent increase in tourist demand will generate a modest 4 per cent increase in total employment. Anyhow, a very important consideration with reference to growth strategies is that many sites can be vulnerable to the physical impacts of tourism. Therefore, there can be significant limits to growth within tourism caused by negative external effects on the product, and often produced by tourism itself. This can affect the quality of the product, in a broad sense, which can lead to lower willingness to pay, lower levels of visitor satisfaction, and an economic impact that is lower than indicated by the traffic volume.

The basis of a tourism development strategy should be to generate income for the tourist region, driven by demand for commodities and services from people resident outside the region. The rational motivation behind investing in tourism development should be that tourism is among the most potentially valuable fields of regional economic development. However, rural economic development has many dimensions that should be examined in conjunction with the regional economic impacts caused by tourist demand:

- Does tourism compete with other industries for scarce resources within the region?
- Are there external effects between tourism and other industries? Does an easier and more profitable strategy exist to increase income to the region, other than developing the tourist industry?
- Is the tourism industry moving towards greater control by international chains? How should the local and regional tourist production system be organised to give the best possible circumstances for local control of the development process and articulation of local values?
- Is it possible to characterise the kind of regions and rural areas that tourism is the right strategy for, and what are the regional conditions for success? How should the development strategies be designed, and what niches in the market give the best payoff?

Tourism can assist rural economic development through the economic impact created by tourist demand for commodities and services. However, when politicians and planners in local and regional administrations emphasise the indirect effects of tourism there is more rhetoric than reality. Consideration should at least be given to the question of whether the economic effects of tourism are greater than those of other industries. The regional economic impact of tourist development should be weighed against the economic potential of other industries. Therefore, tourism development strategies should not be disconnected from the general economic planning of rural regions.

Acknowledgements

This chapter is based on a research project on tourism and site development done by Eastern Norway Research Institute and Oppland College, during the period 1991–95. The aim was to study tourist development in relation to social, political, cultural, and economic processes in rural areas. One part of the project was to study the economic impacts of tourism (Saeter 1993, 94). I wish to thank my colleagues S. E. Hagen and H. Birkelund for their comments on the first draft of this chapter. Financial support from the Norwegian Research Council is also gratefully acknowledged. The usual caveat applies.

References

Akselsen, R.E., 1986, *The travelling business and the local economy: A case study from Hol municipality* (in Norwegian, title translated), The Royal Department of Communications, Oslo

Archer, A. and Fletcher, J., 1990, Multiplier analysis in Tourism, *Les Cahiers du tourisme*, Centre des hautes etudes touristique, Aix-en-Provence, Serie C, No. 103.

Briassoulis, H., 1991, Methodological issues – tourism input–output analysis. *Annals of Tourism Research*, **18**: 485–495

Bull, A., 1995, *The economics of travel and tourism*, 2nd ed., Longmans, South Melbourne

Fletcher, J.E., 1989, Input–output analysis and tourism in Singapore, *Annals of Tourism Research*, **16**: 514–529

Groenewold, N., Hagger, A.J. and Madden, J.R., 1986, The measurement of industry employment contribution in an input–output model, *Regional Studies*, **21**(3): 255–263

Heng, T.M. and Low, L., 1990, Economic impact of tourism in Singapore, *Annals of Tourism Research*, **17**: 246–269

Hovland, N. P., 1989, *Local economic impact of travelling business: examples from the municipality Risoer* (in Norwegian, title translated), report no. 24, Telemark Research Institute, Boe

Leiper, N., 1990, Partial industrialization of tourism systems, *Annals of Tourism Research*, **17**: 600–605

Reiersen, D., 1980, *Economic impacts of tourism – A case study from Kviteseid municipality* (in Norwegian, title translated), paper no. 45/80, Telemark College, Boe

Smith, S.L.J., 1988, Defining tourism – a supply side view, *Annals of Tourism Research*, **15**: 179–190

Smith, S.L.J., 1989, *Tourism analysis*, Longman Scientific & Technical, Longman Group, Harlow

Saeter, J.A., 1993, *Local economic impacts of tourism – A case study of the municipalities Risoer, Roeros, Vaagan and Bykle in Norway* (in Norwegian, title translated), report 17/1993, Eastern Norway Research Institute, Lillehammer

Saeter, J.A., 1994, *Tourism related employment in the municipalities Risoer, Roeros, Vaagan and Bykle in Norway* (in Norwegian, title translated), paper 04/1994, Eastern Norway Research Institute, Lillehammer

Part Five:
Conclusions

15 Conclusion: the sustainability of tourism and recreation in rural areas

RICHARD W. BUTLER AND C. MICHAEL HALL

Introduction

In rural areas, the concept of sustainability has normally been thought of in the limited context of sustainable agriculture. Yet, for rural areas to be sustainable it is inevitable that the whole range of associated activities be integrated and coordinated. Rural communities are rarely capable of being economically sustainable without a diverse economic base, and tourism and recreation are becoming an increasingly important part of that base. This should imply consideration of sustainability in terms of tourism opportunities, their appropriateness and their capability of attracting and sustaining visitation, and how well they fit into the mix of economic and social activities of rural areas and rural populations. The relative lack of attention to the sustainability of tourism in the rural literature, including government publications and policy statements, until recently suggests that this fact was rarely considered as tourism development was being encouraged, nor does it appear that many developments were well thought out in terms of compatibility with other uses and preferences or even in terms of their long-term economic viability.

The present state of flux places new pressure on rural resources and threatens the established and traditional patterns of land use and increases the possibility of conflict over resources. It also disturbs the homeostasis which had evolved between users of the rural environment in certain regions because of the scale, scope and nature of the changes occurring. The uneasy combination of new and traditional forms of tourism and recreation casts increasing doubt on their sustainability in the changing rural environment. Therefore, one of the major aims of research on tourism and recreation in rural areas should be the identification of new frameworks for applying the principles of sustainability and long-term economic viability of tourism. Only in this way can tourism fulfill its long-vaunted economic potential as an effective tool of rural regional development.

The concept of sustainability

Sustainable development is one of the major policy issues in the world today. The concept of sustainability came to public attention with the publication of the World Conservation Strategy (WCS) in March, 1980 (IUCN, 1980). The WCS 'launched sustainability onto the global stage, bringing the cautious but sometimes negative thinking of the conservationist together with the positive but sometimes heedless world of the developer' (Bramwell and Lane, 1993, p. 1). The WCS was not an international treaty but a strategy for the conservation of the earth's living resources in the face of major international environmental problems such as deforestation, desertification, ecosystem degradation and destruction, extinction of species and loss of genetic diversity, loss of cropland, pollution and soil erosion. The international significance of the WCS was illustrated by the more than 450 government agencies from over 100 countries who participated in preparing the document (Hall, 1995).

The WCS defined conservation as 'the management of human use of the biosphere so that it may yield the greatest sustainable benefit to present generations while maintaining its potential to meet the needs and aspirations of future generations' (IUCN, 1980, s.1.6). The WCS had three specific objectives (IUCN, 1980, s.1.7):

- to maintain essential ecological processes and life-support systems (such as soil regeneration and protection, the recycling of nutrients, and the cleansing of waters), on which human survival and development depend;
- to preserve genetic diversity (the range of genetic material found in the world's organisms), on which depend the breeding programmes necessary for the protection and improvement of cultivated plants and domesticated animals, as well as much scientific advance, technical innovation, and the security of the many industries that use living resources;
- to ensure the sustainable utilization of species and ecosystems (notably fish and other wildlife, forest and grazing lands), which support millions of rural communities as well as major industries.

The concept of sustainable development espoused in the WCS emphasised the relationship between economic development and the conservation and sustenance of natural resources. According to Redclift (1987, p. 33) 'The term "sustainable development" suggests that the lessons of ecology can, and should, be applied to economic processes'. Therefore, sustainable development stresses that economic development is dependent upon the continued, well-being of the physical and social environment on which it is based (Barbier, 1987; Butler, 1991).

The report of the World Commission on Environment and Development (WCED) (1987), commonly known as the Brundtland Report, provided further impetus to the concept and practice of sustainable development and firmly established the concept on the policy agenda in order to 'make development sustainable to ensure that it meets the needs of the present without compromising the ability of future generations to meet their own needs' (WCED, 1987, p. 43). Five basic principles of sustainability were identified in the report:

- the idea of holistic planning and strategy-making;

- the importance of preserving essential ecological processes;
- the need to protect both human heritage and biodiversity;
- to develop in such a way that productivity can be sustained over the long term for future generations; and
- achieving a better balance of fairness and opportunity between nations (Bramwell and Lane, 1993, p. 2).

More recently, *Caring for the Earth* (IUCN, *et al.*, 1991, p. 10) redefined sustainable development as 'improving the quality of life while living within the carrying capacity of supporting ecosystems'. Nevertheless, the major thrust of sustainable development remains concern for the long-term health and integrity of the environment, meeting present and future needs and adding to the quality of life of current and future generations.

According to Pinfield (1996, p. 153), 'Sustainable development is seen to be development that is people-centred, seeking to improve the human condition, and environment-centred, seeking to sustain the variety and productivity of the earth'. Sustainable development occurs at the interface between policies for economic development, community and cultural development, and ecological development. Sustainable development therefore seeks to ensure that economic development is contained within socio-cultural and environmental limits.

Sustainability and the rural dimension

Sustainable development remains influential in a number of policy spheres, not least of which is the area of rural policy (Murdoch, 1993; Whatmore, 1993). However, much of the discussion on applications of sustainability has been in individual components of rurality, e.g., attempts at developing sustainable agriculture, rather than a comprehensive approach to integrate the socio-cultural, economic and environmental components of both sustainability and rurality. For example, the Rural White paper entitled *Rural England: A Nation Committed to a Living Countryside* (Department of the Environment and Ministry of Agriculture, Fisheries and Food [DoE/MAFF], 1995), was the first specifically rural policy from a British Government for 50 years (Blake, 1996).

The traditional bucolic image of rural areas is dominated by agriculture both as the means of production and the focus of life with links to the urban communities only in terms of the egress of produce and the occasional leisure foray of urban residents to the country house. Such an image even at the time of the enclosure movement in reality did not exist (see Chapter Three). The countryside, from earliest times, has always been a multi-faceted environment with many varied uses, some tightly integrated, while others coexisted uneasily. Even the seemingly simple production of food was dependent upon a complex set of economic, socio-cultural and environmental linkages and inter-relationships. To this, in historic times, were added non-agriculturally related activities such as mining and small-scale manufacturing, along with other activities, at least peripherally related to agriculture, including forestry, small-scale manufacturing, cottage industries, the sport and leisure of the wealthy, and artists seeking subject matter and inspiration from the countryside. More recently, in addition to the development of agribusiness and plantation forestry, the countryside has become a focus for the tourism and recreational activity of a wider segment of the population as well as the domicile of a far broader range of inhabitants, some of whom have little, if anything, to do with the traditional functions of the countryside. Farm labourers could not survive on the output of a single product agribusiness as they once could on the mixed output of a traditional farm, neither could Robin Hood survive in the new plantation forest of Sherwood with its absence of deer and oak trees. The lack of diversity in the contemporary rural system in many countries is anathema to the concept of sustainability.

As Chapter Three noted, prior to the Second World War, although the widespread shift into commercial agriculture had produced regions of greater or lesser viability, the rural system overall retained a degree of homogeneity and distinctiveness. In many regions and countries this structure has been either destroyed or weakened. Weakness is a result of at least three types of restructuring, namely: the collapse of peripheral areas unable to shift to a more capital intensive economy; the selective and reductionist process of industrialization of the remaining agricultural sector; and the pressures of urban and exurban development. The result is a rural system suffering absolute decline along its extensive margins and the rural-urban interface, with the intervening core area weakened by decoupling of farm and non-farm sectors and the shift of decision making to urban based corporations and governments. Restructuring has created a fragmented and reduced rural system which seems to lack most of the criteria for sustainability in either economic or community terms (Troughton, 1997).

Blake (1996, p. 211) has also recognised that rurality is no longer dominated by concepts of food production and notes that new uses of the countryside are redefining the idea of what constitutes the rural landscape. In Britain, as in many other industrialised countries discussed in this book, these new uses are placing extreme pressures and creating new conflicts not only in terms of rural policy making and their relationship to agriculture but also between themselves. For example, Blake (1996) reports that, according to a Countryside Commission survey, 76 per cent of the English population visited the countryside in 1990. Such a high level of visitation inevitably requires the transformation of villages, and the creation of tourist facilities and infrastructure such as car parks and toilets. However, at the same time, 89 per cent of people now believe that the English countryside should be protected at all costs (presumably as long as this cost would not result in the exclusion of those who wanted it saved). Similarly, the clear-cutting of forestry plantations and apparent devastation of the countryside in Australian states, particularly Tasmania, has created negative perceptions amongst visitors, even though such plantations are planted for wood production rather than recreation and amenity (McArthur and Hall, 1996).

One of the major problems with much of the sustainable development literature is the willingness of academics, planners and policy-makers to assume that apparently contradictory aims of those seeking economic, social and environmental develop-ment can be easily reconciled with goodwill (Curry, 1992). One of the more difficult issues to resolve is often found at the most local level and that is the different desires, expectations and requirements of long-time residents and new arrivals and changing community power structures that may result. The conflict between new and established residents may take a number of forms generally focussing on development related issues. For example, in Elmira, Ontario, established residents were enthusiastic supporters of a proposal for a new bridge and associated road linkages to the village whereas newer settlers, who tended to be either commuters or those involved in 'quaint' tourist activities were generally opposed to the new developments on the basis they would reduce the 'traditional' feel of the village. In Byron Bay in northern New South Wales, Australia, newer arrivals were behind the opposition to the development of a Club Med Resort because of its perceived potential impacts on the environment. In contrast, longer-term residents tended to support the development because of the value they placed on employment generation (Hall, 1995). In addition to the above examples, the recreation and tourism literature is replete with documentation of a wide variety of conflicts between second-home and cottage owners and permanent residents including issues of privacy, access, vandalism, property prices and taxes, crowding and pollution (e.g., Coppock, 1977; Bouquet and Winter, 1987; Gartner, 1987).

There are many other conflicts implicit in the diverse nature of rural areas. Many of these owe their origins to changing tastes and preferences amongst the ever-changing user populations of rural areas and the shifting spatial influences of exogenous economic and political forces. For example, the conversion of former farmland into plantation forests in Australia, New Zealand, the United Kingdom, and mainland Europe is a response to changing economic circumstances for particular rural products and government policies. While the loss of the agricultural heritage was bemoaned at the time, even greater opposition on amenity grounds is often generated when the forests are cut.

In a similar fashion, the frequent loss of the family farm and its associated complex landscape and its replacement by the mono-cultural landscape of agribusiness has aroused opposition from a variety of sources. Organised labour and local government have expressed concern at the loss of employment through the introduction of agribusiness associated with greater efficiences of scale and improved technology, even though, somewhat ironically, many rural areas seek to attract the investment and new employment offered by such new business. Opposition to the spread of agribusiness has also been voiced by wildlife and landscape conserva-tionists who note the loss of variety and habitat, and by hiking and other recreational users over the disappearance of long-established footpaths and other means of access in rural areas (see Chapter Eleven).

Rural areas, because of their relative remoteness from urban populations have long been used for defence purposes. However, in recent years with the cessation of the Cold War much defence land is being considered for return to a more productive use. While identification of ownership is one substantial area of conflict a more widespread issue in the rural context is the purpose for which such land should be made available, whether it be for agricultural, conservation, tourism, residential development or plantation forestry. In this setting decisions will be made according to a variety of economic, social and environmental considerations, ones not normally dealt with by Ministries of Defence.

Accessibility within and to the countryside has long been another source of conflict. Transportation planners at a national scale often seem to view the countryside simply as an area to be transgressed by road and rail links between major cities. Unless strong legislation exists to protect significant landscapes, the tendency is frequently to locate new route ways across reserves and relatively undeveloped lands rather than prime agricultural or residential land because of economic considerations. Transportation within rural areas also represents an area of potential conflict in the context of sustainability. The decline of public transportation in rural areas reflecting in part a declining rural population and changed political philosophies over the appropriate role of government in transportation has meant that 'in rural areas cars are more of a necessity than in cities' (DoE/MAFF, 1995, p. 132). The probable growth in automobile use in rural areas, and the subsequent increase in air pollution and demands for better roads may therefore run against desires for a tranquil and unpolluted rural environment (Blake, 1996). This problem is further exacerbated by the increasing commuting use of rural areas by urban workers, which is clearly related to issues of purchase of goods and services outside of the immediate resident community thereby threatening the viability of existing retail and service outlets in such communities. These conflicts notwithstanding, the complexity that is implicit within them is an essential component of the diversity so necessary for rural sustainability.

Tourism and rural sustainability

The idea of sustainable tourism has received considerable coverage in both academic and policy literature in recent years. However, the vast majority of researchers on sustainable tourism have concentrated on environment-tourism relationships or the impact of tourism on the bio-physical environment, and questions about sustainable tourism development in rural areas are rarely asked and even more rarely answered. Tourism has often been thought to be compatible with principles of sustainable development which may explain the fervour with which academics and policy-makers alike have supported the introduction of the concept into policy-making for tourism in rural and natural areas. Nevertheless, there remains a massive 'implementation gap' between the policy idea and its application in a manner which demonstrably meets the ideals of sustainable development discussed above. One of the major errors which policy makers and academics have made with respect to tourism is to treat the industry in isolation from the other factors which constitute the social, environmental, and economic fabric of rural regions. Tourism, therefore, needs to be appropriately embedded within the particular set of linkages and relationships which comprise the essence of rurality.

True sustainable rural development should include tourism as but one component of the policy mix which government and the private sector formulate with respect to rural development. Tourism needs to be in harmony with the multiplicity of uses, needs and demands which so characterise rural areas in order for it to be deemed as appropriate and potentially sustainable. Analysis of rural areas prior to the deliberate introduction or expansion of tourism requires consideration of the economic, social and environmental 'fit' of tourism with existing linkages and relationships in order to ensure that the full range of development objectives can be met. The days of adding tourism development onto existing regional economic structures in the naive belief that it will contribute to the overall wellbeing of the region should be long past. Without detailed consideration of factors, such as opportunity cost and cumulative effects, and the implementation of a comprehensive monitoring programme which utilises various sustainability indicators (e.g., Local Government Management Board, 1995; MacGillivray and Zadek, 1995), tourism developments may have a variety of unintended effects and fail to achieve their maximum positive potential.

Sustaining rural areas in the way that the majority of observers appear to wish them sustained has as its core the maintenance of an economically viable rural population which is engaged in traditional or related rural activities, in particular family farm based agriculture. Sustainable tourism is therefore as much about sustaining rural culture and identity as it is the physical environment. Any policy response which seeks to use tourism as a mechanism to ameliorate the effects of economic restructuring needs to consider the cultural component of rural change wrought by exogenous forces and the dialectic that exists between the city and the countryside. Tourism both affects and is affected by contemporary rurality. Visitors favour the more traditional rural landscape created by smaller farm holdings, particularly those with horticultural or cash crops, such as orchards, berry farms, vineyards, or vegetable producers, which offer a greater variety of recreational opportunities. Such visitation and consequent purchase of produce at the farm gate may help maintain some family farms by providing supplementary income and thus indirectly sustaining the landscape. In contrast, the landscape created by large-scale agribusiness often has low amenity value and often results in the reduction of public access to the countryside, thereby contributing to the loss of tourist spending in the wider rural region and a loss of tourism income generating activities for other businesses. As well, such a decline in tourist visitation may result in declining sympathy and support for rural preservation programmes and policies. Many regional authorities appear to fail to recognise that it is the visual complexity of the rural landscape, and the subsequent visual fulfillment of rural images and myths, which generate amenity values for locals and visitors alike. In a sometimes desperate search for economic development, a wider tax base, and employment generation, inappropriate policies and development programmes may be followed. Policy measures in one sector, such as the attraction of agribusinesses or large foreign investments to a region, may lead to a decline of the industrial value of the region to other industries, such as tourism and businesses which are based on adding-value to local primary production. An integrated approach to rural resource development is therefore essential if sustainable development is to become more than wishful thinking. As Jenkins (1996) observed with respect to rural Australia, government can best assist rural areas to meet the challenges of economic restructuring and change by supporting the development of leadership and generic skills (education and entrepreneurial skills), and by attaching greater importance to the provision of relevant global and national data which affects decision making, rather than specifically supporting programmes which encourage the production of brochures, walking trails and other small scale local tourism initiatives, such as visitor centres.

Sustainable development will more likely be achieved if all actors can be persuaded that the sustainable approach is in their economic, if not personal, interest. It should be recognised, however, that tourism may not be an appropriate element to be introduced or maintained in all rural areas. To succeed effectively in economic, social and environmental terms, tourism requires specific conditions which meet market needs and current tastes and preferences. Where these are absent, tourism is unlikely to be successful, especially in the long-term. Policy makers, therefore, need to identify and recognise the elements which make up a suitable base for tourism and recreation and which allow them to be successfully integrated into the existing rural fabric of a particular place.

This book has examined a number of themes and issues which policy makers and planners need to address in terms of sustainable rural tourism development: the importance of understanding the broader context of rural restructuring, the formulation and implementation of policy, the imaging of the countryside, and the economic and social dimensions of rural tourism development. Each of these factors needs to be considered if tourism is to be made relevant to the needs of rural people and communities.

Sustainability does not mean freezing the rural landscape. Rather it requires perceiving the countryside as a cultural landscape in which ideas of rurality are socially and politically constructed. Despite attempts by some (e.g., Hoggart 1989, 1990), to do away with the rural, and the increasing recognition that both urban and rural areas are subject to the same global transitions in economic, political and social structures (e.g., Cloke, 1989), notions of 'rural' and 'rurality' remain important not only for the everyday lives of people in the city and the country but also for planners and policy-makers. As Harvey (1989, p. 72) recognised, the rural 'lingers in the realms of ideology with some important results'. Similarly, although Cloke and Goodwin (1993, p. 168) denied that 'rurality is in itself a deterministically casual mechanism', they went on to note that people 'behave as though rural is real to them and is influential in their locational decisions'.

New ways of seeing the countryside become developed with each round of capital that is invested in the countryside (Cloke and Goodwin, 1993). As several chapters in this book have demonstrated, tourism and recreation, along with other forms of consumption, rely on the marketing of a rural idyll in order to attract both visitors and investment. Constructions of rurality therefore play a vital role not only in determining the rate of change in the countryside but also how tourists see the country and how the rural community see themselves.

Understanding the construction of the rural must therefore become an integral part of sustainable rural tourism. 'Rurality' and 'rural' categories of consumption and production are essential to providing the context within which tourism occurs. It is perhaps ironic that rural tourism appears based on images of an unchanging, simpler and problem-free countryside when the reality has been one of change although, admittedly, change has been uneven and has 'taken different forms and has proceeded at different scales at different times in different rural areas' (Cloke and Goodwin, 1993, p. 327). Given its importance in determining tourism flows and the patterns of tourism development, it is also perhaps ironic that the vast bulk of academic research on rural tourism has missed understanding the means by which the rural image is created and sold to the visitor and local alike. It is hoped that this book will go at least some way in helping students of tourism to appreciate that not only is rural change a socially, economically and politically constructed process, but that, increasingly, tourism and recreation are critical, though complex, components of this process.

References

Barbier, E.B., 1987, The concept of sustainable economic development, *Environmental Conservation*, **14** (2), 101–110

Blake, J., 1996, Resolving conflict? The rural white paper, sustainability and countryside policy, *Local Environment*, **1** (2), 211–218

Bouquet, M. and Winter, M., eds., 1987, *Who from their labours rest: conflict and practice in rural tourism*, Gower, Aldershot

Bramwell, B. and Lane, B., 1993, Sustainable tourism: an evolving global approach, *Journal of Sustainable Tourism*, **1** (1), 6–16

Butler, R.W., 1991, Tourism, environment, and sustainable development, *Environmental Conservation*, **18** (3), 201–209

Cloke, P., 1989, Rural geography and political economy. In *New models in geography*, vol.1, R. Peet and N. Thrift, eds., pp. 164–190, Paul Chapman Publishing, London

Cloke, P. and Goodwin, M., 1993, Rural change: structured coherence or unstructured coherence, *Terra*, **105**: 166–174

Coppock, J.T., ed., 1977, *Second homes: blessing or curse?*, Pergamon, London

Curry, N., 1992, Recreation, access, amenity and conservation in the United Kingdom: the failure of integration. In *Contemporary rural systems in transition*, vol. 2, I.R. Bowler, C.R. Bryant and M.D. Nellis, eds., pp. 141–154, CAB, Oxford

Department of the Environment and Ministry of Agriculture, Fisheries and Food (DoE/MAFF), 1995, *Rural England: a nation committed to a living countryside*, HMSO, London

Gartner, W.C., 1987, Environmental impacts of recreational home developments, *Annals of Tourism Research*, **14** (1): 38–57

Hall, C.M., 1995, *Introduction to tourism in Australia: impacts, planning and development*, 2nd. ed., Longman Australia, South Melbourne

Harvey, D. 1989, *The urban experience*, Blackwell, London

Hoggart, K., 1989, Not a definition of rural, *Area*, **20**: 35–40

Hoggart, K., 1990, Let's do away with rural, *Journal of Rural Studies*, **6**: 245–257

International Union for the Conservation of Nature and Natural Resources (IUCN), 1980, *World conservation strategy*, The IUCN with the advice, cooperation and financial assistance of the United Nations Environment Education Program and the World Wildlife Fund and in collaboration with the Food and Agricultural Organization of the United Nations and the United Nations Educational, Scientific and Cultural Organization, IUCN, Morges

International Union for the Conservation of Nature and Natural Resources (IUCN), World Wide Fund for Nature, United Nations Environment Programme, 1991, *Caring for the earth*, Earthscan, London

Jenkins, J., 1996, The role of the Commonwealth Government in rural tourism and regional development in Australia. In *Tourism planning and policy in Australia and New Zealand: cases, issues and practice*, C.M. Hall, J. Jenkins, and G. Kearsley, eds., Irwin Publishers, Sydney

Local Government Management Board, 1995, *The sustainability indicators research project: indicators for local Agenda 21 – a summary*, Local Government Management Board, Luton

McArthur, S. and Hall, C.M., 1996, Evaluation. In *Heritage management in Australia and New Zealand: the human dimension*, C. Michael Hall and S. McArthur, eds., pp.107–126, Oxford University Press, Melbourne

MacGillivray, A. and Zadek, S., 1995, *Indicators for a sustainable future*, New Economics Foundation, London

Murdoch, J., 1993, Sustainable rural development: towards a research agenda, *Geoforum*, **24** (3), 225–241

Pinfield, G., 1996, Beyond sustainability indicators, *Local Environment*, **1** (2), 151–163

Redclift, M., 1987, *Sustainable development: exploring the contradictions*, Methuen, London

Troughton, M.J., 1997, Social change, discontinuity and polarization in Canadian farm-based rural systems. In *Agricultural restructuring and sustainability*, B. Ilbery, Q. Chiotti and T. Rickard, eds., pp. 279–291, CAB International, Wallingford

Whatmore, S., 1993, Sustainable rural geographies, *Progress in Human Geography* **17** (4), 538–547

World Commission on Economic Development (WCED), 1987, *Our common future*, Oxford University Press, New York

Index